DICTIONARY OF FINANCE

DICTIONARY OF FINANCE

By

HARI OM CHATURVEDI

ANMOL PUBLICATIONS PVT. LTD.
NEW DELHI - 110 002 (INDIA)

ANMOL PUBLICATIONS PVT. LTD.
4374/4B, Ansari Road, Daryaganj
New Delhi - 110 002
Ph.: 3261597, 3278000
Visit us at: www.anmolbooks.com

Dictionary of Finance

First Edition, 2002

ISBN 81-261-1244-1

PRINTED IN INDIA

Published by J.L. Kumar for Anmol Publications Pvt. Ltd., New Delhi - 110 002 and Printed at Mehra Offset Press, Delhi.

Preface

The Indian financial system has experienced a strong and widespread growth during the last decade. It has even been more dramatic after initiation of the process of economic liberalization and reforms in the financial and banking sector since 1991. No segment of the financial system, be it financial markets, financial institutions, intermediaries, participants, and the financial instruments has remained unaffected by its growth.

A very important aspect in the growth of the financial system has been the introduction of new financial instruments as well as financing techniques. As a consequence several financial terms which hitherto were unknown to the participants in the Indian financial system. The new instruments and financing techniques include Derivatives, Future Options, Global Depository Receipts (GDRs), American Depository Receipts (ADRs), Note Issuance Facility, Revolving Underwriting Facility, Securitization, Foreign Direct Investment (FDIs), etc. A new branch of Finance, namely Financial Engineering has developed which is concerned with the creation of new financial instruments or development of new financial techniques. Indian Capital market is gearing up to introduce trading in derivatives. A number of new financial institutions such as Securities Exchange Board of India (SEBI), National Stock Exchange, National Securities Depository Ltd. and Securities Trading Corporation of India has been established. Stock exchanges are moving swiftly to the scripless form of trading. A number of Indian companies have started disclosing Economic Value Added during the accounting period, in the annual report. Banks and finance companies now are required to follow norms relating to Capital Adequacy and income recognition. Mutual funds are floating index and sectoral funds and financial institutions are issuing deep discount and zero coupon bonds. Government has shifted from borrowing at administered rates to market determined rates.

Finance, being an area that involves raising and investing money, attracts people from all walks of life. Development of the financial market has further enhanced their interest in this area. Not only people in general, but students who do not opt for finance in their specialization courses at higher level of studies, want to have at least a working knowledge of financial issues. They are curious about trading mechanism at stock exchanges, derivatives, futures, options, venture capital, and the like.

This book is an attempt to offer a shortcut to the understanding and to refresh memory about basic terms from Corporate Finance, Investments, Accounting and Financial Economics. In order to have easy access, terms have been arranged in the form of a dictionary—hence *Dictionary of Finance.* The work of this type is more of editing in nature than of an original writing. A number of books, periodicals and newspapers were consulted in the preparation of this book, spread over a period of several months. I hope students, professionals, investors and people in general will find this book useful.

I am grateful to Dr. B.M. Lall Nigam, Professor, Accounting & Finance, Department of Commerce & Business Studies, University of Delhi, Delhi and Dr. Harmeet Singh, Principal, S.G.T.B. Khalsa Post-Graduate (E) College, University of Delhi, Delhi for taking interest and providing encouragement during writing of this book. My younger brother, Sh. D.D. Chaturvedi, Sr. Lecturer in Economics, Guru Gobind Singh College of Commerce, University of Delhi helped me at various stages in giving proper shape to this book. Dr. Vijay Seth, Reader, Faculty of Management Studies, Professor Sanjay Jain, Indraprastha University, Delhi,

Prof. Y.P. Singh, Department of Commerce & Business Studies, Dr. Ashok Seth, Director, Indraprastha Institute of Management Studies, and Dr. Vineet Kapoor, my colleague at S.G.T.B. Khalsa P.G. (E) College deserve special mention for providing valuable suggestions from time to time.

Finally, I record my appreciation to Sh. J.L. Kumar and Sh. Kripal D. Joshi, Managing Director and Production Manager respectively of Anmol Publications Pvt. Ltd., New Delhi for publishing this book in a very short time.

—Hari Om Chaturvedi

Aa

Abandonment. The complete retirement of a fixed asset after it is removed from service. There are several legal applications : Abondonment of property is the giving up of all control over it with the intention of relinguishing all claim to it. Loss of property is involuntary while abondment is a voluntary act.

Abatement. The cancellation of all or part of a past or prospective expenditure. A reduction or cancellation of an assessed tax. Also, any item of incidental income accounted for as a reduction of general cost.

Ability to Pay. Under this theory, wage levels should increase as profits increase. Those who support this theory rarely recommend the converse, lowering wages as profits decline. Also, a theory of taxation holding that taxes should be based on the taxapayer's ability to pay, the rich paying proportionately more than the poor.

Absorption Costing. The process of costing products or activities by taking into account the total costs incurred in producing the product or service, however remote.

Abstinence Theory of Interest. The concept that interest gained by saving money in an interest-bearing savings account is a reward for not spending the money on goods and services.

Accelerated Depreciation. Depreciation of an asset at a rapid, nonlinear rate, generally during the early years of its useful life.

Acceleration Clause. A section of a written legal document that provides that a balance or remainder of a debt becomes payable immediately under certain conditions, such as failure to make a scheduled payment.

Accelerator Principle. A proposition that investment in real assets such as plant, machinery, inventory etc., be increased to accelerate sales.

Acceptance. Written acknowledgement of the liability by the drawee of a Bill of Exchange on the instrument itself. The drawee accepts his liability by signing on the face of the instrument. It may be co-accepted by a bank as guarantee to make the payment in case drawee does not fulfill his obligation on maturity.

Accepting House. An institution specializing in accepting or guaranteeing bills of exchange. A service fee is charged for guaranteeing payment, enabling the bill to be discounted at preferential rates on the money market.

Accepting Houses Committee. A committee representing the 16 accepting houses in the City of London. Members of the committee are eligible for finer discounts on bills bought by the Bank of England, although this privilege has been extended to other banks.

Acceptor. The drawee of a bill of exchange accepting the bill, i.e., after the drawee has accepted liability by signing the face of the bill.

Accommodation Bill. A Bill of Exchange drawn and accepted for mutual help, without any consideration. The bill is accepted either to accomodate the drawer or for meeting the temporary fund requirements of both drawer and drawee. Duly accepted bill may be discounted with a bank to meet the fund requirements.

Accommodation Endorser. A person or a bank that endorses a loan to another party; for example, a parent company may endorse a bank loan to a subsidiary. The endorser becomes a guarantor and is secondarily liable in case of default. Banks may endorse other banks acceptance notes, which can then be traded on the secondary market.

Account. (1) A statement of indebtedness from one person to another; an invoice. A provider of professional services or of goods may render an account to a client or customer; a solicitor selling a house on a person's behalf will render an account of the sale, which may show that the solicitor owes the seller the proceeds of the sale, less expenses. (2) A named segment of a ledger recording transactions relevant to the person or the matter named. Accounts consist of two sides; increases are recorded on one side and decreases on the other. Accounts may be kept in a written form in a ledger, they may be on loose cards, or they may be on a magnetic medium in a computer. (3) A record maintained by a bank or a building society of the amount of money a customer has deposited or been lent. (4) A period during which dealings on the Stock Exchange are made without immediate cash settlement. There are 24 accounts in the year, most of two weeks duration, but a few last for three weeks to accommodate public holidays. Up to the end of each account transactions are recorded but no money changes hands, which enables speculators to operate with the minimum capital outlay (for shares bought and sold within an account only differences have to be settled). Settlement of all transactions made within an account is made ten days after the account ends.

Accountant. A person trained to keep books of account, which record all the financial transactions of a business or other organization, and to prepare periodic accounts. The accounts normally consist of a balance sheet; a profit and loss account or, in the case of a non-trading organization, an income and expenditure account; and sometimes a statement of sources and application of funds. Other roles of accountants are to audit the accounts of organizations and to give advice on taxation and other financial matters.

Account Day. The day on which all transactions made during the previous account on the Stock Exchange must be settled. It falls on a Monday, ten days after the account ends. Also called *Settlement Day.*

Accounting Concepts. As accounting developed largely from a practical base, it has been argued that it lacks a theoretical framework. Accountants have therefore tried to develop such a framework; although various concepts have been suggested, few have found universal agreement. However, four are deemed to be important; the first, the on-going concern concept, assumes that the business is a going concern until there is evidence to the contrary, so that assets are not stated at their break-up value; the second, the accruals concept, involves recording income and expenses as they accrue, as distinct from when they are received or paid; the third, the consistency concept, demands that accounts be prepared on a consistent basis from one period to another; and the fourth, the prudence concept, calls for accounts to be prepared on a conservative basis, not taking credit for profits or income before they are realized but making provision for losses when they are foreseen. Depreciation and deferred taxation are concepts relating to accounting, but are not often considered when reference is made to accounting concepts.

Accounting Period. (a) The period for which an organization makes up its accounts, usually an annual period. Profit and loss accounts (or income and expenditure accounts) are drawn up to cover that period and balance sheets are prepared for the closing date. It is often a legal requirement that these accounts should be published. However, an organization might make use of shorter accounting periods for internal management purposes, e.g. monthly, quarterly, or six-monthly periods. (b) An accounting period for tax purposes, as defined by the taxation Acts. For unincorporated businesses it is the period for which the businesses prepare their accounts.

Accounting Rate of Return (ARR). The expected net profit to be from an investment, calculated as a percentage of the book value of the assets invested.

Account Payee. The words added to a crossed cheque ensuring that the funds will only be paid to the individual to whom the cheque was made payable.

Accounts Payable. The amounts due to suppliers of goods and services to an organization.

Accrual (Accrued Charge). An amount incurred as a charge in a given accounting period but not paid by the end of that period, e.g. the last quarter's electricity charge.

Accruals Concept. One of the four principal accounting concepts. It is considered good accounting practice to prepare accounts taking note of such accruals. This is also akin to the *matching concept*, which suggests that costs should, as far as possible, be matched with the income to which they give rise.

Accrued Benefits. The benefits that have a accrued to a person in respect of pension, for the service given up to a specified date, whether or not that person continues in office.

Accrued Income Scheme. An arrangement that applies when the owner of interest-bearing securities disposes of them. The interest accrued between the date of the last interest payment and the date of disposal is regarded, for tax purposes, as the income of the transferor. The transferee is able to deduct this sum from taxable income. The scheme does not apply to non-residents or if the transfer is part of a trade. Exemption also applies to individuals (husband and wife being regarded as one) if the total nominal value of the securities held does not exceed £5000.

Accumulated Depreciation. The total amount written off the value of an asset. It is the sum of the yearly instalments of depreciation since the asset was acquired.

Accumulated Dividend. A dividend that has not been paid to a company's preference shareholders. It is, therefore, shown as a liability in its accounts.

Accumulated Profits. The amount showing in the appropriation of profits account that can be carried forward to the next year's accounts, i.e. after paying dividends, taxes, and putting some to reserve.

Accumulating Shares. Ordinary shares issued to holders of ordinary shares in a company, instead of a dividend. Accumulating shares are a way of replacing annual income with capital growth; they avoid income tax but not capital-gains tax. Usually tax is deducted by the company from the declared dividend, in the usual way, and the net dividend is then used to buy additional ordinary shares for the shareholder.

Accumulation Unit. A unit in an investment trust in which dividends are ploughed back into the trust, after deducting income tax, enabling the value of the unit to increase. It is usually linked to a life-assurance policy.

Acid Test. The ratio of an enterprise's current assets minus inventories to its current liabilities. One of several factors used by credit analysts to judge an enterprise's financial position. Also known as the quick ratio.

ACII. Associate of the Chartered Insurance Institute.

Acquisition Accounting. The accounting procedures adopted when one company is taken over by another. This often involves controversial issues as to the way in which goodwill is to be treated.

Actual Cost. Cost data based on transactions that have been completed, as contrasted with costs that have been estimated.

Adjustable Peg. A system that permits changes in the par rate of foreign exchange after a nation has had long-run disequilibrium in its balance of payments. It allows also for short-run variation within a narrow range of a few per cent above and below the par value.

Adjusted Cost Basis. For accounting purposes, the value of property equal to the original cost plus improvements less depreciation.

Adjusting Entry. Any change in an account required either by an auditor or by accounting policy and expressed in the form of a simple or compound journal entry.

Administered Price. A price that is purposely influenced by the government. For example, the interest rate for the use of money is determined by the demand for, and the supply of, loanable capital; it is not generally considered to be determined by a free market.

Administrative Accounting. That part of the accounting process generally associated with management.

Administrative Expense. Expense incurred in the general direction and management of an enterprise; contrasted with expenses incurred by specific functions such as selling or manufacturing.

Ad Valorem. A property tax or import or other duty computed as a percentage rate of the value of the property.

Ad Valorem Subsidy. A fixed-percentage subsidy granted to producers of commodities as a form of financial aid or relief from hardship resulting from economic conditions beyond the control of the producers. The subsidy is calculated on the basis of the current or prevailing market value of the commodity.

Adverse Selection. The insuring of a group of risks that represents an above-average expectation of loss. Also, the tendency of poor risks to seek insurance.

Affiliation. A connection existing between a holding or parent company and its subsidiary, or between two corporations or other organizations owned or controlled by a third.

Agent. One who represent, acts for, and is accountable to another. A contractual relationship may exist between a principal and an agent, forming an agency. The scope of the contract determines whether the agent is "special" (restricted in his "activities") or "general" (equipped with broad powers).

Aggregate Demand. The flow of money and expenditures for goods and services during a given time period. The expectations of aggregate demand influence the aggregate supply.

Aggregate Supply. The amount of goods and services produced by all firms in the economy during a given time period in response to demand expectations.

Agribusiness. The sector of the economy involved with the processes and procedures of agriculture, including farming, services and supplies.

AIDA. Attention, Interest, Desire, Action.

Alienation Clause. A special type of acceleration clause that requires payment of an entire loan balance upon sale or other transfer of title to real property.

Allocate. To spread a cost systematically over two or more time periods, objects, activities, processes, operations, or products. In government accounting, to transfer an appropriation, or a part thereof, from one agency to another.

All-risk Cargo Insurance. Preferred-risk ocean marine insurance covering all risks. Cargo insurance is usually written on a specified-perils basis.

Amalgamation. The act of combining under a single head all or part of the assets and liabilities of two or more business units by merger or consolidation.

Amortize. To write off all or a portion of the cost of an asset; to depreciate or deplete. Also, to retire a debt over a period of years.

Amortized Cost. In accounting, the cost of an asset minus the portions written off or depreciated.

Analytical Forecasting. Forecasting gross national product by estimating the components of demand and then combining them into an overall estimate.

Anchor Lease. A lease, usually favourable, given to a large or well-known retail business in order to attract the public to an area such as a shopping center.

Annual Audit. An audit by a professional accountant that covers transactions for a period of one year.

Annual Closing. In accounting, the posting of closing entries that takes place at the end of a fiscal year.

Annual Transit Policy. Insurance obtained to cover incoming and outgoing commercial shipments. It is applicable to shipments via railroad, railway express, interstate or intrastate motor carriers, coastwise steamers, or the insured's own vehicles. This policy is usually written on a specified-perils basis.

Annuity. A series of periodic and equal payments made at fixed intervals. In the case of retired employee who receives such payments, the annuity is referred to a *pension*.

Annuity Fund. The fund, created as a result of an annuity agreement.

Annuity Method. A method of depreciating an asset.

Anticipated Cost. An addition to operating costs that results from the use of LIFO inventory evaluation during a period of rising prices. Also known as *inventory profit*.

Anticipated Profit. A profit that is recorded before being realized; paper profit. Also known as *anticipatory profit*.

Anticipatory Repudiation. A breach of contract occurring when a buyer of real estate informs the seller before closing escrow that he does not plan to fulfill the transaction.

Antidumping Tariff. A tariff applied by a government to discourage market dumping of imported goods intended for sale in the importing country at prices significantly below those charged for similar goods produced in the country of import.

Applied Cost. In accounting, a cost that has been allocated to a product, process, or other specific activity of an enterprise.

Appreciation. The increase in the value of a specific asset with reference to book value or acquisition cost.

Apropriation. The earmarking of funds for some specific or general purpose; a distribution of net income to various accounts: the amount of future expenditures that has been approved.

Appropriation Account. In government accounting, the account of a government agency to which the amount of an appropriation is credited. Also, a British phrase for the account to which the profit-and-loss balance for the year is carried and taxes and dividends are charged; the balance is transferred to revenue reserves.

Appropriation Period. In government accounting, the period of time, usually one year, for the expenditure or obligation of an appropriation.

Appropriation Section. A section of an income statement that shows the disposition of net income between dividends, surplus reserves, and earned surplus.

Arbitrage. A technique used to take advantage of differences in market prices for shares of stock. If, for example, WXR stock can be bought in New York for $ 10 a share and sold in London at $ 10.50, an arbitrageur may simultaneously purchase WXR stock in New York and sell the same amount in London, making a profit of 50 cents a share, less expenses. The technique also applies to the purchase and selling of commodities. Arbitrage tends to equalize prices of a commodity in different markets.

Artificial Person. An enterprise, business firm, or organization that has powers, either granted by law or by custom, that resemble those of a natural person.

Artisan's Lien. A legal claim against another's property as security by a person who has invested labor upon, or added value to, such property and who has not been reimbursed for the value of the labor and materials.

Asian Development Bank. The first Ministerial Conference on Asian Economic Co-operation was held in Manila (Philippines) in 1963 which suggested the establishment of a Regional Development Bank of Asia. As a result, the Asian Development Bank (A.D.B.) came into existence with 31 member-countries and was formally opened for business on December 19, 1966.

Asking Price. The price at which a good or a security is offered for sale. In some circumstances, such as in local retailing, asking price is taken to indicate willingness on the part of the seller to negotiate the final selling price to some level below the asking price.

Assessment. The process of valuing property for establishing taxation. Any recurrent tax levied by a government authority, such as for property or real-estate taxes. A special tax levied for improvements or repairs to community property under the direct control of a municipal authority; also known as a *special assessment tax* or *improvement tax.* A levy on stockholders, members of an organization, or owners of special beneficial interests for the purpose of raising additional capital.

Assessment Bonds. Municipal bonds that are to be repaid through assessments made against property—usually against the property that has benefited from the improvements financed by the bond issue.

Asset. A physical (tangible) object or a right (intangible) that has economic value to its owner. For balance-sheet purposes, assets are broadly grouped as current, fixed or intangible, and within these groupings are descriptive titles, such as receivables, inventories, investments, plant and equipment, goodwill, and patents.

Assignment Clauses. In insurance, clauses referring to the assignment of proceeds of a policy before a loss occurs. A collateral assignment is sometimes made, in which the policy is assigned as security for a debt. A life insurance policy may be assigned to a lender as collateral for a loan. After a loss has occurred, the benefits may be assigned like any other fund.

Associate Broker. A licensed natural or legal person who acts for another in a real estate or related transaction.

Associated Company. A corporation wherein 50 per cent of the voting capital stock is owned by another. In British usage, a corporation in which another company holds a trade investment.

Assurance. In commercial world 'Assurance' denotes a payment of premium "at regular intervals in return for a fixed sum which will become payable at a stated time."

Assurance does not depend upon a possibility. Examples of Assurance are life and endowment policies. With endowment assurance, payment becomes due on the death of the life assured. With endowment assurance, payment becomes due after the expiry of the stated period. Generally, both are combined in a policy.

Assured. A beneficiary of an insurance policy; a person who would be indemnified by another against a risk of loss.

ATA Carnet. International customs document, recognized by countries that are parties to the ATA Convention, and used by firms that send or take goods abroad on a temporary basis as sales samples or exhibits at international conventions. Goods covered by the ATA carnet are imported and exported free of customs duties.

At Par. In securities trading, at par is the quotation or price that is equal to the face or nominal value of the security being traded; also a fixed transfer rate of foreign exchange.

At Sight. A term used with reference to Bills of Exchange payable on presentation, as opposed to on a particular date.

Attachment. A legal proceeding that accompanies a court action by which a plaintiff may acquire a lien on a defendant's property as a security for the payment of any judgment the plaintiff may recover. It is provisional and independent of the court action and is usually provided for by statute. One person, for example, sues another and, before judgment, attaches property belonging to the one being sued in order to make certain of the payment that may eventually be secured by judicial action.

At-the-close Order. A stock market order to buy or sell that is to be executed at or as near to the close of the trading day as is practicable; any such order or portion thereof not so executed is treated as cancelled.

At-the-opening Order. A stock market order to buy or sell that is to be executed at the opening of the stock or not at all; any such order or portion thereof not so executed is treated as cancelled.

Auction. Selling of goods to public by an auctioneer, normally sold off to the highest bidder. The auctioneer acts as agent for the seller. Sale of goods at an auction may be subject to a reserve price fixed by the seller.

Audit. Examination of a set of books and/or accounts and verification of the correctness by a person or a firm other than the one who prepared them (with the object of ascertaining whether or not the books are properly kept and/or the accounts show a 'true and fair' view of the state of affairs of the enterprise at the date stated) followed by a Report to the persons by whom the auditor was appointed.

Audit Adjustment. An adjusting entry to a journal resulting from an examination by a public accountant.

Audit Bureau of Circulation. An independent organization established in 1914, ABC provides certified evidence of the paid circulation of publications in the United States.

Audit Certificate. The certification of a financial statement by a certified public accountant; an auditor's report.

Audit, Internal. Regular and independent appraisal, by a staff of internal auditors of the accounting, financial and other operations of an enterprise. Although more often limited to the auditing of accounts, in its most useful aspect internal auditing involves the appraisal of operations generally, weighing actual results in the light of planned results. Internal Audit is an effective tool of management control.

Audit Period. The period of time covered by an audit.

Audit, Special. Audit of the affairs of a company undertaken by the Government under special circumstances.

Auditor. A person or a firm of auditor appointed by the members of an enterprise to inspect its accounts and relevant records on behalf of the members. Every company registered under the Companies Act, 1956, is obliged to appoint an official auditor. Members of the Institute of Chartered Accountants of India, New Delhi, are only qualified to act or be employed as auditor of any enterprise in India.

Audit Trail. A notation accompanying a transaction entry or posting that refers to its source records or documents.

Audit Voucher. A voucher that has been examined and approved for payment.

Audit Year. The year covered in an annual or balance-sheet audit; usually the fiscal year.

Auditor's Report. A written declaration prepared by an auditor following an audit conducted by him. Using standard language, it is addressed to the management of the firm whose financial records have been audited, and it contains details of the scope of the audit, comments on operating results and financial condition, a funds-flow statement, causes of changes as compared with preceding years, and procedural suggestions. The auditor may or may not express an opinion about the fairness or unfairness of the data as being an accurate representation of the financial condition of the firm. If the auditor is unable to express an opinion, he explains his reasons for this in a *disclaimer of opinion*.

Authorized Capital Stock. The number of shares at the par or stated value of the capital stock that may be issued by a corporation under its articles of incorporation. In some instances, the stockholders or directors may determine the stated value per share.

Automatic Dividend-Reinvestment Plan. An agreement between a shareholder and a mutual fund, whereby dividends are automatically used to purchase additional shares of stock in the fund.

Automatic Reinstatement. The continuance of total effectiveness of an insurance contract, after a loss has occurred, in an amount equal to the face value of the contract.

Automation. Applying such machines in business and industry which automatically operate or perform a set of interrelated operations with virtually no human labour. Its latest application is computer. The term 'Automation' is derived from the Greek word 'Automotos' which denotes self-moving.

The basic features of automation: (1) Self-direction and self-control; (2) Communication, computation and control; (3) Integrated system. *The benefits*: (1) Ensures speedy and error-free work; (2) Reduces material and labour wastage; (3) Provides exact service at the right time; (4) Brings down investment per unit of output or per employee; (5) provides all-round satisfaction to consumers and clients. *The demerits*: (1) Creates displacement and surplus in an enterprise; (2) Hinders creation of more job opportunities; (3) Involves heavy initial investment and recurring expenses for maintenance.

Available Assets. Assets that are free for general use, free of encumbrance or lien, and not serving as collateral for an obligation.

Avoidable Costs. Those that are incurred as a result of specific action or management decision rather than being an inherent and unavoidable part of the very existence of business or organization.

Bb

Backlog. Orders that have been accepted and entered in the financial sales, and job records of performance but for some reason have not yet been shipped.

Back Order. The portion of a customer's order that has not been shipped against an accepted order that is in backlog.

Back-to-back Loan. A loan from one company to another in a different country, often in a different currency, using a bank or other financial institution as a middle man to provide the loan but not the funding, which comes from a third party. Usually the loan is between a parent company and overseas subsidiaries; a pledge is usually given to honour loans on which there may be a default.

Back-up Credit. An alternative source of funds arranged if an issue of commercial paper is not fully taken up by the market. Back-up credit is provided by a bank for a fee or by the deposit of credit balances at the bank of the issuer. The back-up is often a stand-by facility provided by the bank, which may be drawn upon if the paper is not placed.

Backwardation. First, the difference between the spot price of a commodity, including rent, insurance, and interest accrued, and the forward price, when the spot price is the higher. Secondly, a situation that occasionally occurs on the Stock Exchange when a market maker quotes a buying price for a share that is lower than the selling price quoted by another market maker.

Bad Debt. Amount due from a debtor that is deemed irrecoverable. Such an amount can be treated as a loss and written off in the profit and loss account. Doubtful debts may appear in the balance sheet of an organization as a provision for bad debts.

Bailment. A transfer of possession of goods without the passing of title, as on consignment for safe keeping, repair, or sale. The person making the delivery of the goods is the bailor, the recipient is the bailee. No one can become a bailee without his written consent. A bailor need not be the owner of the goods. A bailee has a property interest in the bailed goods. A bailee may not deny the bailor's title. The bailor must warn the bailee of any hidden dangers within the conditions of the goods. The bailee must return the goods at the end of the bailment. The bailee must exercise ordinary care with the goods. A bailment constitutes a contract, express or implied, that the purpose of the delivery or transfer will be carried out.

Balanced Budget. A budget in which the expenditures forecast for a given period of operations are equal to the expected revenues for the same period.

Balanced Fund. A mutual fund that has an investment policy of balancing its portfolio, usually between bonds and common stocks.

Balanced Loading. Scheduling a mix of work in a department so that other departments are neither overloaded nor underloaded when the work is sent to them for further processing.

Balance Due. The quantity of material or parts ordered on a purchase order or requisitioned on a work order but not yet received.

Balance-of-Stores Record. In production, a double-entry record system that shows at all times the balances of material on order and available for future orders on addition to the balance of inventory items on hand.

Balance of Trade. The difference between the money value of a country's merchandise imports and the money value of its merchandise exports. A country is said to have a balance-of-trade surplus if it exports more than it imports and a deficit if it imports more than it exports.

Balance on Current Account. The net value of a nation's exports of goods and services plus or minus all unilateral money transfers abroad, such as remittances social security payments, and grants in aid.

Balance Sheet. A financial statement showing the amounts of various assets, liabilities and owners funds of an enterprise at a given date.

Balloon Payment. A large final payment on a note. Any final payment that is at least twice the smallest periodic or installment payment is considered to be a balloon payment.

Bank. A commercial institution licensed as a taker of deposits. Banks are concerned mainly with making and receiving payments on behalf of their customers, accepting deposits, and making short-term loans to private individuals, companies, and other organizations.

Bank Bill. A bill of exchange issued or guaranteed (accepted) by a bank. It is more acceptable than a trade bill as there is less risk of non-payment and hence it can be discounted at a more favourable rate, although this does, to some extent, depend on the credit rating of the bank.

Bank Certificate. The certificate, signed by a bank manager, stating the balance held to a company's credit on a specified date. It may be asked for during the course of an audit.

Bank Charge. The amount charged to a customer by a bank, usually for a specific transaction, such as paying in a sum of money by means of a cheque or withdrawing a sum by means of an automated teller machine. However, modern practice is to provide periods of commission-free banking by waiving most charges on personal current accounts.

Bank Draft. An order issued by a seller's bank against a purchaser's bank directing payment of money, usually through an intermediary bank. Bank drafts generally are negotiable and are similar to the cheques drawn against standard checking accounts except that they are drawn by one bank on its account in another bank.

Banker's Acceptance. An instrument used in financing foreign trade. It makes possible the payment of cash to an exporter for all or part of the amount of a shipment made by him.

Bank Note. A promise made by a bank to the bearer of a note, which is intended to serve as money.

Bank Rate. The rate at which the central bank is prepared to lend to the other banks in the banking system.

Bank Statement. The formal, periodic statement of assets, liabilities, and net worth of a bank. Also, the statement issued periodically by a bank to its customer.

Bar Chart. On of the several charts a technical analysts uses for forecasting individual stock performance. Bar charts contain price on the vertical axis and time on the horizontal axis. Time may be represented in days, weeks, or months. On bar charts, the analyst plots a vertical line to represent a range of prices of the stock during the period. The highest point of the vertical line represent the high price of the day (or the week, as the case may be) and the bottom of the line represent the low price of the day (or the week). A small horizontal line accross the bar denote the closing price at the end of the time period. Generally, information regarding volume for the same period are given at the bottom of the chart.

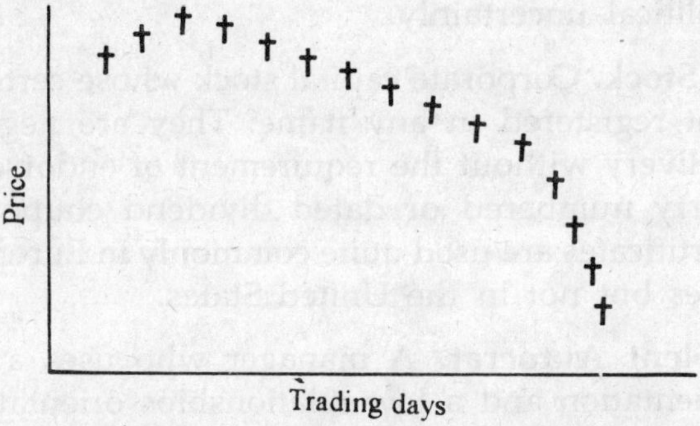

Barter. The exchange of goods or services without the use of money or other medium of exchange.

Base Stock-System. In production, a blend of the fixed-order-quantity and the fixed-reorder-cycle systems. The base stock system uses information regarding customer orders to establish demand at each stock point directly rather than passing the information through a chain of operations and stock points. Orders are placed to replenish inventories to the "base stock" level, which is sufficient for "buffer stock" plus a quantity calculated to cover current use.

Basic Standard Cost. A standard cost that serves as a point of reference from which to measure changes in current standard cost as well as actual cost. Also, a standard cost that is developed from engineering studies, using specific assumptions.

Bazar Bill Rate. The rate of interest that shroffs etc. change on discounting of **Hundis**. The Bazar Bill Rate is not uniform since the unregulated nature of the banking service run by shroffs etc.

Bear. A operator in the stock market who expects stock prices to fall in the near future.

Bear Market. The period of time during which the stock market declines continuously. The likely causes of bear market are—continued secession in the economy and political uncertainly.

Bearer Stock. Corporate capital stock whose certificates are not registered in any name. They are negotiable on delivery without the requirement of endorsement and carry numbered or dated dividend coupons. Bearer certificates are used quite commonly in European countries but not in the United States.

Benevolent Autocrat. A manager who uses a high task orientation and a low relationships orientation where such behavior is appropriate, and who is, therefore, more effective and perceived as knowing what he wants and how to get it without creating resentment.

Bid. An offer to buy. A bid proposal may be presented by a vendor to a potential buyer, in effect stating that the vendor would accept a bid from the potential customer in conformity with the terms of the bid proposal.

Bilateral Contract. A contract that contains mutual promises, with each party to the contract being both a promisor and a promisee.

Bill of Exchange. An unconditional order in writing signed by the drawer and requiring the drawee, the party to which it is addressed, to pay a certain sum in money to order or to a bearer at a fixed or determinable future time. A personal cheque is a bill of exchange drawn on a bank and payable on demand.

Bill of Lading. A receipt for any property received by a common carrier. The form and use of a bill of lading is regulated by the Interstate Commerce Commission.

Bill of Material Repetitions. The number of times a part number is referenced in a bill of material. This information can be useful in determining order quantities for specific part numbers, as for developing kits of materials for production.

Bill of Sale. A written document that confirms that the title or interest of one person in property, merchandise, or goods has transferred to another.

Black Capitalism. An effort begun in the late 1960s to increase the ownership and control of business by black people. Its objective is to improve the job market, the ghetto economy, and the condition and status of the black community.

Black Market. The purchase or sale of foreign exchange or commodities in violation of government restrictions.

Blanket Coverage. An insurance policy that covers two or more items, and in which the full face amount may be applied to any one item. Blanket policies are often used to cover merchandise and goods stored at several different locations, or where the aggregate amount are fairly constant but the locations or values of individual items may be changing.

Blanket Order. An order placed with a vendor, usually for large quantities of materials, such as for an annual supply, against which individual releases are made.

Blanket Rates. In transportation, rates that are generally designed to meet peculiar marketing requirements, usually of agricultural products. Blanket rates cover large geographic marketing areas for specified produce, offering through an average calculation a reduced rate for the entire market areas regardless of the distance between shipping points in that territory.

Blind Entry. In accounting, a journal entry that states only the name of an account and the amounts debited or credited, without explaining the transactions or providing the information essential to an adequate record; a posting in a ledger that is not supported by a by a journal voucher or other evidence.

Blue Chip. Common stock in a company known nationally for the quality and wide acceptance of its products or services, and for its ability to make profits and pay dividends. Usually, such stocks are high-priced and offer relatively low yields; they are considered relatively stable and secure in capital value or market price.

Blue-Sky Laws. A popular name for the laws enacted by various states to protect the public against securities frauds. The term is believed to have originated when a judge commented that a particular stock had about the same monetary value as a patch of blue sky.

Board for Financial Supervision (BFS). A body set up by the Rserve Bank of India (RBI) in November 1994 for the purpose of supervision and surveillance of the financial system. Specifically, the board's ambit includes commercial banks, financial Institutions and non-banking financial companies. It is headed by the Governor of RBI and will have a term of two years. The Board will ensure compliance with the guidelines and regulations relating to capital adequacy, credit management, income recognition, treasury operations, etc. It will receive operational support from RBI's Department of Supervision. The Board has an Advisory Council consisting of persons who are proficient in economic, banking, legal and financial matters. The functions of the Board will also help in improving supervisory policy and skills.

Bond. An IOU or promissory note issued by a corporation. A bond is evidence of a debt on which the issuing company usually promises to pay the bondholder a specified amount of interest for a specific length of time, with the face amount of the bond to be repaid on the expiration date. A bondholder is a creditor of the corporation, not a part owner as is a stockholder.

Bond and Preferred Stock Fund. A mutual fund whose policy is to invest in bonds and preferred stocks.

Bonded Block Loading. An effective and secure method for loading freight; the items are stacked in the manner of overlapping "bricks".

Bonded Debt. Outstanding bonds that are evidence of a debt.

Bonded Warehouse. A warehouse, usually at a port of entry, in which imported goods can be stored until duties have been paid or the goods have been reexported.

Bond-Yield Equivalent. Zero-coupon bonds and deep discount bonds are issued at a discount to their face value, discount being the return on investment. This return is received at maturity. However, one does not know the annual yield on his investment which can be calculated using the following formula:

$$\text{Annual Yield} = \frac{\text{Face value—Issue price}}{\text{Issue price}} \times \frac{365}{\text{Term of maturity}}$$

The above formula is also very useful for computation of annual yield on treasury bills and commercial paper.

Bonus Account. A savings account that pays a higher than normal rate of interest.

Bonus Formula. The formal provisions in an incentive bonus plan that determine the total funds available for bonus purposes in a given year. Individual bonus awards are made from this total pool.

Bonus Pool. The total amount of bonus funds generated by an incentive plan in a given year and available for awards. In most companies, the pool approximates the total bonuses that would be paid if all participants received "normal" awards.

Book Inventory. A statement of inventory that is not the result of a physical count. It is accomplished by adding the units and cost of incoming goods to previous inventory figures and deducting the units and cost of outgoing goods.

Bookkeeper. A person who keeps the books in which the financial transactions of an enterprise are recorded. This work may be specialized, as in the case of the person who maintains the general ledger or works on accounts receivable or accounts payable. A bookkeeper may also be a public accountant, although the function of bookkeeping does not usually require the professional level of training and education of a public accountant.

Book Value. The net amount at which an asset or a group of assets appears on the books of account, as distinguished from the market value or an intrinsic value. Also, the face amount of a liability less any unamortized discount and expanse.

Book Value Per Share. An indicator of the financial status of an enterprise, BV/share represents the sum of the common stock, paid-in surplus, and retained-income accounts of the balance sheet, divided by the number of common shares outstanding.

Bordereau. In insurance accounting, a tabular register or report that contains abstracts of insurance that has been written.

Boston Ledger. A type of ledger in which the record on each account moves horizontally in columnar sections assigned to consecutive accounting periods. Several accounts may be kept on a single page. This form of ledger may eliminate the need to prepare a separate trial balance.

Boycott. An effort discourage people from dealing with a particular firm, or to discourage nations from dealing with a particular nation.

Broker. An agent, often a member of a stock exchange firm or an exchange member himself, who handles the public's orders to buy and sell securities or commodities. A commission is charged for this service. Generally, a natural or legal person who, for compensation or in expectation of compensation, acts for another in a real estate or commercial transaction.

Brokerage. A commission that accrues to a broker for having brought about an arrangement or transaction between a buyer and a seller. The commission may be paid by either the buyer or the seller, or in part by both, in accordance with custom or regulation. Also, the business or establishment of a broker.

Broker's Loan. Loan obtained from a bank by a broker or dealer in securities for the purpose of purchasing or carrying securities or, most often, for carrying a customer's margin account.

Budget. A financial plan; an itemized estimate of expected revenues and expenditures for a specific future period of time. The term may also be applied to any proposed detailed plan for the utilization of manpower, material, or other resources.

Budgetary Control. It is one of the tools of overall management control. Budgetary Control is "a process of finding out what's being done and comparing actual results with the corresponding budget data in order to approve accomplishments or to remedy differences by either adjusting the budget estimates or correcting the course of differences.

Budget, Cash. It is a forecast of cash receipts and disbursements against which actual cash experience is measured. This is perhaps the most important single control of a business. Cash budgeting indicates availability of excess cash, thereby making possible planning for profit-making investment of this cash.

Budget Deficit. An excess of total expenditures over total revenues in a company's or national budget. Some economists hold that a deficit in the U.S. national budget is not detrimental to the economy if the gross national product increases during the budget period.

Budget, Fixed Costs. The Budget which exclusively refers to Fixed Costs. Since Fixed costs are determined by policy, some accountants want them to include in a separate budget as Fixed Costs Budget. It is argued that such costs are uncontrollable by functional and departmental heads and, therefore, no purpose is served by showing them in each functional budget as part of the costs which come within the responsibility of appropriate manager.

Budget, Flexible. Budget which is elastic in nature. It indicates a number of possible outputs and different cost structures in contrast to Fixed Budget which shows one volume of output and related costs in a manufacturing industry. Since it is very unlikely that the volume depicted in the forecast and Budget will be the one obtained in practice, the Flexible Budget is the only one which can enable costs to be controlled effectively.

Budget, Functional. Budget prepared to indicate performance and cost for each function in a department. Functional Budget is prepared in addition to Departmental Budget with a view to controlling more effectively a function as Administration, Production, Purchase, Sales, Research and Development. The budget for, say, the Machine Shop is clearly a Departmental Budget, yet, because this budget relates to production, the figures must also be summarised in the Functional Budget for Production.

Budget, Master. The principal or supreme budget and the budget of all budgets of an enterprise. It puts together all others into one overall integrated budget. Its purpose is to harmonise and collate the different sectional budgets of the enterprise for top management control.

Budget Mortgage. A mortgage loan under whose terms each monthly payment made by the borrower covers not only the interest and a payment on the principal but also one-twelfth of such annual liabilities as taxes and insurance. The lending firm keeps these payments in a reserve account and pays the charges as the become due. Also known as *budget loan.*

Budget Summary. Budget Summary takes into account Master Budget, Balance Sheet Budget and Income Statement to present a complete budgetary programme in quantitative and financial terms. Budget summary thus aims at assisting overall management control in an enterprise.

Budget Surplus. An excess of total revenues over total expenditures. The effect of a surplus in the national budget is to reduce the level of economic activity.

Builder's Risk. Fire insurance written to cover the constantly increasing value of a building under construction. It may be written for a small initial face value and increased each month on the basis of regular reports from the insured. Alternatively, it may be written for an amount presumed to be the final value of the building when completed, with the rate being adjusted periodically.

Bulk Freight. Material that is shipped loose rather than in packages or containers, as coal in a hopper car or sulfur in the hold of a ship.

Bulk Sales Law. A law in some states that requires the sale of a business to be advertised beforehand for the protection of its creditors. Also known as *ten-day escrow law*.

Bull. One who believes that the stock market prices or activity will rise. For example, a bullish operator on a stock exchange or commodities market expects prices to rise and buys in the hope of selling at a later time for a gain.

Bullion. Refined gold or silver in the form of bars or ingots.

Bunker Charge. An extra charge that may be added to ocean freight charges, justified usually by increased fuel costs.

Burden. The costs of manufacture or production that are not readily identifiable with specific products; examples are factory overhead, indirect costs, and employee fringe benefits.

Burglary Insurance. Basic protection against loss due to crimes committed by outsiders rather than by employees of an organization or authorized visitors. It applies only when there is physical evidence of forced entry. Coverage is provided for specific goods or property and damage incurred in the course of the burglary.

Burning Ratio. In insurance accounting, the ratio of an actual loss by fire to the total value of the combustible property.

Business Agent. In labour relations, the highest official in a union or labor organization operating on a local basis. The business agent is usually salaried and is either elected or appointed to perform the principal work of the local union, such as negotiating contracts, settling grievances, and building membership rolls.

Business Interruption Insurance. A type of insurance that covers the insured for loss of earnings sustained as a result of fire.

Business Life Insurance. Insurance on the life of a member of a partnership or on the officer or stockholder in a corporation payable so as to finance purchase by surviving owners of the insured's interest at his or her death. Insurance on the life of a sole proprietor payable so as to finance the purchase of the business by an outside interest at the owner's death. Insurance on the life of a key employee for the benefit of the enterprise.

Business Manager. It is widely held that the aim of business manager is to earn profit. Profit is only a measure of a 'surplus' of sales over expenses in carrying out some type of business. In reality, in business and non-business organisations, the managers are expected to create profit, i.e., a 'surplus'. Apart from that, managers are primarily concerned with establishing an environment in which people can attain group goals with the least amount of time, money, materials and personal dissatisfaction. Thus, the aim of managers is basically the same in business and non-business organisations. It is also the same at every level: the Managing Director of a business unit, Inspector General of Police, Dean of a Hospital, Cricket Manager and Principal of a College and Vice-Chancellor of a University as managers have the same aim.

Business Risk. The risk associated with unstable operating income, which arises largely from instability in the demand for the firm's products and services, an unstable variable cost ratio, and high fixed operating costs.

Buyer. In a retail business, an executive who undertakes the purchasing and stocking of various items for the store.

Buyer's Market. A market where supply is greater than demand, giving buyers considerable influence over prices and terms of sales. Prices generally tend to move downward in a buyer's market.

Cc

Call Loan. A loan that may be terminated at will be either party; primarily a loan made by a bank to a stockbroker. A loan that has been terminated in this way is known as a *called loan.*

Call Price. The price at which a callable bond is redeemable.

Callover. A meeting of commodity brokers and dealers at fixed times during the day in order to form a market in that commodity. The callover is usually used for trading in futures, in fixed quantities on a standard contract, payments usually being settled by differences through a clearing house. Because traders usually form a ring around the person calling out the prices, this form of market is often called *ring trading.* This method of trading is also called *open outcry,* as bids and offers are shouted out during the course of the callover.

Call Risk. The risk that the borrower will call back Bonds on fall of yields so that he can refinance at a lower rate of interest. This puts investor to a disadvantage on two counts—1. The appreciation in price is discouraged because of the callability at the call price. 2. Reinvestment of funds received on redemption will yield low returns.

Cancellation Price. The lowest price at which the manager of a unit trust may offer to redeem units on a particular day. The cancellation price is calculated on the basis of a formula laid down by the Securities and Investment Board.

Capital. 1. The total value of the assets of a person less liabilities. 2. The amount of the proprietors' interests in the assets of an organization, less its liabilities. 3. The money contributed by the proprietors to an organization to enable it to function; thus share capital is the amount provided by way of shares and the loan capital is the amount provided by way of loans. However, the capital of the proprietors of companies not only consists of the share and loan capital, it also includes retained profit, which accrues to the holders of the ordinary shares. 4. In economic theory, a factor of production, usually either machinery and plant (physical capital) or money (financial capital). However, the concept can be applied to a variety of other assets (e.g. human capital). In general, the rate of return on capital is called profit.

Capital Account. 1. An account recording expenditure on such items as land and buildings, plant and machinery, etc. 2. A budgeted amount that can only be spent on major items especially in public-sector budgeting. 3. An account showing the interest of a sole trader in the net assets of the business he or she runs.

Capital Asset. An asset in continuous use or possession, including land, buildings, equipment, leaseholds mineral deposits, goodwill, patents, trademarks, and copyrights.

Capital Budget. In finance, the portion of a budget, or a separate budget, dedicated to proposed future additions to capital assets and their financing. In municipal accounting, it is a plan for issue of additional shares, or by a resolution of the board of directors.

Capital Gain. The amount by which the sale price of a capital asset exceeds its cost.

Capital Levy. In finance, a nonrecurring tax on capital. The term may be used in connection with a special nonrecurring tax that is placed on new capital values acquired during a particular accounting period. In this concept, the capital levy is similar to a capital-gains tax except that it is levied on appraised instead of realized gain.

Capital Loss. Loss from the sale of a capital asset. For tax purposes, a capital loss is reduced by the amount of any offsetting capital gains. Up to $ 1,000 of net capital loss is deductible from an individual's income tax during the year reported. If the capital loss is more than $ 1,000, as much as $ 1,000 may be deducted annually thereafter until the full amount has been deducted. (These are rules are regulations of the U.S. Internal Revenue Service and are subject to change).

Capital Market. Collectively, securities exchanges, underwriter, and investment banks, usually concentrated in some financial center that may be a major city such as New York, Chicago, or London.

Capital/Output Ratio. A concept with two facets: (1) the "total" capital/output ratio is the economy's total stock of real capital divided by the level of its income or output; (2) the "marginal" capital/output ratio is the change in an economy's income or output resulting from a unit change in its stock of real capital; a ratio of 3/1 means that three units of additional capital produce one unit of additional output.

Capital Rationing. In corporate finance, capital rationing occurs any time there is a budget ceiling, or constraint, or the amount of funds that can be invested during a specific period of time, such as a year. Such constraints, are particularly prevalent in firms that have a policy of financing all capital expenditures iternally. Another example is when a division of a large company is allowed to make capital expenditures only up to a specific budget ceiling, over which the division usually has no control. By imposing the capital rationing constraint, the firm attempts to select the combination of investment proposals that will provide the greatest profitability.

Capital Surplus. That part of the paid-in capital of an enterprise that is not assigned to capital stock. Contributions by stockholders in excess of par or stated value of shares, also known as *paid-in surplus,* are capital surplus.

Capital Value. Investment in capital goods (fixed assets), measured in terms of cost or other value.

Career-Average Pension. A form of pension in which the benefit earned each year is calculated in terms of that year's income. This contrasts with pensions based on some form of final average pay, often the average of the five-year period immediately preceding the employee's date of retirement.

Carryback. The right, sometimes extended under tax regulations, to average out gains and losses over more than a one-year period. This enables the taxpayer to offset gains in one year with losses that have been accrued in an earlier year. The effect is to reduce the tax for the period in which gains were recorded.

Carrying Over or Budla. It denotes the facility given to a speculator to avoid or at least to defer the loss, arising due to unfavourable fluctuation in prices of shares and securities, by means of a postponement of the transaction to the next settlement. For this concession the party making it charges 'Budla Brokerage' from the other party.

Budla or Carry Over is effected by means of two new bargains. A Bull transaction is carried over by a sale for current settlement and re-purchase for the next settlement. A Bear transaction is carried over by a purchase for the current settlement and re-sale for the next settlement. The result is that the original bargain is completed for the current settlement and a new transaction at a new price is opened up for the next settlement. The party effecting the 'budla' is in the same position, but to complete the transactions he requires finance.

Carryover Clause. In real estate, a provision in an "exclusive listing" (one that is given only to a single real estate sales agent) that, under specified and negotiated circumstances, assures the sales agent that he or she will be eligible to receive a commission should the real estate be sold after the tenure period of the exclusive listing period. It is usual to assign an exclusive listing for a specified period of time after which, if the property has not been sold, the listing may be offered to one or more other sales agencies that may simultaneously endeavor to sell the property.

Carry-over Day. Stock Exchange term. Accounts are made up at stated intervals. The first day of each new account is known as the Carry-over day or Contango.

Cash Asset. Cash can any asset that can be immediately converted into cash without disrupting day-to-day operations. Also known as *cash resource.*

Cash Basis of Accounting. The method of accounting whereby revenues and expenses are recorded on the books of account when received and paid without regard to the period to which they apply.

Cashbook. A book of original entry for cash receipts and disbursements.

Cash Cow. A profitable business with regular cash flow becasue of the sustained demand or popularity of its product. Examples are Colgate-Palmolive's Colgate toothpaste and Reckitt & Colman's Dettol.

Cash Discount. A reduction in the amount of an invoice given for prompt settlement of a sales debt.

Cash Dividend. A dividend paid in cash rather than in property, Stocks, bonds, or any other substitute for cash.

Cash Flow. The cash inflow and outflow of an enterprise between two given dates or accounting periods. According to the AICPA, cash flow in financial analysis means net income after adding back expense items that currently do not *use* funds, such as depreciation, but it may also involve deducting revenue items that do not currently *provide* funds, such as the current amortization of deferred income. It corresponds to the *funds derived from operations* in a statement of source and application of funds.

Cash Journal. In accounting, a cashbook; a columnar journal in which all transactions are entered, whether or not cash is involved.

Cash Sale. The delivery of goods or services with immediate receipt of cash in payment. In stock market terms, a transaction on the floor of the stock exchange calling for delivery of the securities the same day. In "regular way" trades, the seller is to deliver on the fifth business day after the purchase or sale has been made.

Casualty Insurance. Insurance providing coverage for a variety of specific situations in which chance, accident, or neglect may result in provable loss. Some of the usual types are: (1) burglary, robbery, theft, and larceny insurance; (2) automobile insurance; (3) workmen's compensation insurance; and (4) disability or accident and health insurance.

Ceiling Price. The highest price obtainable or permissible in the sale of particular goods or services.

Certificate. In stock market terminology, the actual piece of paper that is evidence of ownership of stock in a corporation. Watermarked paper is used to discourage forgery. The certificate is usually registered by the corporation or the transfer agent in the name of the owner of the certificate.

Certificate of Deposit. Time deposit which, by agreement with the purchaser, is kept on deposit for a specified minimum time period in the bank that sold it. Many CDs are negotiable, and, because they offer both liquidity any yield, can be sold in a secondary market. Banks began to offer CDs in the 1960s at rates competitive with other money market instruments.

Certificate of Incorporation. The document issued by an authorized official of state government (usually the secretary of state) establishing the existence of a corporation.

Certificate of Origin. A certified statement of where goods originated, often required for imported goods.

Certificate of Public Convenience and Necessity. Authority granted by a government regulatory body to operate as a common carrier.

Certificate of Release. A notice by a lender that a mortgage has been paid in full.

Certificate of Title. A written opinion of the condition of a title, based on available records and without guarantee. Certificates of title are used in several fields of business, such as real estate, marketing, and any other area of activity that involves proof of ownership of real property or goods.

Certificate Cheque. A depositor's cheque guaranteed by the issuing bank to be fully covered by funds being in suspension in the account of the depositor who has drawn the cheque.

Certified Public Accountant. An accountant who has been

registered/licensed to practice public accounting and is permitted to call himself a certified public accountant and use the initials CPA after his name.

Certified Transfer. When a shareholder wants to sell only part of his holding, he sends the share certificate with the transfer form to the secretary of the company. The transfer form is then endorsed by the secretary showing that the certificate has been deposited.

Certiorari. A writ of a higher or appellate court to call up the records of an inferior court or other authority that has exercised a judicial function.

Chain of Title. In real estate, history of the conveyances and encumbrances affecting a title from the original grant or patent, or as far back as records are available.

Chain Store. A shop, or store, which is one of many, each in a different location. Examples in India are Bata—manufacturing and selling shoes; Kwality—producing and selling variety of icecreams, etc. Structurally, these shops are organised on a branch basis.

Chairman of a Company. Normally the senior person in a company, and often merely a figurehead who takes no active part but presides as chairman at meetings of directors. An active Chairman is often both Chairman and Managing Director of the company.

Chairman's Report. A report submitted annually on the activities of a company duly signed by the Chairman. It is circulated at the Annual General Meeting and included in the Annual Report. It generally contains tribute to the staff, and discusses the performance of the year and the prospect for the future.

Chamber of Commerce. A registered organisation of industrialists and businessmen. Such organisations are run by an elected council. Federation of Indian Chamber of Commerce and Industry (FICI), Associated

Chamber of Commerce (ASSOCHEM) are two national organisations in India.

Chamber of Shipping. An organisation of ship-owners and others interested in shipping trade, and performing functions similar to a Chamber of commerce. In other words, this organisation is looking after the interest of shippers and ship-owners, advising them on different issues, and making representations on their behalf.

Chance of Loss. In insurance, the relative probability of specific property being destroyed. If the property is certain to be destroyed, the chance of loss is 100 per cent. If the property cannot be destroyed, the chance of loss is zero. The greater the chance of loss, the more likely a person or a company will be to seek insurance.

Changeover Cost. The sum of the setup and tear-down costs for a manufacturing operation.

Charge. In two major senses this term is used in commerce—first, as a synonym for price concerned with sale of goods or services; second, in the context of mortgages and the lending of money. on security. The creditor is said to have a 'charge' on the property, real or personal, provided as Security for the loan.

Charge Account. Another Name for a Credit Account offered by a retailer with a view to attracting more trade by giving customers extended credit items.

Chargeable Gain. A Capital Profit on which tax is payable.

Charter Party. A form of contract between merchant and shipowner.

Chart of Accounts. A systematic listing of accounts by name and number serving as an index for recordkeeping and as rapid account identification for posting and other uses in bookkeeping.

Chattel Mortgage. A mortgage on tangible personal property of a movable nature, such as automobiles or large appliances.

Cheap Money. The value of a particular currency is low compared with the value of goods and services. It describes a condition wherein the general price level is high and a relatively small amount of goods or services may be obtained for a relatively large quantity of money. Also, cheap money is money lent at low interest rates. The term is sometimes used to signify inflated currency.

Check

1. In data processing, partial or complete testing of the accuracy of machine operations or of the correctness of a computer program.
2. Also, a bill of exchange drawn on a bank and payable on demand. The British spelling is *cheque.*

Checkoff. A procedure by which an employer, with written permission of a worker, withholds union dues and other assessments from his or her paychecks and transfers the collected funds to the union. This provides security for the union from the standpoint of prompt collections from its members.

Check Register. In accounting, a journal in which checks are recorded as issued. In data processing, a register used to store information temporarily so that it may be checked against the result of a succeeding transfer of the same information.

Christian Socialism. A movement in the late nineteenth century by various church groups to preach the "social gospel" and promote social legislation and reform that seeks to improve the well-being of the working classes by appealing to Christian ethical and humanitarian principles.

Circulating Capital Good. A capital good that is destroyed in the course of use by a single use. Coal and similarly expendable fuels are examples.

Class Rates. Insurance rates established for large general classes of risks, according to the construction, occupation, and location of the insured property. Also known as minimum rates and tariff rates.

Clearing House. A central agency for the collection, classification, and distribution of information. In finance, an establishment maintained by banks for settling mutual claims and accounts among the members of the establishment.

Clear Title. A title to goods or property that is free of all encumbrances.

Close. The actions that result in adjustments of entries and in the placing of the books of account in order at the end of a month (or any accounting period of less than one year) so that trial balances can be drawn and financial statements prepared.

Closed Account. An account the sum of whose debits and credits are equal.

Closed Corporation. A corporation whose stockholders are few in number and who are generally active in the management of the business.

Closed-end Company. A company that maintains an investment service for a limited group of stockholders, often specializing in a particular type of security, without redemption privileges. Its shares may be listed on a stock exchange.

Closed-end Investment Company. An investment company that has a fixed number of shares of stock outstanding. These shares are traded like other shares of common stock and are not redeemed by the investment company.

Closed-end Mortgage. A mortgage that has no provision for an increase of the loan to satisfy additional financing needs. Opposite of *Open-end Mortgage.*

Closed Mortgage. A mortgage that cannot be paid off before maturity.

Closed Shop. A firm which agrees that a person must be a labor union member before being employed and must remain a member of the union while employed. Closed shops were outlawed which permits only a union shop, when agreed to by the employer and the union.

Closing Statement. A financial summary given to the buyer and seller at the close of a transaction involving the exchange of property for a specific consideration. The statement accounts for all funds received and expended by the escrow holder.

Coinsurance. A coinsurance clause (often found in property insurance) which assumes that the insured will carry insurance equal to a certain percentage of the value of the property. In the event of loss, the insured will recover any partial loss in the proportion that the amount of insurance actually carried bears to the amount of insurance required by the coinsurance clause. The effect of coinsurance is to limit the amount that will be paid on partial losses if the insured does not carry the required amount of insurance.

Collateral. Personal or real property pledged as security for an obligation.

Collateral Trust Bonds. A debt issue that is secured by collateral such as other securities deposited with a trustee.

Collective Agreement. A collective bargaining contract agreed upon by management and a union, describing wages working conditions, and other matters of mutual interest.

Collective Bargaining. Refers to Negotiation between a company's management and a union, which represents the company's employees as its bargaining or negotiating agent, for the purpose of agreeing on mutually acceptable wages and working conditions for the employees.

Collective Farms. Agricultural cooperatives in the Soviet Union, consisting of communities of farmers who pool their resources, lease land from the government, and divide the profits among themselves according to the amount and kind of work done by each. This type of farming, which is subject to detailed government regulation, dominates agriculture in the Soviet Union.

Colour of Title. In real estate, a title that appears to be good but is not. Also known as *apparent title.*

Command Economy. An economic system in which an authoritarian government exercises primary control over decisions concerning what and how much to produce; the government may also decide for whom to produce.

Commercial Bank. A modern term for the joint stock banks functioning with commercial outlook. Functions of a commercial bank comprises: (1) Mobilisation of savings; (2) Financing economic enterprises with short-term loans; (3) Discounting of bills, hundis, etc.; (4) Creation of deposit; (5) Purchasing of shares and securities as an agent of the client; (6) Collection and payment of bills of the client; (7) Money transfer from one place to another by banker's draft; (8) Issue of Letter of Credit and Traveller's Cheque; (9) Dealing in foreign exchange; (10) Administration and execution of estates. At present in India, commercial banks exist in both private and public sector.

Commercial Floater Contract. An insurance policy issued to cover business property that is in the hands of the owner. Several of the most common commercial floaters are: contractor's equipment, installment sales physicians's and surgeons, salesmen's, agricultural mobile equipment, livestock, and paraphernalia.

Commercial Law. The branch of law that that relates to business enterprises and commercial transactions, including contracts, negotiable instruments, estates and trusts, sales, debtors, creditors, corporations, real estate, and securities.

Commercial Paper. Any form of negotiable instrument, such as a check, draft, or bill of exchange.

Commission. Compensation paid to an agent, broker, or employee, related to services performed; usually based on a percentage of the gross amounts involved.

Commission Merchant. An agent or factor through whom goods, wares, and merchandise are sold or to whom they may be consigned for resale, for a compensation referred to as a commission.

Committee Deed. An instrument used for transfer, with court approval, the title to property of an infant or an insane person.

Committee of Incompetent. A court-appointed guardian or guardians of the persons or estate of one adjudged incompetent or insane.

Commodity. Another word for an economic "good"; an article of commerce.

Commodity Rates. A system of freight charges that takes into account the special characteristics of a particular commodity moving between specified points, as related to volume and distance.

Common External Tariff. A customs duty of tariff, charged in common by the member nations of a common trading area and customs union on goods imported from nonmember states.

Common Market. An association of trading nations resulting from the agreement to: (1) impose no trade restrictions, such as tariffs or quotas, among its participants, (2) establish common external barriers to nonparticipants, and (3) impose no national restrictions on the movement of labor and capital among participants.

Common Stocks. Securities representing ownership interest in a corporation. If the corporation has also issued preferred stock, both common and preferred have ownership rights, but the preferred normally has prior claim on dividends and, in the event of liquidation, on assets. Holders of common stock assume the greater risk, but generally exercise more control and may gain greater reward in the form of capital appreciation in addition to dividends. Claims of both stockholdings are junior to claims of bondholders or creditors of the company. The terms "common stock" and "capital stock" are often used interchangeably when the company has no preferred stock. The British term for common stock is *ordinary shares*.

Common Stock Fund. An investment company whose investment policy is to seek profits by investing in common stocks.

Communication. The word 'communication' is derived from the Latin word 'communis' which means 'common' that stands for sharing of ideas in common. The term 'communication' has varied meanings. It refers to various means of transmitting information from one person to another or from one place to another. It also refers to the act of inducing others to interpret an idea in the manner intended by the writer or the speaker.

Companies, Register of. The Register which is maintained by the Registrar of Companies. Name, address, business, and other details of every company are recorded in this Register. Name of the companies are struck off from the Register if the Registrar has reasonable cause for believing that they are not in business.

Company. A Body corporate registered by the Registrar of Companies of a country and whose regulation is governed by the provisions of Company Law existing in the country concerned. In the eye of law, a company is a legal person who can sue and be sued. Companies may be public limited and private limited. They are administered by a group of directors called 'Board of Directors'.

Company, Bubble. A company that has never had any real business or intended to trade honestly, or a company formed with the intention of defrauding the public.

Company, Chartered. A Company established by the Royal Charter of England. These were once more common than they are today—they were used for developing international trade. One well-known company still in existence is the Hudson's Bay Company.

Company, Compulsory Winding-up. It is, in other words, winding up by the court. Circumstances in which a company in India may be wound up by the Court are laid down in Section 433 of the Companies Act, 1956 (as amended) and may be stated as follows: (1) If the company has, by special resolution, resolved that the company may be wound up by the Court; (2) If default is made in delivering the Statutory Report to the Registrar or in holding the Statutory Meeting; (3) If the company does not commence its business within a year from its incorporation, or suspends its business for a whole year; (4) If the number of members is reduced, in case of a public limited company, below seven, and in the case of a private company, below two; (5) If the company is unable to pay its debts.

Company, Joint Stock. These companies grew out of investment by several people on the basis of agreement that profits would be shared by them according to their contribution in the capital. At that time no regulations were practically existing to regulate their functions formally. After the scandal of the South Sea Bubble, however, those early attempts at company formation were abandoned. And from then only the necessity of adequate legislation to effectively control the companies was felt.

In all centuries, joint stock companies are controlled by the Companies Act of respective countries. The Act keeps in view the responsibility of the company to shareholders, creditors, employees, customers, society, state and to the company itself.

Company, Finance. A Company whose business is speculative lending, higher purchase finance. In stricter sense, the term could be applied to financial institutions.

Company, Holding. A Company which controls one or more other companies (subsidiaries), either through the composition of the Board of Directors or by virtue of holding more than 50 per cent of the Nominal Value of the Equity Share Capital, i.e., ordinary shares carrying voting rights.

Special provisions have been laid down in the Companies Act, 1956, for the holding companies in India. A Holding Company is required to publish Group Accounts in the form of (1) a Consolidated Balance Sheet, (2) a Consolidated Profit and Loss Account.

Company, Investment. A Company engaged in using its funds to acquire shares or securities instead of carrying business on its own account. They are not trusts in true sense. For Investment Companies are neither trustees nor there exists any Trust instrument.

Company, Objects. The Memorandum of a Company must contain the object or objects. The general practice is to make the object clause so comprehensive as to include every conceivable lawful act since subsequent alternation of this clause is difficult. Any activity which is outside the expressed provisions of the object clause is considered ultra vires. But the objects which have not been stated in the Memorandum but are conducive or incidental to the main purpose are within the implied jurisdiction of the company. Except in the case of a trading concern, it must also mention the territory to which the objects of the company would extend.

Company, Private (Limited). A Company registered as Private Limited and, hence, comes under the restriction on the right to transfer its shares, limitation on membership not exceeding 50, and cannot invite the public to subscribe for shares. Most of the companies registered in India are private limited. Companies Act, 1956, monitor the functioning of these companies. Under this Act, it is a statutory requirement that such a company must write [Pvt.] on its letterhead, seal, stamp, etc.

Company, Public (Limited). A Company registered under the Company Law of a country unless it satisfies the conditions necessary to constitute it as a private company. Eventually, no restriction exists on the transfer of its shares, no limitation on the number of members and on public issue of capital. In India, Companies Act, 1956, regulate and control the functioning of public limited companies. Under this Act, such a company must have at least 7 shareholders and the Board of Directors should have 3 directors at the minimum and 12 at the maximum, excluding Additional Directors nominated by the Government.

Company, Regulated. An Obsolete type of company originally formed to regulate particular trade(s).

Company Reports. Statutory and Non-statutory Reports which have to be maintained by the companies. Statutory Reports e.g., Auditor's Report, Directors' Report, Report on the Annual Accounts, Additional Director's Report, etc. are required to be maintained under the

Company Law of a country. Non-statutory Reports are not required by any law. Such reports are: (1) Report of directors to shareholders on certain proposals or problems to be submitted at the general meeting; (2) Report of ad hoc committees or standing committees of the board on special matter; (3) Special secretarial report.

Company, Shell. A Company that exists only in name. Occasionally, after a company has ceased to trade and has disposed of all assets and liabilities, it defers applying to be struck off from the Register and sells its name to another business which can thereby minimise the cost of setting a new company.

Company, Unlimited. It is nothing but Large partnerships registered under the Company Law of a country and the members, like partners of recognised as a separate legal entity (i.e. may enter contract as a person separate from its members), and (ii) that the liability of members is limited to the nominal value of the shares they have taken up.

Company, Winding-up. Winding up of a company means its dissolution or liquidation. Several consequences follow when a company is wound up. These consequences are that the company's rights, liabilities and assets are determined, contributions from its members are realised, the creditors are paid off and the balances, if any, are divided among its members in proportion to their respective rights. In this way, the corporate existence of a business is being terminated.

Winding-up of a business may take place due to several reasons as financial bankruptcy, reconstruction, amalgamation, fulfilment of its specified objects, and so on. As such bankruptcy or insolvency is not the sole cause of winding up of a company.

There are three ways or modes of winding-up of a

company in India as provided by Section 425 of the Companies Act, 1956, as amended. The winding-up of a company may be either—(i) by the Court (compulsory Winding up) under Section 433, (ii) Voluntary Winding up (by the members and/or creditors) under Section 484, and (iii) Subject to supervision of the Court under Sections 522-526 of the Companies Act.

Compensating Errors. A Book-keeping term for two separate errors, one on the Debit side and one on the Credit side, which happen to cancel each other out.

Competition. Rivalry among buyers and sellers of goods, services, or resources. Competition tends to be related to the freedom with which buyers and sellers may enter or leave a marketplace.

Competitive Bidding Theory. The theory that the optimum bid in a competitive bidding situation may be determined by balancing the probability of success of each possible bid and the expected profits from each bid.

Competitive Price. The price that is established in a market through the independent actions of a number of buyers and sellers. Also, the price per unit of a commodity sold under conditions of perfect competition.

Complementary Goods. Two or more commodities that related because a change in the quantity demanded of one causes a direct change in the quantity demanded of the other, within a consumer's given budget. For example, if a price decrease in bread causes a consumer to increase his quantity demand for bread and this, in turn, raises his quantity demand for butter, than bread and butter are complementary within his budget.

Completion Bond. An obligation under notary seal posted as a guarantee by a contractor of completion of a project according to conditions described in the contract. Also called *Performance Bond*.

Compound. To add interest to principal at periodic intervals, thereby establishing a new basis for subsequent interest calculations.

Compound Duty. A customs duty consisting of a specific duty to which an ad valorem tax is added.

Compound Interest. The interest made by a lender or a creditor for the loan of money; calculated by the periodic addition of simple interest to principal. The new base thus established becomes the principal amount for computing the interest for the next accounting period. Individuals or organizations placing funds on deposit with a bank or other financial institution that offers savings accounts in effect become lenders to or creditors for the financial institution.

Compound Journal Entry. A journal entry having three or more elements and often representing several transactions.

Compromiser. In organizational behavior, a manager whose style is to use a high task orientation and a high relationship orientation in a situation that requires a high orientation to only one or to neither. This manager is perceived as being a poor decision maker, as one who allows various pressures to influence him too much, and as avoiding or minimizing immediate pressures and problems rather maximizing long-term production.

Comptroller General. The head of the General Accounting Office, an arm of the legislative branch of the federal government. The GAO reports directly to the Congress on the financial position and accounting systems of government agencies and, at the request of Congress, provides critiques related to agency organization and management.

Concentration Banking. A means of accelerating the flow of funds of a firm by establishing strategic collection centers. The purpose is to shorten the period between the time a customer mails in his payment and the time when the company has the use of the funds. The selection of the collection centers is usually based on the geographic areas served and the volume of billings for a given area. When payments are received, they are deposited in the collection center's local bank, eventually reaching the bank or a branch of the bank in which the company maintains its major account.

Conditional Sale Contract. A legally enforceable agreement for the purchase of property on an installment payment basis. The buyer does not receives clear title to the property until all payments have been completed. Also known as instalment sale contract.

Conglomerate. A corporation that diversifies its operations by acquiring enterprises in widely varied industries.

Consignment. Shipping of goods for future sale (or for other purposes) without removal of title or transfer of title from the consignor to the consignee. During the period of consignment the consignee is accountable for the goods, although the goods remain a part of the consignor's inventory until the goods have been sold and title has been transferred to the purchaser. The consignee may become the eventual purchaser or act as an agent in the transaction between the consignor and the buyer of the goods.

Consolidated Balance Sheet. In accounting, a balance sheet in which the assets and liabilities of a controlling company are combined with the corresponding financial data of economic units of the total organization in such a way as to present a combined fiscal report, as though all units of the organization were acting as a single unit.

Consolidated Financial Statement. The statement of the financial condition of two or more economic units of an enterprise, presented in a combined format as though they were one unit, the specific data for one unit not identified separately from those of any other in the same enterprise.

Consolidation. The preparation of a balance sheet or other financial statement into a single format that combines the data of related enterprises, which may be affiliates, divisions, or subsidiaries of a parent or holding company.

Constant-cost Industry. An industry that experiences no increase in resource prices as its production expands, despite new firms entering the market. This happens only when an industry's demand for the resources it employs is an insignificant proportion of the total demand for those resources.

Constant-dollar Value. A dollar value adjusted for fluctuations in purchasing power in order to make possible meaningful comparisons of physical output volumes in a statistical series. To obtain constant-dollar values, current dollar values may, for example, be divided by the price-index number for that year.

Consumer Goods. Merchandise, inventory, or real goods bought or used primarily for nonbusiness, personal family, or household purposes.

Contingency Table. A table designed for the purpose of analyzing, or discovering associations between, qualitative characteristics. It is distinguished from a correlation table, which is restricted to the study of quantitative characteristics.

Contingent Annuity. A periodic payment that is dependent upon some contingency, such as the death or disablement of a person.

Continuous Budget. A moving projection of financial operations for a series of accounting periods immediately ahead. At the end of each period, the part of the projection that has just been completed is removed and a new projection for a period of equal length is added to the series.

Contract. In law, a transaction involving two or more individuals whereby each becomes obligated to the other, with reciprocal rights to demand performance of what is promised. Also, the total legal obligation that results from the parties' agreement as affected by law. A promise or a set of promises that the law recognizes as a duty and that, if breached, has a legal remedy.

Contractual Liability Coverage. Insurance written to cover liability that the insured has voluntarily assumed under a contract with a third party: related to bodily injury and property damage protection.

Contra Entry. An item of an account that partially or totally offsets one or more items on the opposite side of the same account.

Control Account. An account that contains the totals of one or more types of transactions whose details appear in a subsidiary ledger or its equivalent. Its balance equals the sum of the balances of the detail accounts.

Controllable Cost. In accounting, a cost that varies with changes in production. Also, any cost that may be directly controlled and regulated by the management of the unit of an enterprise to which the cost is allocated.

Controller. An accountant whose technical skills and activities are dedicated to a single organization or unit of an organization and who is generally the manager of the bookkeeping and financial recording and reporting functions. Sometimes spelled *comptroller.*

Controller's Deed. An instrument transferring the title to real estate; issued by the state, usually when property is sold due to tax delinquency.

Convenience Goods. Products bought for personal consumption, usually, through retail outlets located near the consumer's residence. Such goods are generally staple items of low unit value, purchased frequently and in low volume. Examples are soft drinks, tobacco, newspapers, ice cream.

Convenience Store. A retail sales establishment, generally located away from major shopping centers and open for long hours every day of the years. Usually stocks a limited range of basic grocery items, and prices are often higher than those found in supermarkets. Only national brand items are stocked to assure rapid turnover of inventory, much of which is perishable. Convenience stores depend for their success on their locations and long hours, providing convenience for the shopper.

Conventional Financing. A loan made without government participation.

Convertible. A bond, debenture, or preferred share that may be exchanged by the owner for common stock or another security, usually of the same company, in accordance with the terms of the issue.

Cooperative. A form of organization whose purpose is to gain for producers or consumers, depending on the type of member organization, the profits or savings that would otherwise accrue to middlemen. Its capital is contributed by the members, who are the stockholders.

Corporation. An artificial being created under law: an association of shareholders, or even a single shareholder. Corporations are legal entities entirely different and distinct from the shareholder (s), with the capacity of continuous existence or succession. As legal entities they may take, hold, and convey property, sue and be sued, and exercise such other powers as may be conferred on them by law, just as natural persons may. A Corporations liability is normally limited to its assests, and its stockholders—unlike those of a *Joint Stock Company*—are protected against personal liability for the affairs of the corporation.

Corpus. The principal or capital of an estate, fund, or trust, as distinguished from the income received.

Correction Deed. A document that corrects an error, even if typographical, in a recorded instrument that transfers the title to real estate.

Cost Accounting. The branch of accounting that deals with the classification, recording, allocation, and summarization of cost factors in the planning or operation of an organization.

Cost and Freight. The price quoted for materials delivered to and unloaded at a named location. The buyer assumes responsibility for all insurance coverage. Abbreviated C & F, usually followed by the name of the destination, such as a city.

Cost Center. A department, division, unit, or other clearly identifiable segment of a business that has no capacity for income, but that for purposes of financial control and analysis is treated budgetarily as an entity. Thus, expenses may be used as a measure of the center's performance.

Cost-effectiveness. A technique introduced by the U.S. Department of Defense and adopted by management in the private sector for analyzing specific expenditures to determine whether the same expenditure could be used more effectively in another direction, or so ascertain whether the expenditure can be reduced without negatively affecting the expected benefit.

Costing. The technique of determining the cost of activities, processes, products, or services.

Cost, Insurance, and Freight. The price quoted for materials delivered to and unloaded at a named location. The seller assumes responsibility for securing all insurance coverage.

Cost Ledger. A subsidiary ledger for the accumulation of accounts used in computing or summarizing the cost of goods manufactured or of services produced.

Cost of Reproduction. The estimated cost, under present economic conditions, of replacing an asset as it was when it was new.

Cost-Plus. An expression used to indicate that the eventual purchase price on the completion of delivery of goods or services to the buyer will be determined on the basis of actual costs plus a predetermined and mutually agreed-upon fee, which may be a lump sum or a fixed percentage of total costs.

Cost-Plus Contract. A contract based on a cost-plus purchase price. Used frequently in government procurement or when it is difficult to estimate costs, as in a contract has the disadvantage that it gives the seller little incentive to keep costs to a minimum.

Cost Standard. In Accounting, a predetermined cost estimate with which actual costs may be compared as a measure of performance. Also known as *Standard Cost.*

Coupon Bond. A bond with interest coupons attached. The coupons are clipped as they come due and are presented by the holder for payment of interest.

Coupon Yield. The yield in percentage terms that is stated on the face of a bond. Determined by dividing the annual interest payment in dollars by the par value of the security and converting this figure into percentage terms.

Coverage. In insurance, the face amount of an insurance policy or the amount of compensation provided by the insurer in the event of specified losses on the part of the insured; all the risks and perils covered by an insurance policy. In marketing, the number of persons or the percentage of a demographic entity that is reached by a medium of communications.

Covering Warrant. In government finance, a document issued by the Secretary of the Treasury and countersigned by the Comptroller General that accompanies a deposit of cash receipts within the federal government.

Credit. The ability to buy or borrow in consideration of a promise to pay within a specified time period following delivery. In accounting, a bookkeeping entry that records the reduction or elimination of an asset or an expense, or the creation of or addition to a liability or item of net worth or revenue. Credit entries are made on the right-hand side of an account. Also, the amount recorded in a credit entry; the balance of a liability, net worth, revenue, or valuation account. As a verb, to record a credit by a bookkeeping entry.

Credit Instrument. A written or printed financial document that serves either as a promise or an order to transfer funds from one person to another, or from one firm to another.

Credit Insurance. Intended to cover losses arising out of credit customers' inability to pay their debts, but only to the extent that losses for the year due to this cause exceed normal losses for the year. Generally written for a 12-month period.

Credit Life Insurance. If a credit purchaser dies, his estate or heirs are subject to the debt. It is customary for commercial banks, finance companies, and credit unions to require borrowers to buy a credit life insurance policy whose face value is at least equal to the amount of the loan. The creditor is named as the beneficiary, and premium payments are included in the borrower's monthly loan payments.

Credit Memorandum. A document notifying a purchaser of goods or services that the supplier has decreased the amount of payment owed. The notice is usually made after an invoice has been rendered and partial payment of the invoice amount has been made.

Creditors' Equity. The total amount of liabilities to outsiders other than stockholders.

Credit Union. A cooperative whose purpose is to promote thrift and to make small loans to members. A credit union may be federally incorporated and under the jurisdiction and audit of the Federal Deposit Insurance Corporation (FDIC).

Creeping Inflation. A slow but persistent upward movement in the general level of prices over a long period of years, typically at an average annual rate of up to 3 per cent.

Crop Insurance. Insurance against failure of or damage to a crop. The risk most frequently insured is loss from hail.

Cumulative Dividend. A dividend on cumulative preferred stock that is payable, under the terms of the issue, at stated intervals and before any distribution is made to the holders of common stock.

Cumulative Preferred Stock. Stock having a provision that if one or more dividends are omitted, the omitted dividends must be paid before dividends may be paid on the company's common stock.

Curable Depreciation. In real estate, deterioration, damage, and wear and tear that are potential causes of equipment or property obsolescence or loss of value, and that are customarily repaired by the owner.

Curb Exchange. Former name of the American Stock Exchange, second largest exchange in the United States. The name comes form the market's origin on a street in downtown New York City.

Current-Asset Cycle. The period of time required for sales to equal current assets.

Current Dollars. A value expressed in dollars and reflecting actual prices of the current year. Economic data are often quoted in current dollars.

Current Liabilities. Debts and financial obligations of a company that are due and payable within one year.

Current Maturity. The portion of a long-term obligation that is to be retired during the next twelve months; usually classified as a *current liability.*

Current Ratio. One of many ratios used to measure the performance of an enterprise and its management; determined by dividing current assets by current liabilities.

Current Yield. The yield of a security determined by dividing its annual interest or dividend payment by the current market price and converting this figure into percentage terms.

Custodial Services. Services rendered by custodians. These include safe keeping of securities, collecting income and information about rights and bonus issues of the companies whose shares are held by the custodian on behalf of investors. These services are rendered by institutions such as Stock Holding Coporation of India Ltd., some banks and finanical institutions.

Customs Duty. A tax that is levied on goods transported from one political jurisdiction to another, especially a tax on goods imported from a foreign country. Such a duty is distinguished from a *customs tariff,* which is a comprehensive schedule of such duties.

Cycle Count. Regular counting (as often as daily) of items in stores on a rotating basis that assures that each item is counted at least once each year.

Cyclical Stock. The equity share of a company whose performance is directly related to economic activity in general. For example, the share of a company dealing in stell, rubber or chemicals is generally regarded as a cyclical stock. Such securities usually move up during a period of vigorous economic activity, and decline as the economy slackens.

Dd

Damages. A sum of money claimed or awarded as compensation for loss or harm suffered by a person or by his property or reputation.

Dated Billing. Also, dating. The practice of giving credit beyond a stated period by forward dating of an invoice.

Dated Securities. Debt instruments issued by the government maturing after a *definite* period. Classified into long-dated, medium-dated and short-dated securities. Long-dated securities have a maturing period exceeding 10 years, medium dated mature between 5 to 10 years, and short-dated securities have a life less than 5 years. Recently, government has stopped issuing securities with more than 10 years life.

Daybook. In accounting, a diary of business activities; a chronological record of the transactions conducted by an enterprise. Entries in the daybook are subsequently entered in a journal and posted to a ledger. Daybooks have become virtually obsolete.

DDP. Trade terms under which the seller must deliver the goods to a named place and must bear all the cost and risks involved in getting them there.

Dealer. In the securities business, an individual or a film acting as a principal rather than as an agent. Typically, a dealer buys for his own account and sells to a customer from his own inventory. The dealer's profit or loss is the difference between the price he pays and the price he receives for the same security. The dealer's confirmation must disclose to his customer that he has acted as principal. The same individual or firm may function at different times either as a broker or as a dealer.

Debenture. A instrument issued by a company acknowledging a debt usually but not necessarily secured by a charge on the company's assets such as land buildings. The instrument contains a provision for the payment of interest at a fixed rate, called the *coupon rate*, and an undertaking to repay the debt on a specific date or at intervals or at the option of the company. In comparison to preference and equity shareholders, debenture holders have a prior claim against earnings (for the payment of interest) and assets in the event of liquidation.

Debenture Capital. Proceeds from the sale of debentures.

Debenture Redemption Reserve (DRR). The reserve created for the purpose of redemption of debentures by companies. As per SEBI guidelines it is obligatory for all companies raising capital through issue of debentures to create a *Debenture Redemption Reserve* equivalent to 50% of the amount of issue before redemption commences. These guidelines are to facilities the servicability and repayment of debentures on times. Creation of Debenture Redemption Reserve is not required for issue of debentures with a maturity period of 18 months or less.

Debit. In accounting, a bookkeeping entry or posting that records the creation of or addition to an asset or expense, or the reduction or elimination of a liability; an entry on the left side of an account. The balance of an asset, expense, or debit valuation account.

Debit Memorandum. A document other than an invoice showing the reason and authority for creating a debit. When issued by a bank, it has the effect of reducing the depositor's or customer's account. It may be issued by a customer to his supplier for goods returned to the supplier.

Debt Collection. Literally the term means Collection from debtors of debts incurred. But it has additional reference to some business enterprises concerned with the collection of debts on behalf of other people or enterprise.

Debt Discount. The difference between the face value of a loan and the net amount received by the borrower. When the discount relates to a loan, such as a bank loan, that represents a current liability, it is treated as a prepaid expense.

Debt-Equity Ratio. The ratio of total debt (short-term and long-term) of a firm to its net worth (shareholder's funds). Shareholder's fund include preference share capital. It is a measure of the relative proportion of debt and equity in financing the assets of a firm. A low debt-equity ratio implies the use of more equity than than debt which means a larger safety margin for creditors since owners equity is treated as a margin of safety by creditors and vice-versa.

Debt Limit. In municipal government accounting, the maximum amount of indebtedness that a government unit may incur; established by constitution, statute or charter.

Debt Service. The payment of matured interest and principal.

Debt Service Coverage Ratio (DSCR). The ratio of net profits after taxes plus depreciation plus interest payments on term loans to the sum of interest and loan repayments:

$$\text{DSCR} = \frac{\text{Profits after taxes} + \text{Depreciation} + \text{Interest charges}}{\text{Interest charges} + \text{Loan repayments}}$$

The ratio indicates how many times interest charges

and loan repayments are covered gross cash accruals. Therefore, this ratio is used to make an assessment regarding financial ability of the borrower to meet its debt obligations.

Debt Service Ratio. The term used in the context of a country's ability to service its external debt. It is a ratio of annual exports revenues from goods and services to repayment obligations of the principal and interest on external debt for the year.

Decision Accounting. This is not separate accounting system, but the accounting information which helps arrive at a decision. For example, decisions on capital expenditure, whether to make or buy, what price to charge, whether to subcontract, and other important matters, may all be assisted by the employment of accounting information. Evidently, Decision Accounting calls upon all other systems to provide information which indicates to management the project likely to maximise profit or minimise loss.

Decision Making. A decision is an act of choice wherein an executive forms a conclusion about what must be done in a given situation. In other words, a decision is the selection of the best course of action from among a set alternatives. The word 'decision' is derived from the Latin word 'Deciso' meaning 'cutting away or cutting off or 'in practical content' to 'come to a conclusion.'

Declaration of Restrictions. In real estate, a recorded list of encumbrances imposed by a subdivider that limit the use of a tract. Deeds to individual lots make reference to this document.

Declared Dividend. A dividend that has been authorized by the board of directors to be paid to the stockholders of record on a specified date.

Declining-balance Method. A method of depreciation in which the annual charge for depreciation is arrived at by applying a fixed percentage to the remaining value of the life of an asset. One of several methods other than the straight-line method for calculating the cost of the lost usefulness or the used-up life of an asset. Usually modified by a quantifier—for example, "double" or "triple" declining-balance method.

Dedicated Manager. A manager who tends to dominate others. He gives many verbal directions to subordinates. His time perspective is immediate. He identifies with superiors and with the technical organizational system. He emphasizes technological rather than human demands. He judges subordinates on quantitative performance and superiors on skill in using power. He believes in punitive corrections. His subordinates often complain about the lack of information. His main weakness is that he argues with others when matters could be solved in other ways. He fears loss of powers.

Deductible Clauses. Insurance clauses that eliminate coverage for minor losses, thereby reducing the relatively high costs of processing and investigating small claims and restraining the growth in premium costs to the insured. There are two forms of deductible clauses found most frequently in property and liability insurance policies; the straight deductible and the franchise deductible.

Deed, Warranty. A deed containing a covenant of guarantee, in which the grantor assures that the title is free from defects, that the property is free of encumbrances other than those listed, and that the grantor agrees to protect the grantee against any loss by reason of the existence of any other title or interest in the property at the time the deed is executed.

Deed of Confirmation. A deed used for correction of errors in other deeds.

Deed of Reconveyance. The transfer of a legal title from a trustee to a trustor after a deed-of-trust debt has been paid.

Deed of Release. A deed used to free land, or a portion thereof, from a mortgage. Also known as *release of mortgage.*

Deed of Trust. A deed to real property held by a trustee to secure the performance by the grantor or another of an obligation owed to the beneficiary of the trust.

Deferred Compensation. Payment that a corporation is committed to make to an executive at some future date, normally, after retirement. The compensation can be in the form of a deferred bonus, a portion of salary, or an additional amount that might have been stipulated in an employment contract. Deferred compensation plans are voluntarily participated in by executives.

Deferred Revenue. Income or revenue received before it is earned. Examples include rent received in advance, transportation fees paid for in advance, and theater tickets paid for in advance.

Deflation. A decline in the general price level of all goods and services, equivalent to a rise in the purchasing power of money, as contrasted with inflation. Also, a statistical adjustment of data by which an economic time series expressed in current dollars is converted into a series expressed in constant dollars of a previous period.

Deflationary Gap. The amount by which the theoretical volume of spending necessary to maintain full employment or to absorb all available goods and services at prevailing prices exceeds actual private spending and government expenses.

Demand Deposit. The promise by a bank to pay immediately an amount specified by the customer who owns the deposit. It is thus checkbook money, permitting transactions to be paid for by check rather than with currency.

Demand Schedule. A table showing the number of units of a commodity that buyers would be willing and able to purchase at various possible prices during a given period of time. All other factors remaining the same.

Democratic Leadership. A style of management in which the leader plays a permissive role, sharing the functions of leadership with the members of the group by encouraging their participation in goal setting and in planning and directing the activities of the group.

Demurrage. A penalty charge against shippers or receivers for delaying carrier equipment beyond allowed free time. The term has been in use since early in the seventeenth century, when it meant the delay of a vessel beyond its scheduled sailing time and the payment for the delay. It was later extended to include rail transport.

Depletion. Lessening in value as a result of the using up of an asset; the use of a natural resource at a rate greater than its replacement rate.

Depositary. An institution such as a bank that accepts cash deposits from customers; also, an individual or organization that receives any type of property for safekeeping. "Depositary" and "depository" may be used interchangeably; at one time "depositary" was a person and "depositary" a place.

Depreciated Cost. The cost of an asset less the accumulated depreciation; the book value of a fixed asset.

Depreciation. The used-up portion of the life of a fixed asset; expired or lost utility; the process of estimating and recording lost usefulness. According to the AICPA. depreciation is a process of allocation, not of valuation.

Depreciation Accounting. A branch of accounting that deals with systematically distributing or allocating the cost or other basic value of a fixed asset over its estimated useful economic life by means of periodic charges to expense or against revenue.

Depreciation Base. The recorded cost of a fixed asset or fixed-asset group that is to be recovered through depreciation, not including the estimated amount that may be recovered from sale or salvage of the asset.

Depreciation Expense. The portion of the cost of a fixed asset or fixed-asset group that is charged against operations for an accounting period. Also, any provision for depreciation.

Depreciation Fund. Assets in the form of money or marketable securities that have been set aside or reserved for the purpose or replacement of fixed assets that are depreciating.

Depression. A phase of the business cycle characterized by industrial and commercial stagnation, scarcity of money and goods, low prices, poor expectations, and mass unemployment. Similar to a recession, but more severe and lengthy in its effects and duration.

Derivative Securities. Refers to securities such as options and futures whose value depends upon value of other assets that underlie them.

Deterministic Inventory Models. In manufacturing, inventory models used where the actual demand for a time period is known. Such a model may be employed, for example, by a company that produces to a specific backlog.

Devaluation. An official act that makes a domestic currency cheaper in terms of gold or foreign currencies, generally to increase a nation's exports while reducing its imports.

Dilution. In finance, the weakening of an equity position caused by a reduction in the value of a corporation's stock.

Diminishing Returns. The principle that as more of a variable factor is applied to a fixed factor, the output increases less than proportionately. An input whose quantity a business can vary at will is the variable factor of production; an input that cannot be increased is the fixed factor.

Dinar. Basic unit of currency in Algeria, Bahrein, United Arab Emirates, Iraq, Jordan, Kuwait, Libya, People's Democratic Republic of Yemen, Tunisia, and Yugoslavia.

Director. A person selected by shareholders to establish company policies. The directors appoint the president, vice presidents, and all other operating officers. They also decide, among other matters, if an when dividends shall be paid.

Direct Overhead. Factory, selling, or any other expense that may be charged directly to the processing or manufacturing of a specific product or service.

Direct Placing. A placing of shares in a company direct to investors, without recourse to underwriters to back the deal or to public subscription.

Direct Reduction Loan. A loan repayable in consecutive equal monthly installments, paying interest and principal sufficient to retire the debt within a definite period. "Direct" means that after the monthly interest amount has been deducted from the amount of the payment, the remainder is applied directly to the reduction of the principal of the loan.

Direct Taxation. Taxation, the effect of which is intended to be borne by the person or organization that pays it. Economists distinguish between direct taxation and indirect taxation. The former is best illustrated by income tax, in which the person who receives the income pays the tax, thereby suffering a reduction in income. The latter is illustrated by VAT in which the tax is paid by traders but the effects are borne by the consumers who buy the trader's goods. In practice these distinctions are rarely clear-cut. Corporation tax is a direct tax but there is evidence that its incidence can be shifted to consumers by higher prices or to employees by lower wages.

Disbursement List. A printed list containing the identity and quantity of part and assemblies to be withdrawn from stock and dispatched to the starting point of manufacture or assembly on a given day.

Discounted Cash Flow. A method of analyzing investments in which future cash flows are discounted, or converted to their present values.

Discount Rate. The interest rate charged by Reserve Banks on loans to members banks. The interest is discounted when the loan is made, rather than collected when the loan is repaid.

Discretionary Account. An account in which a client gives his stockbroker or someone else power of attorney as to the purchase and sale of securities and commodities, including selection, timing, amount, and price to be paid or received. This discretionary power may be with or without specific limits.

Discretionary Income. Income over and above that required for the basic consumer needs of food, clothing, and shelter.

Discretionary Order. Power given to stockbroker to act on behalf of a client with respect to the choice of securities to be bought or sold, the total amount to be bought or sold, and whether any transaction shall be for the purpose of buying or selling.

Dishonor. To fail to pay or accept a bill or other negotiable instrument.

Dispatch Earning. An economy or saving in shipping costs as a result of promptly discharging cargo at its destination.

Disposable Personal Income. Income remaining after payment of personal taxes.

Diversifiable Risk (or Unsystematic Risk) Risk associated with factors causing movement in specific firm or industry. This risk is avoidable by diversification.

Divided Account. In the sale of securities through underwriting syndicates, a divided account is one in which the liability of the members of the syndicates is limited to their percentage participation. If the member sells all the securities alloted him under his participation, he has no liability, regardless of whether or not other members are able to sell their allotments.

Dividend. The dividend is generally expressed as an amount per share on the par value of the share. The size of the dividend payment is determined by the board of directors of a company, who must decide how much to pay out to shareholders and how much to retain in the business; these amounts may vary from year to year. In many countries it is usual for companies to pay a dividend every six months, the largest portion (the *final dividend*) being announced at the company's AGM together with the annual financial results. A smaller interim dividend usually accompanies the interim statement of the company's affairs, six months before the AGM. Dividends are paid by dividend warrant.

Dividend Equalization Reserve. A reserve formerly created to smooth out fluctuations in the incidence of taxation so that dividends could be maintained. Such reserves are now normally referred to as *deferred-tax accounts*.

Dividend Limitation (Dividend Restraint). An economic policy in which the dividends a company can pay to its shareholders are limited by government order. It is usually part of a prices and income policy to defeat inflation.

Dividend Mandate. A document in which a shareholder of a company notifies the company to whom dividends are to be paid.

Dividend Waiver. A decision by a major shareholder in a company not to take a dividends, usually because the company cannot afford to pay it.

Dividend Warrant. The cheque issued by a company to its shareholders when paying dividends. It states the tax deducted and the net amount paid. This document must be sent by non-taxpayers to the Inland Revenue when claiming back the tax.

Documentary Bill. A bill of exchange attached to the shipping documents of a parcel of goods. These documents include the bill of lading, insurance policy, dock warrant, invoice, etc.

Documents Against Acceptance (D/A). A method of payment for goods that have been exported in which the exporter sends the shipping documents with a bill of exchange to a bank or agent at the port of destination. The bank or agent releases the goods when the bill has been accepted by the consignee.

Dollar. The standard monetary unit of Antigua and Barbuda (EC$), Australia ($A), Bahamas (B$), Barbados (BDS$), Belize (BZ$) Bermuda (Bd$), the British Virgin Islands (US$), Brunei (B$), Canada (Can$), Cayman Islands (CI$), Dominica (EC$), Fiji (F$), Grenada (EC$), Guam (US$), Guyana (G$), Hong Kong (HK$), Jamaica (J$), Kiribati ($A), Liberia (L$), Micronesia (US$), New Zealand ($NZ), Puerto Rico (US$), Saint Kitts and Nevis (EC$), Singapore (S$), the Solomon Islands, (SI$),

Taiwan (NT$), Trinidad Tobago (TT$), Tuvalu ($A), the USA (US$), the Virgin Islands (US$), and Zimbabwe (Z$), in all cases divided into 100 cents.

Dollar Cost Averaging. A system of buying securities on the stock market at regular intervals with a fixed dollar amount. Under this system, the investor buys by the dollar amount rather than by the number of shares. If each investment is of the same number of dollars, payments may buy more shares when the price is low and fewer when it rises. Thus, temporary downswings in price benefit the investor if he continues periodic purchases in both good times and bad and if the price at which the shares are sold is more than their average cost.

Dollar Pool. The fund of dollars and other currencies held to enable UK residents to buy foreign securities, domestic property, etc. It was abolished in 1979 when UK exchange control was abandoned.

Dormant Partner. A partner who plays an inactive role in the management of a business and who is not known to the public as having an interest in the enterprise.

Double Indemnity. An insurance policy provision insurance policy that the insurer will pay twice the face amount of the policy if the insured dies as a result of an accident.

Double Insurance. Coverage of the same property or risk by two insurance policies.

Double Taxation. Short for double taxation of dividends. The federal government taxes corporate profits once as corporate income. Any remaining profit distributed as dividends to shareholders is taxed again as income to the receiver-shareholder.

Dow-Jones Industrial Average (DJIA). A quantitative measure of the performance of the stocks of corporations listed on the New York Stock Exchange. The DJIA is based on 30 industrial stocks, which some critics contend are not truly representative of the majority of issues traded daily. The 30 stocks are blue chip stocks that behave differently from the norm. Regardless, the DJIA is often used as a barometer of the performance, rise, and decline of the stock market.

Downstairs Merger. A merger in which a parent corporation becomes a subsidiary.

Down Tick. In the stock market, a transaction made at the same price as the preceding sale but lower than the preceding different price. Indicated at each trading post on the floor of the NYSE by a minus sign next to the last price of the stock traded. Also called *minus tick.*

Draft. A written order draw by one party, the drawer that orders a second party, the drawee to pay a specified amount of money to a third party, the payee.

Drawback. A refund of duty paid on imported goods that are subsequently shipped out of the country.

Dualism Concept. In accounting, the recognition of Credit and Debit as the two basic elements of transactions both within and outside a business enterprise.

Dual-Purpose Fund. A closed-end fund that sells income shares and capital shares. Owners of income shares receive all the income the company obtains through dividend and interest payments. Owners of capital shares receive the profits the company obtains from capital gains.

Due Bill. A statement of charges for services rendered, containing details of the services and terms and dates when the amounts due are considered payable. In transportation, a due bill covers additional charges when an original bill for freight charges was too low or in error. Sometimes used to indicate a receipt signed for ocean bills of lading delivered with specified credit privileges.

Due Date. In purchasing, the expected date or receipt for a part: in manufacturing, the expected completion date of a part.

Due-Date Rule. In manufacturing, the sequencing of jobs to be run on the basis of due dates, taking the earliest due date as the first job to be run.

Duration. The weighted average maturity of bond or debenture where the weights are the relative present values of each payment. In simple terms, it is the average time within which a bond's cash inflows are received. It takes into account the amount and timing of every cash inflow, rather than the time span till the final inflow. This measure, a contribution of F. Macualay in 1938, is computed from the formula given below.

$$\text{Duration} = \sum_{t=1}^{n} \left\{ t \times \frac{\text{Present value of cash flow in time } t}{\text{Present value of the security}} \right\}$$

Here, n is the term to maturity and t stands for different periods.

Duty. A charge assessed by a government on imported or exported goods.

Duty Free. Description of goods exempted from customs duty.

Ee

Eearmarking. Setting aside specific tax revenues for specific services or projects.

Earned Income. Income received as payment in connection with one's occupation. Under current regulations, most forms of executive compensation, including salaries, bonuses, and gains from nonqualified stock options, are classified as earned income.

Earning Per Share (EPS). The net profits of a company expressed on a per (equity) share basis. It is arrived at by dividing the figure of profits after taxes and dividends paid on preference shares, if any, by the number of equity shares outstanding. Therefore, it does not reveal the potential impact of dilution in earnings on account of securities such as convertibles or warrants that may be outstanding. Moreover, an improvement in EPS does not necessarily indicate a more productive use of the total amount of funds available with a firm.

Earnings Report. A statement issued by a company showing its earnings or losses over a given period, usually one fiscal year. It lists the income earned, expenses, and net results. In order to facilitate comparison with the performance of previous years, it is usual practice to display current earnings along with a statistical report or analagous data for the preceding years, often going back as far as years. Also known as *income statement or profit and loss statement*.

Easement. In real estate, an intangible, usually nonprofitable, right of one person to the use or enjoyment of the property of another. *Public easements* deal with the rights of the general public.

Economic Activity. The production and distribution of goods and services. Also, the contribution of persons to the production and distribution of useful goods and services.

Economic Entity. A unit of an organization, not necessarily a legal entity; for example, a profit center of a corporation.

Economic Life. In accounting, the period during which a fixed asset is capable of yielding services that are useful to its owner.

Economic Man. In classical economics, an imaginary individual in a capitalistic society—a worker, entrepreneur, consumer, or invester—conceived of as motivated by economic forces. Thus this individual will always act to obtain the greatest satisfaction for the least sacrifice or cost. Satisfaction may take the form of profits to an entrepreneur or investor, leisure hours to a worker, or pleasure to a consumer from the goods and services purchased.

Economic-man Theory. The theory that employee motivation depends almost entirely on financial incentives. During the mid-1940s, as the behavioral sciences developed, the theory was discounted on the basis that there are other kinds of motivation, some of which may be more important to the individual than the financial incentive.

Economics. A social science concerned chiefly with the way society chooses to employ its limited resources to produce goods and services for present and future consumption.

Economic Sanction. A Call by a nation or of many to impose boycotts and embargo on trade with another who either refuses to respect treaties or advocate policies and actions which are not acceptable to the former. It is generally the common practice in an attempt to disrupt the economy of the offending nation. Such economic sanctions were employed by the U.K. and other countries against Rhodesia with a view to forcing it to retract from nationalist policies which followed its unilateral declaration of independence.

Economy, Mixed. An Economic system which has emerged from an attempt to integrate the good features of capitalism and socialism. Under this system, production and consumption of goods and services are not only regulated by the market forces and price but by the state also. The State, as such, enters production and distribution of goods and services. Economic development is aimed at achieving through planned efforts by the state. Restrictions are imposed on using property not beneficial to the society. Social welfare and equitable distribution of national wealth are given top priority in economic planning and policy formulation of the government.

Efficient Frontier. The Set of efficient portfolios.

Efficient Portfolio. A portfolio that offers the highest expected return at a given level of risk or the lowest risk at a given level of expected return.

Eighty-twenty Rule. In marketing, an empirical rule reflecting the common experience that relatively small proportion (20 per cent) of items in a company's catalogue generate a large proportion (80 per cent) of the company's total activity in sales. The rule also states that approximately 20 per cent of the customers are responsible for 80 per cent of the sales volume. Some managers claim the same is relatively true of the sales effort, that 20 per cent of the sales force produces 80 per cent of the orders.

Ejectment. A statutory action to recover the possession or real property.

Elevating Charge. Services charge performed in connection with floating or mobile elevators; also, a charge assessed for handling grain through stationary grain elevators.

Embargo. A government order prohibiting goods from entering the country. May be placed against a nation, prohibiting any of its products from entering the country, or against a specific product regardless of its national source.

Emolument. The return from personal labor received or accrued in the from of compensation, such as a salary, wage, fee, commission, award, price concession, or other personal benefit.

Employee Contribution. The money individual employees pay to participate in company benefit plans, especially common in the areas of insurance, pension, and savings plans. The usual practice is to deduct employee contributions directly from their paychecks.

Employment. Indicates Regular occupation. Opportunities of regular occupation depend on a country's overall economic development achieved. In any country, employment opportunities are created broadly by industrial sector, agricultural sector and service sector. With the expansion of those sectors employment opportunity increases, in the sense that new jobs are created for people.

Endorsement. Insurance companies usually print standard contracts in large quantities. An endorsement is a separate document or additional clause physically attached to the standard policy form for the purpose of amending the standard contract. Also known as a *rider,* especially when the amendment is contained on a separate sheet of paper attached to the original contract.

Enterprise. A business undertaking. Unless otherwise qualified, the entirely of an organization rather than a unit or subdivision. Also, that quality of business management identified with energy, initiative, resourcefulness, and adaptability.

Entity. Existing, in being. For legal purposes, the artificial person created when a corporation is organized in an entity separate from the stock-holders. The estate of a deceased person while in administration, a partnership, and the status of marriage are other examples of legal entities.

Equalizing Dividend. A dividend paid to correct inequities caused by changes in established regular dividend dates. As an example, when two companies are merged and each has a different dividend date, an equalizing dividend may be paid.

Equation of Exchange. An expression of the relation between the quantity of money (M), its velocity of circulation (V), the average price of finished goods and services (P), and the physical quantity of those goods and services (Q):

$$MV = PQ$$

The equation in fact states that the total amount of money spent on goods and services (MV) is equal to the total amount of money received for goods and services (PQ).

Equilibrium Income Level. The particular level of income in an economy at which aggregate demand and aggregate supply are in balance.

Equilibrium Level of Output. The particular level of output in an economy at which aggregate demand and aggregate supply are equal.

Equilibrium Price. A price that equates the quantity demanded with the quantity supplied. It balances the behavior of buyers with that of sellers, thus clearing the market.

Equilibrium Quantity. The quantity of a good that is bought and sold when a market is in equilibrium.

Equipment Trust Certificate. A type of security issued—generally by a railroad—to pay for new equipment. Title to the equipment, such as a locomotive, is held by a trustee until the notes are paid off. The certificate is usually secured by a first claim to the equipment.

Equitable Owner. One who has conveyed the title to property in trust but retains the right to use and enjoy the property.

Equity. In finance, right or claim to an asset. A holder of an equity may be a creditor, part owner, proprietor, or stockholder. Also, an interest in the property or in a business that is subject to claims of creditors. Generally used as a statement of the amount or percentage of ownership interest.

Equity Financing. The sale of capital stock by a corporation for cash or other things of value to the operation of the corporation.

Equity Receiver. A person appointed by a court of equity at the request of the owner, or of creditors, to take control of a property with the intention either to reorganize it and operate it until it can be returned to the owner or to discontinue operations and distribute any remaining assets.

Equity Risk Premium. The rate by which expected (or actual) rate of return on equity shares exceeds the expected (or actual return) on a risk-free asset.

Equity Security. A transferable certificate of ownership; sometimes used in connection with capital stock, stock warrants, or indebtedness convertible into stock. Also a controlling company's interest and holding of stocks, bonds, notes, and other formal evidences of ownership or indebtedness of a subsidiary.

Equity Transaction. Any transaction that has the effect of increasing or decreasing net worth.

Errors and Omissions Excepted (E. & O.E.). These initials are commonly included at the end of an Invoice. The idea is to absolve person issuing the invoice from clerical error. However, the legal support to it is doubtful.

Escalation Clause. A clause often included in a contract which may take some time to complete. Such a clause, if accepted with the contract, enables the contractor to increase the price when incidence of inflation causes costs to rise. The rate of increase, etc. is detailed in the clause with appropriate notes. Escalation Clause may be found incorporated in the Tender submitted for construction work.

Escudo. The standard monetary unit of Cape Verde (CV Esc) and Portugal (Esc); it is divided into 100 centavos.

Estate. The sum total of a person's assets less liabilities (usually as calculated at death for the purposes of inheritance tax). Or a substantial piece of land, usually attached to a large house.

Estate Duty. A former tax on the estate of a deceased person at the time of death. This tax applied in the UK from 1894 to 1974, when it was converted to capital-transfer tax. The latter tax became inheritance tax in 1986, when it reverted to a form of taxation similar to the former estate duty. The tax is levied on the assets less the liabilities of the deceased, taking into account (to forestall avoidance) certain gifts made in a defined period before the death.

Eurobond. A bond issued in a eurocurrency, which is now one of the largest markets for raising money (it is much larger than the UK stock exchange). The reason for the popularity of the eurobond market is that secondary market investors can remain anonymous, usually for the purpose of avoiding tax. For this reason it is difficult to ascertain the exact size and scope of operation of the market. Issues of new eurobonds normally take place in London, largely through syndicates of US and Japanese investment banks; they are bearer securities, unlike the shares registered in most stock exchanges, and interest payments are free of any withholding taxes. There are various kinds of Eurobonds.

Eurocheque. A cheque drawn on a European bank, available in 39 countries, which can be cashed at any bank or bureau de change in the world that displays the EC sign (of which there are some 200000). It can also be used to pay for goods and services in shops, hotels, restaurants, garages, etc., that display the EC sign (over 4 million). The cheques are blank and are made out for any amount as required, usually in the local currency. They have to be used with a Eurocheque Card which guarantees cheques for up to about £100. In most cases, a commission of 1.25% is added to the foreign currency value of the cheque before it is converted to sterling and there is a cheque charge (for cheques drawn on UK banks).

Euroclear. One of two settlement houses for the clearance of eurobonds. Based in Brussels, it was set up in 1968 by a number of banks. The other settlement house is Centrale de Livraison de Valeurs Mobilieres.

Euro-commercial Paper (ECP). Commercial paper issued in a eurocurrency, the market for which is centered in London. It provides a quick way of obtaining same day funds by the issue of unsecured notes, for example in Europe for use in New York.

Eurocurrency. A currency held in a European country other than its country of origin. For example, dollars deposited in a bank in Switzerland are eurodollars, yen deposited in Germany are euroyen, etc. Eurocurrency is used for lending and borrowing; the *eurocurrency market* often provides a cheap and convenient form of liquidity for the financing of international trade and investment.

Eurodeposit. A deposit using the currency of another country, i.e. a transaction in the eurocurrency market.

Eurofrancs. The monetary franc dealt in and traded outside France but within the member states of the Common Market.

Euromark. The monetary mark dealt in and traded outside the Federal Republic of Germany but within member states of the Common Market.

Euronote. A form of euro-commercial paper consisting of short term negotiable bearer notes. They may be in any currency but are usually in dollars or ECUs. The *euronote facility* is a form of note issuance facility set up by a syndicate of banks, which underwrites the notes.

Event Studies. Studies that measure the impact of price sensitive events on stock's returns.

Exact Interest. In accounting, simple interest based on a year of 365 days, as compared with ordinary interest and a base of 360 days. The ratio of exact interest to ordinary interest is 0.9863878; the reciprocal is 1.0138.

Excess Deductions Account. Generally, an accounting record that taxpayers who claim losses from farming operations are required to keep for federal income-tax purposes.

Excess Freight. Freight in excess of that shown on the original carrier billing.

Excess Issue. In manufacturing, the quantity of parts issued to a shop order in excess of the quantity required by the bill of material.

Excess-line Insurance. Insurance obtained by a firm or individual through a foreign or alien insurance company. Lloyd's of London is well known for writing excess-line insurance coverage.

Excess Return. The excess of the actual rate of return on a security over the return on a riskfree asset.

Exchange Cheque. A cheque given in exchange for cash or for another cheque.

Exchange Distribution. In securities trading, a method of disposing of large blocks of stock on the floor of an exchange. Under certain circumstances, a member broker can facilitate the sale of a block of stock by soliciting and getting other member brokers to solicit orders to buy. Individual buy orders are lumped together and crossed with the sell order in the regular auction market. A special commission is usually paid by the seller; ordinarily the buyer pays no commission.

Ex-Dividend. In securities transactions, synonym for "without dividend." The buyer of a stock selling ex-dividend does not receive the recently declared dividend.

Executive. In organizational behavior, descriptive of a manager who uses a high task orientation and a high relationships orientation in a situation where such behavior is appropriate and who is therefore more effective. Such a manager sets high standards, treats everyone somewhat differently prefers team management, and is therefore often perceived as a good motivating force.

Executive Routine. A computer routine that controls the loading and relocation of routines and in some cases makes use of instructions that are unknown to the general programmer. Also knows as *supervisory routine.*

Exemplary Damages. In a tort action, the sum assessed as punishment by the jury, above the compensatory damages, in order to make an example of the wrongdoer as a deterrent to others who might consider similar conduct. Injuries caused by willful, malicious, wanton, and reckless conduct will subject the offender to exemplary damages.

Exercise Provisions. The clauses in a stock option award governing the timing, amounts, and costs at which the option can be exercised by the recipient.

Export-Import Bank of India (EXIM Bank). Established in 1982, a bank in India with an authorised capital of Rs. 200 crores. It is the principal financial institution for the country's foreign trade and for co-ordinating the working of similar institutions. This bank offers financial assistance for exports of capital and engineering goods, turnkey and construction projects, consultancy services, and selling of joint ventures abroad—involving deferred payment terms.

Export-Import Merchant. A merchant who specializes in international trade, selling domestically produced goods in markets overseas, or purchasing goods made overseas and reselling them to customers in the domestic market.

Ex-Rights. In securities transactions, synonym for "without the rights." Corporation raising additional capital may do so by offering their stockholders the right to subscribe to new or additional stock, usually at a discount from the prevailing market price. The buyer of a stock selling ex-rights is not entitled to the rights.

Extended Cost. In accounting, the cost of a unit of material or of a single product multiplied by the quantity of the material or product.

Externalities. The benefits or costs accruing to some individual or group not involved directly as a buyer or seller in a market transaction.

Extraordinary Depreciation. Depreciation caused by unusual wear and tear, obsolescence, unexpected disintegration, or an inadequacy beyond what can be attributed to loss of physical or useful life through ordinary circumstances.

Extraordinary Item. The term used for an item of profit or loss appearing in Profit and Loss Account of a firm which is non-repetitive in nature. Examples include substantial gains on sale of land and building or gains from market purchasing of debentures issued by the company.

Ff

Face Value. The nominal value of a security. The value of a bond, which appears on the face of the bond, unless the value is otherwise specified by the issuing company. Face value is ordinarily the amount the issuing company promises to pay at maturity; it is not an indication of market value. The face value helps to know the share of ownership in a company.

Factor. An individual or a firm that buys trade receivables with or without recourse. The profit to the factor as a result of the transaction derives from a commission and from interest payments on advances the factor may make against receivables. As an agent in the sale of merchandise, a factor may hold possession of the goods in his own name or in the name of his principal. He is authorized to sell and to receive payment for the goods.

Factor Beta. A relative measure of the sensitivity of the return on a common factor with the return on the market portfolio. Mathematically, it is the covariance of the factor returns with the market return divided by the variance of the market rate of return.

Factor Model (or Index Model) A return generating process that attributes the return on a security to the sensitivity of that security's rate of return to the movements of various common factors.

Factor's Lien. In law, the right of a factor to keep possession of goods consigned to him for the purpose of reimbursing himself for all advances previously made to the consignor of the goods.

Factory Ledger. A subsidiary ledger that contains the operating costs of a manufacturing establishment, such as materials, labor, and factory overhead.

Factory Mutual Company. An insurance company that provides coverage exclusively for factory property.

Factory Overhead. Also known as manufacturing or factory or works overhead. It is the indirect cost of production that includes indirect material, indirect labour and other indirect-expenses, incurred for operating the manufacturing or production division of a factory.

Fallacy of Composition. The erroneous assumption that what is true of one part is necessarily true of the whole. This is a common problem in economics: what is good for a firm or single family may not be good for the aggregate of all firms or families.

Farm Mutual Company. An insurance company that insures farm property exclusively.

FAS. *Free Alongside.* Indicates that the buyer assumes responsibility for materials after they have been delivered to a vessel and are ready for loading.

Fee Simple Estate. In law, complete ownership of land. Such an estate passes upon the death of the owners to the heirs, free from any conditions. Opposed to an *estate for life,* in which all rights to the land cease with the death of the owner. Also known as *estate in fee simple.*

Fiduciary. A person in a position of trust and confidence, as a broker with respect to a principal. The broker as a fiduciary owes a loyalty that cannot be breached under the rules of agency.

FIFO. Acronym for *first in, first out*; in accounting, a method of inventory costing based on the assumption that costs should be charged against revenue in the order in which they are incurred. Thus inventory is valued on the basis of actual cost at the time of acquisition and, as consumed, is charged to cost of sale accordingly.

Fill-or-Kill Order. A market or limited-price order to a stockbroker that is to be executed in its entirety as soon as it is presented to the exchange. If not so executed, the order is treated as canceled.

Final Average Pay. An individual's earnings during the final period of employment or participation in a compensation plan, typically the last three, five, or ten years' average pay. It is used particularly in the calculation of pension benefits.

Financial Assets. Intangible assets, such as shares and debentures, that represent a claim against real assets or against income generated by these assets, or a claim against a government.

Financial Risk. In the securities market, the uncertainty of future returns from a security because of changes in the financial capacity of the organization that issued the security. Sometimes called *business risk.*

Finished Goods. Products that are ready for shipment to a customer. Also known as *end item* and *end product.*

First in System, First Served. A rule used in decision-making for production scheduling that is based on the due dates for orders waiting in line. The order that has the earliest planned due date will be assigned first.

First Mortgage. A mortgage that has priority as a lien over all other mortgages. Also called *senior mortgage* and *first loan.*

Fiscal Drag. A large budgetary surplus that might be created by the tax system as the economy approaches full employment. It may act as a brake on the expansion of the economy.

Fiscal Monopoly. A government monopoly created to generate revenue. Commodities such as salt and tobacco, for example are sometimes reserved for sale by the government, and their profits are used for public purposes.

Fiscal Year. Any 12 months in sequence selected as an accounting period, not necessarily corresponding with the calender year. The fiscal year of the U.S. government, for example, ends September 30 of each year.

Fixation. In the behavior of an individual, fixation occurs when a person repeats the same negative pattern over and over again, despite experiences that show that it accomplishes nothing. Frustration can freeze old and habitual responses and prevent the use of new and more effectual ones. Common symptoms of fixation in business are the inability to accept change and stubborn refusal to accept new facts when experience shows the old ones to be untenable.

Fixed Charge. A regularly recurring expense, such as rent or interest, that the company must pay. A fixed expense is deducted from income before earnings on equity capital are computed.

Fixed Cost. An operating expense that does not vary with the volume or activity of business or of production. Also known as *fixed expense*, or *constant cost*

Fixed-Reorder Cycle. In manufacturing, a system of inventory control that operates by placing orders for replenishment of stock at regular intervals. The size of the reorder is varied to absorb the variations in usages, so that the maximum inventory is maintained at a predetermined level.

Flat. A security market term referring usually to the sale of a bond. A bond is sold "flat" if its trading price includes consideration of all unpaid accruals of interest. This is the common form of trade for bonds that are in default of interest or principal. All other bonds are usually dealt in "and interest," which means that the buyer pays the seller the market price plus interest accrued since the last payment date. When applied to a stock loan, "flat" means without premium or interest.

Flexible Budget. A budget with alternative provisions that are based on varying rates of activity.

Float. In finance, moneys, usually in the form of checks, en route to the payee but not yet credited to the payee's account. The payor of the check may have, in the process of effecting payment, deposited the check with a corresponding bank. In effect the deposit may not have yet been made in the payee's bank nor credited to the payee's account. The payee, therefore, may not draw against the deposit that is in "float". However, at its own discretion the payee's bank may waive this restriction. The word "float" is also used to indicate transmittal documents that are en route to a destination wherein they are to be exercised.

Floater Policy. A type of insurance policy or contract covering property that "floats" or moves about from place to place, or goods of a class in which the particular items change or shift in quantity over relatively short time periods.

Floating Address. An address written in such a way that it can be easily converted to a machine address by indexing, assembly, or some other means.

Floating Capital. That portion of the capital of a business firm that is not invested in fixed or capital assets but in current and working assets.

Floating Coverage. A type of insurance coverage common for property that is being transported from one place to another. Such property includes airplanes, boats, and other goods that are of necessity moved from place to place.

Floating Debt. Current liabilities: Short-term obligations. Floating and funded debts represent the total liabilities to outsiders.

Floating Exchange Rates. Foreign exchange rates determined in a free market by supply and demand.

Flood Insurance. Such insurance is generally difficult to obtain in areas subject to flooding because of the frequency of catastrophic losses. A federal flood insurance program has been authorized to make such protection available at reasonable rates.

Floor Broker. A member of a stock exchange who executes orders on the floor of the exchange to buy or sell any listed security.

FOB. Abbreviation for *free on board*. FOB indicates the point at which the buyer assumes responsibility for the goods. For example, FOB *factory* means that the buyers assumes responsibility for the goods when they leave the factory. FOB *railroad* means that the buyer assumes responsibility after the goods have been placed on railroad cars.

Forced-Sale Value. The amount derived from a sale of assets or goods on an urgent basis, usually where the seller is under legal or economic compulsion to sell.

Foreign Corporation. In state corporation laws, a corporation that has been created under the laws of a state or country other than the one in which the corporation is officially located. In federal law, a corporation established under the laws of another country.

Foreign Exchange Rate. Price of one currency in terms of the currency of another country.

Forfeitures. Funds relinquished by a terminating employee in a qualified profit-sharing or thrift plan. These funds are sometimes used by the company to reduce future company contributions to the plan, or they may be allocated to current participants to increase their shares.

Forgery. The alteration or false writing of an instrument with the intent of deceiving and injuring another person; for example, signing someone's name to a cheque without his or her consent.

Formula Pension. The category of pension covering most salaried employees, under which a rate formula is applied to individual earnings to calculate the employee's pension.

Franc. Basic unit of currency in Belgium, Burundi, France, Guinea, Luxembourg, Malagasy Republic, Mali, Rwanda, and Switzerland.

Franchise. An agreement whereby one enterprise, the franchisor, extends to another, the franchisee, the right to conduct a certain type of business operation in accordance with policies, practices, procedures, and merchandise created and owned by the franchisor.

Franchise Deductible. A clause found most frequently in ocean marine insurance policies for property and liability coverage. It provides that if losses are less than a specified amount such as a percentage of the value of the property, nothing will be paid. If the loss exceeds the percentage, the insurance company pays the full amount of the loss.

Franchise Tax. A tax on the right of a corporation to do business under its corporate name.

Fraud. Deceitfulness and is a primarily connected with a Contract.

Fraud, Agreement to Commit. Agreement to commit a fraud is illegal and not enforceable at law.

Fraudulent Preference. An act of bankruptcy. An insolvent debtor's deliberate preference of one creditor or surety.

Free Currency. Money that may be exchanged for the money of another country without legal restrictions.

Free Exchange Rates. Rates of Exchange in the foreign currencies which are governed by normal forces of supply and demand, without any sort of state supervision or control at a national or international level.

Freehold. A property without any encumbrances except to the state. There may, however, be such encumbrances as Easements, etc. The term 'Freehold land and buildings' is more commonly used in accounts to denote freehold land owned by the business, and buildings on it. If anyone has the freehold to land he has the best title of becoming its absolute owner. This term is related with property e.g., land, building, etc.

Free of Capture or Seizure. In time of hostilities Marine Insurance policy may contain a 'Free of Capture or Seizure' clause, disclaiming responsibility for those losses.

Free Port. A restricted area at a seaport for the handling of duty-exempted import goods. Also known as *Foreign Trade Zone.*

Freepost. Another Name for the postal facility whereby a person can obtain a reply by post without any cost to the other party.

Free-Trade Area. An association of trading nations whose participants agree to impose no restrictive devices such as tariffs or quotas on one another, but are free to impose whatever restrictive devices they wish on nonparticipants.

Free Trade Zone (FTZ). The trade centre in a country,

earmarked by the Government, which is kept out from any restrictions on trade among different countries of the world arising from the differences in comparative costs.

Freezing. Freezing denotes Creation of blockade in order to prevent a person or an enterprise to use the owner's fund, assets, etc. This term is also used in connection with accounts, wages, salary, dearness allowance, etc.

Freight. In consideration of letting the ship or space within it, the Charge paid by a charterer to a ship-owner. The amount of charge is payable only after the delivery of goods.

Freight Allowed. This expression means that shipments will move freight-collect and, unless otherwise specified, that an amount equal to the charges paid by the buyer to the carrier will be deducted from the total cost of the goods when the seller's invoice is paid.

Freight Consolidator. An independent contractor who receives many small shipments for the account of one industrial company and combines them into one carload or truckload.

Freight-in. Freight paid on an incoming shipment. An element of cost of the goods or materials received.

Freight Liner. A door-to-door Container Service offered by Railways and Road transport of a country. It ensures speed and efficiency. Containers can be booked in advance against a fixed charge from the place of origin to destination. The containers conform to international standards. They are owned by the services rendering concern but packed and loaded by the user at his own premises and then sealed.

Freight-out. Freight charges paid or allowed by the seller on goods or materials shipped out.

Full-Faith-and-Credit Debt. In municipal accounting, the debt of a municipality or municipal enterprise, the ·epayment of which is a direct obligation of the municipality.

Full Liability. A liability of a sole person or company, not shared with others.

Functional Authority. A part from the line and staff, a third form of authority also exists in an organisation known as the functional authority.

Functional Authority permits a number of specialists to exercise authority within their area of competence. It is the right and power given to a specialist or a department to issue orders or instructions to other departments. It is binding on the line authority.

Functional Finance. The doctrine in commerce that the government should pursue whatever fiscal measures are necessary to achieve noninflationary full employment and economic growth, without regard to budget balancing. The federal budget is viewed as a functional and flexible tool for achieving economic objectives, rather than as an accounting statement to be balanced periodically.

Fundamental Analysis. A form of security analysis that attempts to determine the intrinsic value of securities on the basis of information available on underlying economic variables. The estimated intrinsic values are compared with current market prices for taking investment decisions.

Funded Debt. Outstanding bonds or notes that are evidence of a debt.

Funded Pension Plan. A pension plan that has a fund specifically set aside for the payment of promised funds to retirees. The fund consists of company contributions, employee contributions (where they are part of the plan), and the income from investments of the fund.

Funded Reserve. Any of several types of reserves for pensions, bonuses, the retirement of preferred stock, or any other prospective liability against which certain assets have been accumulated, set aside, or earmarked.

Funding Bonds. Bonds that are issued for the purpose of retiring current or long-term indebtedness or to finance current expenditures.

Funding Company. The name given to a type of a financial company that offers investors a package of mutual fund shares and life insurance.

Fungibles. An instrument covertable into another of similar description. For example, a Global Depository Receipt (GDR) is convertible into its underlying shares. Fungibility may be one-way or two-way. In one-way fungibility, recoversion of the converted securities is not allowed. In India, fungibility is one-way since GDR may be cancelled and changed to shares, however, vice-versa is not allowed. In two-way fungibility, companies are allowed to reconvert the shares released into GDRs for placement, with foreign investors.

Futures Market. A market to trade contracts for future delivery of certain commodities or securities. (See also comodity futures and financial futures)

Gg

GDR. Global Depository Receipts.

Gambling. Means playing game for money or a prize. Specifically, this is an agreement whereby one party pays a sum if an event occurs on consideration of the other party paying a fixed sum if it does not. The subject matter of the agreement is nothing but a sum of money. And neither party has any personal interest in the event or stands to lose anything other than the money.

Gantt Chart. A pictorial method for displaying and monitoring a process; project, or production schedule so as to evaluate performance against a timetable. Gantt charts, if properly maintained, can serve as valuable tools for planning, scheduling, and controlling the various aspects of a production situation.

Garnishee. A person upon whom a garnishment is served. He is the debtor or a defendant and has money or property that the plaintiff is trying to reach in order to satisfy a debt from the defendant.

Garnishee Order. A legal Order made on a person owing money to a judgement debtor instructing him not to pay the debtor until the debtor made good the claims against him.

Garnishment. A legal proceeding by which a plaintiff seeks to reach the money or property of the defendant that is in the hands of a third party. A garnishment differs from an attachment in that by an attachment an officer of the court takes actual possession of property through a writ. In a garnishment, the money or property is retained by the plaintiff until final adjudication.

Geared Investment Trust. An investment trust tnat borrows money, usually to increase its investment in equities. The shares of a geared investment trust tend to rise faster in rising markets and fall faster in falling markets than ungeared trusts.

Gearing Adjustment. An adjustment in current-cost accounting to allow for the fact that in inflationary times profits may accrue to a company from its fixed-interest capital, so that the whole cost of capital maintenance need not fall on the profits available to the ordinary shareholders.

General Agreement on Tariffs and Trade (GATT). A trade treaty that has been in operation since 1948, to which 95 nations are party and a further 28 nations apply its rules de facto; thus some 90% of world trade is governed by GATT regulations. Its objectives are to expand world trade and to provide a permanent forum for international trade problems. Special attention is given to the trade problems of developing countries. The Tokyo round concluded in 1979, agreed many tariff reductions, non-tariff measures, and a revised anti-dumping code. The Uruguay round, begun in 1986, is conducting negotiations on non-tariff measures, subsidies safeguards, etc. The Uruguay round reached stalemate several times in 1991 and 1992. The GATT office is in Geneva.

New WTO (World Trade Organisation) has replaced the GATT. Under the GATT India has received significant tariff concessions from several countries in return for equivalent concessions extended by her.

General Arrangements to Borrow (GAB). The special arrangements made by the Group of Ten (G10) to enable the International Monetary Fund to increase its lending to members of G10. They came into effect in 1962 and were augmented in 1983 when Switzerland, though not a member of the IME, joined the GAB, enabling it to extend its loan facilities to non-members.

General Average Loss. Dating back many centuries, it applies to ocean marine cargoes, regardless of whether or not insurance is carried. It is one of the perils covered by modern ocean marine insurance policies. A general average loss is incurred in time of emergency for the common welfare of the vessel, and involves sacrificing a part of the cargo or the hull in order to save the entire ship. The expenses of the loss are shared proportionally by all parties involved.

General Average Sacrifice. A sacrifice made by the master of the ship for the benefit of the shipowner, charterer, and cargo-owners. The term is related with Marine Insurance.

General Expense. An administrative expense, not identified with a specific process, product, or service generated by the operation of the facility. Also known as *burden.*

General Fund. In finance, moneys available for expenditure that are not earmarked for any specific program or project.

General Merchandise Warehouse. This operation stores and ships a great variety of merchandise rather than specializing in one type, provided that controlled environmental conditions are not required.

General Mortgage. A mortgage that involves all the properties of a mortgagor.

General Mortgage Bond. A bond that is secured by a blanket mortgage on the company's property, but that is often outranked by one or more other mortgages.

General Overhead. In accounting procedures, the expense of administration and selling.

General Partner. An active member of a partnership who has unlimited liability for the actions of the partners. An enterprise formed as a partnership with one or more partners is required by law to have at least one general partner for liability purposes.

General Reserve. Denotes the profit of a business, instead of distributing to its owners, retained within the business. General Reserves, sometimes referred to as Revenue Reserves are indicated separately in the accounts of companies.

General Store. A type of retailing institution that usually sells a limited selection of a wide range of goods. The general store is distinguished from the Department Store in that its limited selections of goods in each line are not departmentalized. Also called *General Merchandise Store.*

General Warranty. In real estate, a covenant in a deed whereby the grantor agrees to protect the grantee against any claimant.

Ghetto. Historically, a section of a city in which people of specific races or religious beliefs were required to live and to earn their livelihoods. Currently, an economically depressed urban area in which members of minorities live.

Giffen Goods. Cheap necessary foodstuff the sales of which increase with the rise in the price of that foodstuff. This is also known as "Giffen Effect."

Gift Cheques. Decorative cheques made available by certain banks for use on festive occasions. The main beneficiary of such a cheque is the issuing Bank which normally charges high to the account of the donor.

Gift Deed. An instrument that transfers the title to real estate for which the consideration is love and affection, rather than material consideration.

Gilt-Edged Bond. A high-grade bond issued by a company that has demonstrated its ability to earn profits over a period of years and pay its bondholders their interest without interruption.

Give-up. The splitting of a stockbroker's commission with participating brokers following a large trade; now forbidden by the stock exchanges.

Glass Insurance. Property insurance coverage including plate glass windows, glass signs, motion picture screens, glass bricks, glass doors, showcases, countertops, and insulated glass panels. The comprehensive policy is generally used to provide all-risk coverage, excluding damage due to fire, war, and nuclear destruction. It is assumed the firm's fire insurance contract will cover damages and losses due to fire.

Going Value. An owner's equity in a business enterprise, as established by accounting records and reports; equivalent to net worth.

Gold Certificate. In the United States, a form of paper money in circulation from 1865 to 1933. The certificate represented gold bullion that fully secured the certificate. From 1933 to 1955, gold certificates were issued, in a revised form, only to Federal Reserve Banks for reserve purposes. Since 1955, the reserves have been indicated only by bookkeeping entries in a record known as the Interdistrict Settlement Fund.

Go No-go Gage or Go Not-go Gage. In manufacturing, a type of limit gage utilized to measure the dimensions of a mechanical part to determine whether or not the part is within allowable limits. Not necessarily intended for use in determining the exact variance or departure from the mean dimensional tolerance, it is used to sort defective and non-defective parts with respect to tolerances or limits.

Good. A single element of wealth; a commodity: an item of merchandise, raw material, or finished goods.

Good Title. A title to land or property that is free from encumbrance, such as mortgages and liens, as disclosed by a complete abstract of the title taken from the records in the recorder's office.

Goodwill. One of the intangible values of a business beyond its net worth. Good-will may include such assets as general reputation, brand name recognition, technical know-how, location, and the historic ability of the company to retain its accounts on the basis, for example, of services. The value of goodwill in establishing the marketable worth of a company is difficult to establish and depends on subjective judgment and negotiation, but it can have a considerable effect on the gross value of the company in a merger or sale-of assets situation.

Government Bond. A financial obligation of a government. In the United States, U.S. government bonds are regarded as the highest-grade issues in existence.

Government Monopoly. A monopoly both owned and operated by a federal or local government. Examples include the central banks of most countries and water and waste disposal systems.

Graduated Lease. A lease of property that provides for a variable rental rate, often based on future determination such as a periodic appraisal. A feature primarily of long-term leases.

Graduated Life Table. In insurance calculations the tabular counterpart of a mortality curve or of a survivor-life curve.

Grant. A transfer of real or personal property or goods by deed or writing. Also, the instrument by which such a transfer is made also. The property so transferred.

Grant, Bargain, and Sell. In real estate, a phrase sometimes used in a deed to pass title, meaning the grantor promises that he or she has good title to transfer, free from encumbrances, and warrants it to be such.

Grant Deed. In real estate, the instrument used most often in California to transfer the title to property. The deed carries implied warranties.

Grantee. One who acquires the title to property or goods by deed.

Granter. One who conveys the title to property or goods by deed.

Gray Market. A market in which scarce commodities are purchased and sold using business methods that are generally disapproved of even though they are not strictly illegal.

Greenback. A form of paper money issued by the U.S. Treasury in 1862. Eventually the total issue was $ 450 million. Some greenbacks were retired under the Resumption Act of 1875, but more than $ 346 million were left in circulation, and subsequent legislation provided for a constant reissue of the currency. In 1900, under the Gold Standard Act, a gold reserve of approximately $ 150 million was established to ensure the redeemability of the greenbacks. It is estimated that about $ 300 million worth of greenbacks are still in circulation.

Green Revolution. A term descriptive of the development of high-yielding varieties of seed grains, which has had a dramatic impact on the agricultural output of developing nations.

Gross. In accounting procedures, an amount or quantity that is not yet reduced by related deductions or expenses. As an adjective, the term may applied to income, sales, expenses, and similar items of accounting. In retail marketing, a *gross* is 12 dozen (144) of an item of merchandise.

Gross Domestic Product (GDP). Calculated by subtracting payments of wages, interest, rent, profits, and other items paid abroad as income from Gross National Product (GNP). Nations in which foreigners have a heavy investment or whose citizens have extensive holdings abroad usually find the GDP concept a more revealing gauge of economic activity than the GNP.

Gross Income. The total of revenues before deductions are taken for any items of expense. Also known as gross revenue, *gross earnings*, and *gross sales* when the reference is to the total of goods or services sold.

Gross Loss. The excess of the cost of goods or services sold over the amount of sales; opposite of gross profit. Also known as *loss*.

Gross Margin. The excess of sales revenues over the direct costs of the products sold. Also known as *price margin*.

Gross Merchandise Margin. In retail accounting, net sales less the cost of merchandise.

Gross National Debt (GND). The total national debt outstanding. It includes that part of the debt held by government units in trust, in investment, or in sinking funds.

Gross National Disproduct (GND). The sum of all the social costs or reductions in benefits to society that result from producing the gross national product.

Gross National Expenditure (GNE). The total amount spent by the four sectors of the economy—household, government, private business, and international—on the nation's output of goods and services. It is equal, by definition, to the Gross National Product.

Gross National Product (GNP). The value in current prices of all final goods and services produced by the economic system over a time period, usually one calendar year. It is the best known and most widely used single measure of the performance of a nation's economy. It includes personal consumption expenditures for goods and services, gross private domestic investment, government purchases of goods and services, and the net export of goods and services. Depreciation is not considered in calculating the GNP.

Gross Operating Spread. In retail accounting, gross merchandise margin minus the cost of merchandise procurement.

Gross Profit. Net sales less the cost of goods sold before considering selling and general expenses, incidental income, and income deductions. In an enterprise engaged in manufacturing, gross profit is the excess of net sales over direct costs and factory overhead, and is to be distinguished from marginal income, which is the excess of net sales over direct costs only.

Gross Requirements. In production procedures, the total requirements for a part or assembly; quantity on hand is not considered.

Gross Sales. The total amount of sales revenue, before deductions are taken for returns and allowances but after deducting trade discounts, sales taxes, excise taxes based on sales, and cash discounts. Also known as *gross revenue*.

Gross Weight. The combined weight of goods and their container. Also, the total weight of a freight vehicle and its cargo.

Group Account. A British accounting term for a consolidated statement.

Group Dynamics. The study of the behavior of group and

of the interacting behavior of individuals as members of the group.

Growth Fund. A mutual fund established with the objective of appreciating capital of investors by investing in shares which are likely to rise significantly.

Growth Stock. Stocks of companies whose earnings are expected to grow much faster than the economy for at least several years. This may be due to the expanding market for its goods or services, growth in the market share owing to product quality or innovative management.

GTC Order. Initials stand for *Good Till Canceled.*

Guarantee. One to whom a guaranty is given. A promise by one persons to make good for the failure of another who is liable for a debt or the performance of a contract or duty. The obligation involves in a guaranty. Also, an alternative spelling for guaranty.

Guaranteed Bond. A bond whose interest, principal, or both are guaranteed by a company other than the issuer. Usually found in the railroad industry when a large company, leasing a section of trackage owned by a small company, may guarantee the bonds of the smaller company.

Guaranteed Stock. Preferred stock on which dividends are guaranteed by another company, under much the same circumstances as a bond is guaranteed.

Hh

Half Commission Man. Stock Exchange denotes a person who is neither a stock-broker nor a stock-jobber. In return for a share in the commission, he introduces clients to a broker.

Hallmark. The Mark made on gold or silver after an Assay test indicating their genuine quality. At present there are two qualities of silver and four of gold. The British Hall-mark is accepted internationality as a guarantee of standard. There are four marks—(i) the Maker's mark, (ii) the Hall or Assay-office mark, (iii) the Quality mark, and (iv) the Date letter.

Halo Effect. Term connected with one of the limitations of performance appraisal of individuals in any enterprise. It is generally believed that no system of performance appraisal is absolutely immune of subjectivity. Of the many reasons, Halo effect is one important factor.

Hazard. The various factors or the primary factor contributing to uncertainty in a given insurance situation. The risk of loss to any particular person or company may be calculated as the total of all hazards present. A hazard may be anything that may conceivably bring about a loss, whereas the word *peril* is used to denote the factor that actually caused the loss.

Head-end Business. The transportation of property such as mail, baggage, and express in the cars immediately behind the locomotive of a passenger train.

Head Tax. A tax that may be levied on immigrant aliens entering at any port of the United States.

Hedge Fund. A type of mutual fund whose investment policy is to seek profit through the purchase of relatively high risk investments, often using borrowed capital to increase profit potential.

Hidden Amenities. Conditions of agreeable living or beneficial influence arising from the location of or improvements to property, which are not noticed at once but which enhance property value; such conditions include superior materials and workmanship.

Hidden Reserve. The amount of the understatement of net worth that may result from a variety of accounting practices, for example, classifying additions to fixed and other assets as expense. Disclosure of hidden reserves is required for any substantial amounts that may be so classified. Also known as *secret reserve.*

Hire Purchase. The equivalent of instalment buying in the United Kingdom. The buyer pays an initial deposit, takes possession of the goods or receives the benefits of the services, and then makes regular payments that cover the remainder of the purchase price plus interest or carrying charges. The buyer does not take title to the goods until the last periodic payment or installment is paid in full.

Hoffman-Neill Rule. A method for appraising property, no longer in use.

Hold-Back Pay. Wages witheld by an employer for the purpose of calculating payroll periods. For example, employees may be paid for Friday for all work up to the previous Tuesday of a given weekly period, the difference between the wages earned between Tuesday and Friday being "held back" but owed to the employee.

Holding Company. A company that owns the securities of one or more other companies, in most cases with voting control. Also knows as *controlling company.*

Holding Period. The length of time over which an investor is expected to hold or has held an asset.

Hold Order. In manufacturing, a written order directing that certain operations or work activities be interrupted or canceled, pending a change in design or material.

Hold Point. A stock storage point for semifinished inventory.

Hold Track. A railroad where cars are placed while awaiting disposition orders from shippers or receivers.

Horizontal Merger. A merger involving firms that produce closely related products and sell them in the same market. The usual objective is to round out a product line that is sold through the same distribution channels, thereby offering joint economies in sales and distribution.

Hotchpot. In accounting, a combining of the properties of two or more persons to enable an equal redistribution of the properties.

Hot Money. Investment of large amounts of short-term funds in international capital markets by banks financial institutions and wealthy individuals. These are quickly withdraw if fluctuations in interest or exchange rates is anticipated. Therefore, is is not a reliable source of financing.

Household Goods Warehouse. A warehouse that specializes in storing household articles and furniture. Such enterprises often operate fleets of moving vans and offer the service of moving the goods of entire households to any point in the United States. Some such warehouses offer delivery service to virtually any point in the world.

Housekeeping. In data processing, the setting up of constants and variables to be used in preparing a computer program.

Human Resource Development. A term connected with one of the operative functions of Personnel Management. Human Resource Development is essentially a part of corporate manpower planning, aims at educating, training and retraining the employees of the enterprise. This improves enterprise's performance, relieves shortages of people in particular department and prevents obsolescence of individuals.

Hundi. Indigenous bills of exchange are known as "Hundi" which are mostly of 60 days duration. The rate at which the banks are prepared to discount first class Hundis is known as the "Hundi Rate." It is negotiable instrument written in an Indian language. Hundis are governed by customary law.

Hundred Percent Location. A retail business location considered optimum for attracting business.

Hyperinflation. An economic situation in which prices are rising with little or no increase in output.

Hyper-market. Very large Super Markets are nowadays called Hyper-market.

Hypothecation. This refers to the pledging of assets as security for funds borrowed. Bank lending for working capital involves a hypotheciation of investontories and book debts. Under this arrangement, the current assets remain with the borrower, but in case of default, the bank may seek recovery of the loan by instituting a lawsuit to seize the hypothecated assets, which can later be sold.

Ii

IASC. International Accounting Standards Committee.

IBRD. International Bank for Reconstruction and Development.

ICICI. A private sector term lending institution set up in 1955 by the Government of India in collaboration with the world bank. It name is changed recently from Industrial Credit and Investment corporation of India Ltd to ICICI Ltd. Its activities include granting of term loans, particularly foreign currency loans, providing lease finanice, management of public issues of companies and providing venture capital. It has co-promoted a number of other important institution as SCICI for financing shipping industry, Credit Rating and Information Services of India Limited (CRISIL), a credit rating agency and Technology Development and Information Company of India (TDICI) to promote indigenous technology. With a view to be a global financial player it is entering into new thrust areas such as banking, financial adivisory services, mutual funds and insurance sector (when it opens up for private sector).

Identity Equation. An equation stating an equality that is true by definition. For example, the total output of an economy (its gross national product or GNP) is equal to the sum of consumption, investment, and government expenditures in a closed economic system; that is. GNP = C + I + G.

Idle Capacity. In manufacturing, unused productive potential, in reference to machinery, operations, or a factory's facilities that are not in use or are used only partially. Idle capacity may be expressed in units of output capability that could be realized through full usage, or in hours available for use.

Idle-Capacity Cost. In according, the variance that can be attributed to the failure to use facilities at projected rates.

Imperfect Competition. A classification of market structures that falls between the two extremes of perfect competition and Monopoly. It consists of monopolistic competition and oligopoly.

Implicit Costs. The costs of self-owned or self-employed resources that are not entered in a company's account books. Rental receipts wages that a self-employed proprietor forgoes by owning and operating his or her own business are examples.

Implied Contract. A contract that is inferred from actions of the parties who fulfill promises without the existence of an expressed contract.

Implied Easement. In real estate, an easement that is not recorded but is apparent through continued use.

Implied Warranty. Ocean marine insurance policies contain three implied warranties; (1) seaworthiness of the vessel, (2) no deviation from the prescribed course, and (3) the legality of the enterprise. In business transactions, an implied warranty is a guarantee assumed by law to exist although it is not specifically stated in a document.

Impoverished Style. A style of managerial leadership that exerts a minimum effort to get the required work done with the minimum of control considered to be appropriate to sustain organization membership.

Imputed Cost. In accounting, a cost that is indirectly estimated and that is attributed rather than directly measured.

Inactive Stock. An issue traded in relatively low volumes on an exchange or in the Over-the Counter (OTC) market. Volumes may be no more than a few hundred shares a week and are sometimes even less. On the New York Stock Exchange many inactive stocks are traded in 10-share units rather than the customary 100.

In-and-out Trade. A security market expression for the purchase and sale of the same security within a short time period, a day, a week, or a month. An in-and-out trader is generally more interested in day-to-day price fluctuations than in dividends or long-term growth.

Income Bond. Generally, an income bond promises to repay principal as stipulated but to pay interest only when earned. In some cases unpaid interest on an income bond may accumulate as a claim against the corporation when the bond becomes due. An income bond may also be issued in lieu of preferred stock.

Income Fund. A type of investment company whose main investment goal is to obtain liberal current income for shareholders of the fund.

Income Tax. A direct tax on income. The principal direct tax in most countries, it is levied on the incomes of either individual taxpayers or households. It lends itself particularly well to levying ability to pay taxes and to progressive taxation. Its defects are that it may discourage work and risk bearing investment. The tax is calculated on the taxpayer's taxable income, i.e., gross income less any income-tax allowances and deductions. If the allowances and deductions exceed the gross income in a fiscal year, no income tax is payable; if tax has been deducted at source it will normally be repayable.

Incontestable Clause. A clause is an insurance policy stating that after a certain period of time the policy may not be contested except for the nonpayment of premiums.

Inconvertible Paper Standard. A monetary system by which a nation's unit of currency cannot be converted into any metal or other precious substance in terms of which it may or may not be defined. Historically, this standard has existed on a domestic basis in all countries since the worldwide abandonment of the gold standard in the 1930s.

Indemnity. The legal protection or security whereby a person or an organization is obligated to make good a loss or damage another has suffered. The compensation for that loss or damage. Also, legal exemption incurred by one's actions.

Indented Bill of Material. In manufacturing, a bill of material that has the highest-level assemblies positioned on the left-hand margin of the reporting document and subsequent lower levels indented sequentially to the right. Also referred to as an *indenture.*

Indenture. In financial transactions, a written agreement under which debentures are issued, setting forth maturity date, interest rate, and other terms. In real estate proceedings, a deed executed by both parties to the transfer of title to land or property.

Independent Contractor. A person or firm whose time and efforts in fulfillment of a contract are not regulated by others.

Index Fund. A passively managed mutual fund in a diversified portfolio of shares representative of some market index, such as the Sensex.

Indian Standards Institution (ISI). A Central Government enterprise established in 1947 to determine and improve the qualitative standards or agricultural and industrial products, raw materials, machinery, spare parts, etc. This institution gives certificate to products which satisfy the qualitative standard fixed for the same. The institution also allows the producers to use ISI stamp on products approved and certified. ISI-stamped product ensures quality and thus facilitates domestic and foreign trade.

Indirect Cost. In accounting, a cost or expense attributable not directly to the processing or manufacturing of a specific product or service but indirectly to a more general activity of the enterprise, and a cost or expense that also does not necessarily vary with the quantity or volume of output. Indirect costs generally include a variety of factory operating costs, such as supervision, building depreciation, depreciation, maintenance, utilities, general administration, and marketing expenses.

Indirect Tax. A tax that can be shifted either partially or entirely to someone other than the individual or firm responsible for paying the tax. Examples are sales taxes, excise-taxes, and taxes on business or rental properties.

Inducement to Break a Contract. If a person induces another to break a contract, he is committing an actionable wrong. But this does not apply to any contract between the employer and employee of an enterprise, when such contract is the result of voluntary arbitration. Nor a person can be stopped to persuade another to break a contract in a lawful manner.

Induction. Frequently used in Personnel Management with particular reference to Recruitment and Hiring of personnel. Induction involves imparting to the new employee the whole concept of the enterprise within the shortest possible time and clarification of the particular person's job in the context of the whole enterprise. It acts as the first step in a proper communication policy to build up a two-way channel of information between management and the employee. It thus creates confidence of the new employee in the enterprise, promotes a sense of belonging and loyalty to the enterprise, apprise him with information and knowledge about the enterprise, and the information which he needs for self-guidance in regard to terms and conditions of employment, welfare provisions, grievances and disciplinary procedure, working routines and so on. The first impression obtained from induction bears a lasting effect in forming an opinion in regard to his employer.

Industrial and Investor Bank. A bank that acts as the bridge between capital-users and capital-savers. Such a bank is viewed as the entrepreneur of entrepreneurs.

Industrial Broker. A natural or legal person who acts for another in a transaction and who specializes in industrial real estate.

Industrial Credit and Investment Corporation (I.C.I.C.I.). On the recommendation of a three-man Mission, sponsored by the U.S. Government and the World Bank in 1953 to set up a special institution of quasi-government character like the Industrial and Commercial Finance Corporation of U.K., a private limited company known as the Industrial Credit and Investment Corporation of India was registered in January, 1955.

The Authorised Capital of the Corporation is Rs. 25 crores and Paid-up Capital Rs. 5 crores subscribed wholly by domestic and foreign private investors. This apart, the Corporation initially obtained an interest-free Loan of Rs. 7.5 crores from the Government of India. At the end of 1955, the World Bank granted a long term loan of 10 million dollars (around Rs. 5 crores) to the Corporation which was guaranteed by the Government of India.

Underwriting operations constitute its main function. While promoting new ventures, it also endeavours to provide a part of the 'equity capital' required by them. The funds of the Corporation is also made available to purchase capital assets in the form of land, building and machinery. Since 1969, the Corporation has started providing foreign currency loans to proprietary and partnership concerns either directly or in association with State Financial Corporation and banks. The I.C.I.C.I. entered the foreign capital market for the first time, directly, in 1973 by issuing Bonds of Swiss Francs 8 million in the European capital market. The Corporation has also enlarged its sphere of activities by forming a 'Merchant Banking Division' to provide services at the project level in backward areas.

Industrial Development Bank of India (I.D.B.I.). The Industrial Development Bank of India is a specialised financial institution to provide long-term finance to industry. It is functioning with the object of providing direct loans, subscribing to shares and debentures to industrial ventures, underwriting of shares and bonds and guaranteeing of loans and deferred payments. In 1964, the I.D.B.I. was established as a subsidiary of the Reserve Bank of India with Authorised Capital of Rs. 50 crores and Issued Capital of Rs. 30 crores.

The main function of the I.D.B.I. is to finance industrial enterprises in both public and private sectors. Financial assistance is provided to manufacturing, mining, shipping and other transport industry, hotel industry either directly or through specific financial institutions in the form of : (i) Direct assistance as grants, loans and advances. It subscribes in shares, debentures or bonds. The bank guarantees loans raised by industries in the open market from scheduled and non-scheduled banks. It accepts commercial bills and promissory notes. (ii) Indirect assistance. The bank often refinances term loans repayable within 3 to 25 years given by the

I.F.C.I., S.F.C.s., and other financial institutions. Term loan given by the scheduled banks and State Co-operative banks is also refinanced by it. It can refinance export credit also. (iii) Special assistance. Under the Act of 1964 this institution can create special fund known as the Development Assistance Fund. This fund can be used to finance those concerns unable to secure finance either because of heavy investiment or low rate of return. (iv) General activities.

Industrial Dispute. Ordinarily, it means any dispute between employer and employees, or between employer and workmen, or between workmen, which is connected with employment or non-employment or the terms of employment or with the conditions of labour, or of any person.

In India, this term has been defined by the industrial Disputes Act. Section 2-A (which was added to the Act by an amendment made in 1965) defines "industrial dispute" as all differences between an individual workman and his employer connected with, or arising out of, his discharge, dismissal, retrenchment or termination notwithstanding that no other workmen nor any union of workmen is a party to the dispute.

Industrial Espionage. Denotes Attempts by one company to obtain access to unpublished information of another. Such information may relate to new invention to labour-saving devices, production method, cost-reduction techniques, proportion and component of ingredients to a product, financial policy and status, and so on.

Industrial Estate. A Planned industrial area, with factories organised to provide varied employment. Such an estate provides necessary zoning, land, shopping facilities, waste disposal outlets and other infrastructure facilities.

Industrial Finance. Finance required by the industrial units for the purposes of Fixed as well as Working Capital. For the promotion, growth and development of an economic enterprise, irrespective of size, nature and ownership, finance of both nature is required for short-term and long-term period.

Industrial Finance Corporation of India (I.F.C.I.). Industrial Finance Corporation of India was established on July 1, 1948 as a shareholder's Corporation under an Act of Parliament. The Central Government guaranteed the shares of the Corporation. Though the Authorised Capital of the Corporation was initially Rs. 10 crores, in 1972 it was increased to Rs. 20 crores. Currently the commercial banks hold 20% of the shares of the I.F.C.I., Another 8% is held by the cooperative banks. The Life Insurance Corporation of India holds 22% of the shares, and the rest 50% is held by the Industrial Development Bank of India. To enhance its resources, the Corporation is authorised to issue bonds up to 5 times the paid up capital and to accept deposits from the public repayable after not less than five years. The bonds and debentures are guaranteed by the Central Government.

Industrial Goods. Various kinds of materials used or consumed by a business, and those that are used in the production of other goods.

Industrial Life Insurance. Designed for individuals who are financially unable to buy ordinary life insurance. As with ordinary insurance, industrial life insurance may be whole life, limited-payment life, or endowment.

Industrial Relations. Rules and regulations governing the relations between a labor union and management. They often deal with such matters as contract negotiation, the type of recognition accorded the union, the financial arrangement for collecting membership dues from employees, the methods of controlling the quantity and kind of union membership through apprenticeship requirements, licensing provisions, initiation fees, seniority rules, and the handling of grievances.

Industrial Revolution. The era in history when man applied his innovative talents to the industrial (manufacturing and service) environment and consequently achieved technological advancement. It began in England around 1750-1755 A.D.

Industrial Training Institutes (I.T.I.). Training Institutions established by the Ministry of Labour and Employment, Government of India, to impart vocational practical training in different trades. The object of these institutions is to prepare young people for self-employment and employment in industries.

Industrial Union. A labor union that admits to membership people who work within an industry, irrespective of their occupation or craft.

Industrial Unit, Sick. An Industrial undertaking running with financial loss regularly. The BIFR (Board for Industrial and Financial Reconstruction), India, has viewed a sick unit as an industrial company (registered for not less than seven years) which has at the end of any financial year accumulated loss equal to equal to or exceeding its entire worth and has also suffered cash losses in such financial year and the financial year immediately preceding such financial year.

Inferior Good. A commodity whose purchases and consumption decrease relative to other commodities as the incomes of consumers rise. Examples of inferior goods are potatoes, used clothing, and other commodities sometimes referred to as *poor man's goods.*

Inflation. Although this is a term in Economics, in modern trade and commerce the term is frequently used. Popularly, inflation refers to a rise in price level or, which is the same thing, fall in the value of money. Renowned economist Kemmerer states: "Inflation is too much money and deposit currency—that is too much currency in relation to the physical volume of business being done." This is what Coulburn also means when he defines inflation as: "Too much money chasing too few goods." The implication is that prices rise due to an increase in the volume of money as compared to the supply of goods. But prices may rise due to other factors also—such as rise in wages and profits.

Inflation may be of three kinds: (i) Demand-pull inflation: The most common cause of inflation is the pressure of ever-rising demand on a stagnant or less rapidly increasing supply of goods and services. The expansion in aggregate demand may be the result of rapidly increasing private investment and/or expanding government expenditure for war or for economic development. (ii) Cost-push inflation: In certain circumstances, prices may be pushed up by wage increases forced upon the economy by labour leaders under the threat of strike. Cost can also be raised by manufacturers through a system of fixing a higher margin of profit. Again, the Government is, at times, also responsible for raising the cost through imposing new taxes and raising continuously the rates of existing commodity taxes. Thus, rise in wages, in profit margin, and in taxation—all these are responsible for cost-push inflation. (iii) Sectoral inflation: It is not always necessary to have a general increase in demand to bring about inflationary pressure. Sometimes, the increase in demand may be confined to some sector of the economy; this increase in demand and the consequent rise in the price in a particular sector may spread to other sectors. The "sectoral demand" thesis emphasises the fact that prices are highly flexible upwards but relatively rigid downwards. There may be a rise in prices in the agricultural sector where there is scarcity but there may be price stability in the industrial sector where there is an excess supply. But in course of time, prices all over the economy will assume an upward trend. Inflation is also classified as Open and Suppressed. The other classifications are Creeping; Running and Galloping Inflation.

Inflationary Gap. The amount by which actual private spending and government expenses exceed the theoretical amount of spending necessary to maintain full employment or to exceed the theoretical amount of spending that is adequate to absorb all available goods and services without appreciably raising the price level.

Innovation. Denotes the Introduction of a new process, a new product or a new market. The first employer or the enterprise who innovates, gets extra income which lasts till the process, product or market becomes common to all.

Innovation Theory. Put forth by Joseph Alois Schumpeter, this theory attributes business cycles and economic development to innovations that forward-looking entrepreneurs adopt in order to reduce costs and increase profits. Once an innovation proves to be successful, other entrepreneurs follow with the same or similar techniques and methods, and these innovations cause fluctuations in investment that in turn cause business cycles. The innovation theory has also been used as a partial explanation of how profits arise in a competitive capitalistic system.

Input-output Analysis. A tabular display of data that serves the major purpose of emphasizing the intricate relationships among the various sectors or industries of the economy and how each affects the others. Wassily W. Leontief is largely responsible for input-output analysis, which he presented in a simplified version in his article "Input-Output Economics" (*Scientific American*, October 1951.)

Insider Dealings. Transactions in shares and securities by people who possess special knowledge affecting the value of those shares. Such people are generally the company directors and auditors who may have prior knowledge of events likely to influence the market value of shares in their companies.

Insolvency. Also known as Bankruptcy, meaning that a person or firm is unable to pay its debts when they become due.

Insolvent. In law, an insolvent debtor is one whose property and other assets are insufficient to pay all his or her debts.

Inspection Ticket. In manufacturing, a sheet, card, or other document used to report that an inspection functions has been performed.

Instalments, Delivery and Payment. If according to a contract, delivery or payment is to be by instalments, problems crop up from a failure to comply with the instalment system. Failure of one instalment discharges the other party. The court will generally ascertain the intention of the defaulting party in case of delivery. If obvious intention to continue to fail to deliver the instalments is established, the case will be treated as one of breach of contract. Other things being equal, if there is merely a failure on one instalment in part or whole then the complainant can obtain damages.

Institutional Infrastructure. A collective term for Enterprises providing intelligence and assistance in setting up new business and industrial establishment.

Insurable Interest. An interest of such nature that the insured party would be financially injured by the occurrence of the event insured against. An insurable interest is required in all lines of insurance before a contract is legally valid.

Insurance. A legal contract in which an insurer promises to pay specified amount to another party, the insured, if a particular event (known as the peril), happens and the insured suffers a financial loss as a result. The insured's part of the contract is to promise to pay an amount of money, known as the *premium* either once or at regular intervals. In order for an insurance contract to be valid, the insured must have an insurable interest. It is usual to use the word insurance to cover events (such as a fire) that may or may not happen, whereas assurance refers to an event (such as death) that must occur at sometime.

Insurance Broker. A person engaged in obtaining insurance for those who apply to him or her for this service. It is usual for individual brokers to represent several insurance companies so that they are in a position to obtain the best insurance to suit the needs of their clients.

Insurance, Credit. Insurance which covers losses from Bad Debts. Normally, insurance companies do not offer this service but leave it to specialist enterprises.

Insurance, Double. A risk insured twice is called Double Insurance. But the insured cannot get compensation from two insurer, nor can obtain reimebursement more than the actual loss suffered. And if a risk is insured with two companies, both of them, in the event of paying compensation, will share the loss either equally, or proportionately to the value of risk insured.

Insurance Underwriter. A member of a syndicate or an individual firm concerned with assessing and arranging insurance coverage.

Insured Deposit. A deposit in a bank or other financial institution that is insured by the Federal Deposit Insurance Corporation or any other federal-or state-sponsored insuring agency. If the institution fails, deposits are insured against loss up to specified maximum limits per account.

Insuring Clause. In an insurance policy, a description of the risk assumed by the insurer.

Intangible Asset. In accounting procedures, any asset having no physical existence; examples are goodwill, patents, trademarks, formulas, licenses, franchises, and research-and-development costs. Some tax authorities define intangible assets as any asset other than cash or real estate.

Integrated Pension Plan. A pension plan that adjusts the employee's pension benefits downward to reflect the company's contribution to social security.

Inter-American Development Bank (IDB). Formed in 1959, the IDB promotes economic and social development partly through the provision of technical assistance among its member nations; Argentina, Barbados, Bolivia, Brazil, Chile, Colombia, Costa Rica, Dominican Republic, Ecuador, El Salvador, Guatemala, Haiti, Honduras, Jamaica, Mexico, Nicaragua, Panama, Paraguay, Peru, Trinidad and Tobago, United States of America, Uruguay, and Venezuela.

Interest. In financial transactions, the price a borrower pays to a lender for the use of the latter's money. It is calculated as a periodic percentage of the principal amount of the loan; however, payments of interest do not alter the principal amount of the loan.

Interest, Compound. Interest calculated not as a fixed amount per annum based on the capital to which it applies, but on an accumulating balance consisting of both capital invested and the interest already earned.

Interest Cover. Number of times that the total fixed interest payable can be met out of the current income of a business concern. The break-even point indicates when the income before tax becomes equal to total fixed interest payable before tax.

Interest, Gross. A term used in Economics to denote the total amount paid by the borrower to the lender as the price of a loan. A part of the Gross Interest consists of (i) Payment of risk (the greater the risk, the higher is the extra payment required by way of insurance), (ii) Payment for labour (extra charges are made when the creditor has to incur extra labour or inconvenience for collecting the money).

Interest, Net. A Term used in Economics to signify true interest. It is the payment for the loan irrespective of any other considerations. In other words, Gross Interest minus payments for risk and labour is the Net interest.

Interest on Calls. If the Articles of Association of a company provides, interest is charged for Calls in Arrears. This is called Interest on Calls.

Interest, Simple. Interest calculated on the original capital sum, and not including interest on unpaid interest.

Interline Waybill. In transportation, carriers' waybill used whenever more than one carrier is involved in a single shipment of goods.

International Champer of Commerce (ICC). Set up in 1919 as the international focal point for chambers of commerce.

International Development Association (I.D.A.). There were many economically sound projects in developing countries which the World Bank did not finance as a matter of policy. Some such projects aim at creating "social capital", e.g. construction of roads and bridges, slum-clearance and urban development, sanitation, etc. which could make an important contribution to the development of a backward region. But these projects require finance on extremely flexible terms. The International

Development Association was founded in 1960 as an affiliate of the World Bank to make soft loans and, in general, to supplement the development effort of the I.B.R.D.

The financial assistance which the I.D.A. grants has three distinct characteristics. First, the I.D.A's credit is interest-free; only a nominal service charge annually on the amount withdrawn and outstanding will be made with a view to meeting I.D.A's administrative expenses. Next, the repayment period is very long—fifty years. Finally, amortisation of the loan generally will begin only after a ten-year period of grace. The repayment of the principal is in very small percentages, from one to three per cent a year after the period of grace is over.

Members of I.D.A. are to two kinds. Part I members consist of countries subscribing and providing nearly 95.6 per cent of total resources of I.D.A. Part II members consist of less developed countries subscribing and providing 4.4 per cent of the total resources of I.D.A. Its investable funds mostly come from industrialised and developed members, and transfers from the net earnings of the World Bank.

International Finance Corporation (I.F.C.). The International Finance Corporation was set up in 1955 due to the need for a special international financial agency to provide capital for private enterprise, in undeveloped member-countries without government guarantee.

The main objective of the I.F.C. is to assist economic development of less developed countries by encouraging the growth of productive private enterprises by helping to mobilise domestic and foreign capital for this purpose. To achieve this objective, the I.F.C. intends: (1) Investing in private productive enterprises in association with private investors and without government guarantee of repayment; (ii) Serving as a clearing house to bring together investment opportunities, private capital of both foreign and domestic origin, and experienced management; and (iii) Stimulating productive investment of private capital both foreign and domestic.

The Corporation has been guided by certain principles in its operations. First, the I.F.C. makes its investment in partnership with private investors from capital exporting countries or from the country in which the enterprise is locating or from both. Next, the Corporation's investment will never be more than half of the capital needed for an enterprise. The minimum investment which the I.F.C. will make in any enterprise is fixed at $ 10,00,000 or its equivalent but no upper limit has been fixed. Further, privately owned industrial enterprises, contributing to the economics development of the country, will primarily be eligible for loans. Fourth, the rate of investment in each case would be a matter of negotiation depending on the risks and other terms of investment. Lastly the I.F.C. will not seek or accept a government guarantee for repayment of any of its investment.

The International Finance Corporation functions as an affiliate of the World Bank. Memberships in the Bank is a prerequisite for membership in I.F.C. To the total Subscribed Capital of the I.F.C., each country's subscription is proportionate to its subscription to the Capital of the World Bank. The biggest subscriber of the Corporation is the U.S.A.

International Monetary Fund (I.M.F.). One of the outcomes of the Bretton Wood Agreements in 1944. The Fund was formed in 1946 and commenced exchange transactions in March 1947.

The objectives of the Fund as enunciated in the Articles of Agreement are : (i) To promote international monetary co-operation through a permanent institution which provides the machinery for consultation and collaboration on international monetary problems, (ii) To facilitate the expansion and balanced growth of international trade and to contribute thereby to the promotion and maintenance of high levels of employment and real income of member-countries; (iii) To promote exchange stability and to avoid competitive exchange depreciation; (iv) To provide for multilateral convertibility of currencies and to remove all exchange controls and restrictions; and (v) To help members with funds to correct their balance of payments deficits.

The initial Capital of the Fund was $ 8,800 million. Each member of the Fund was assigned a subscription quota based on its national income and its position in international trade. The quotas ranged from $1 million for Iceland to $ 2,750 million for the United States of America. The fund has been particularly interested in the less developed countries of the world and has been assisting them to have a healthy balance of payments and to maintain monetary stability at home. In recent years underdeveloped countries have also started looking to the Fund for assisting their economic development schemes.

Intrinsic Value. The Value contained in the substance from which an article is produced. In trade and commerce the term is most often used in relation to metallic currency.

Invention. From business point of view the term means finding out something new or a new method of producing a thing, or a new product.

Inventory. The stock of goods that a business firm has on hand, including raw materials, supplies, work in process, and finished goods.

Inventory Shrinkage. Losses that result from such nonproductive processes and actions as deterioration, disposal as scrap, and pilferage.

Inventory Turnover. In accounting, the number of times inventory is cycled annually. A ratio of the performance of a company, inventory turnover is calculated by dividing the material cost of annual sales by the average inventory level.

Investment Adviser. A person who on a professional service basis gives advice to another person on investment situations. Investment advisers are required to register with and report their activities to the Securities and Exchange commission.

Investment Bank. In the United States, a term for a bank that specializes in the acquisition of new issues and their resale in small batches to investors. In the United Kingdom, these functions are handled by a *merchant bank* or *issuing house.*

Investment Company. A generic term that describes a company handling mutual funds or closed-end funds, or any of several other types of companies engaged in the business of investing the money of their shareholders in securities and in other organizations.

Invisible Hand. An expression used by Adam Smith in his book *The Wealth of Nations* (published in 1776) in which he contends that the desire for personal profit within the framework of a competitive economic system works like an *invisible hand* to guide the system toward the greatest welfare for all.

Invoice. A document that shows the quantity, price terms, character nature of delivery, and other related details for goods sold or services rendered.

Issue. 1. The number of shares or the amount of stock on offer to the public at a particular time. 2. The number of banknotes distributed by the Bank of England at a particular time.

Issue by Tender (sale by tender). A method of issuing shares on the stock exchange in which an issuing house asks investors to tender for them. The stocks or shares are then allocated to the highest bidders. It is usual for the tender documents to state the lowest price acceptable. This method may be used for a new issue or for loan stock but it not frequently employed.

Issue Date. The date from which interest accrued on a security is calculated.

Issue Price. The price at which a new issue of shares is sold to the public. Once the issue has been made the securities will have a market price, which may be above at a premium on) or below (at a discount on) the issue price. In an introduction, offer for sale, or public issue, the issue price is fixed by the company on the advice of its stockbrokers and bankers; in an issue by tender the issue price is fixed by the highest bidder; in a placing the issue price is negotiated by the issuing house or broker involved.

Issuing House. A financial institution, usually a merchant bank, that specializes in the flotation of private companies on a stock exchange. In some cases the issuing house will itself purchase the whole issue, thus ensuring that there is no uncertainty in that amount of money the company will raise by flotation. It will then sell the shares to the public, usually by an offer for sale, introduction, issue by tender, or placing. In the USA this function is performed by an investment bank.

Itemized Appropriation. In finance, an appropriation of funds with detailed specifics for the disposition or application of the funds.

Jj

Job Analysis. Examination of a job, its component parts and the circumstances in which it is performed. Purpose and slant of job analysis very between job evaluation, vocational guidance, personnel selection, training, training, equipment, design, etc. Can be known as job study.

Jobber's Turn. The difference between the price at which a former jobber on the Stock Exchange was prepared to buy and the price at which the jobber was prepared to sell.

Jobber. In the distribution of goods, an individual or a firm that intervenes between a wholesaler-distributor and the retailer. Jobbers may act exclusively as brokers or sales agents, carrying no inventory of the goods purveyed, or they may so organize and finance their activities as to provide warehousing facilities for the goods. The arrangement between the wholesaler and the jobber with respect to commission varies according to the extent of the services provided by one to the other.

Jobbing Backwards. Looking back on a transaction or event and thinking about how one might have acted differently, and one known then what one knows now.

Job Classification. The process of describing the duties, responsibilities, and characteristics of a job, point-rating it (sometimes through the use of formulas based on time studies of workers already in such jobs), and then grouping the jobs into graduated classifications with corresponding wage rates and wage ranges.

Jot Lot. A collection of diverse things, such as stocks or shares, sold together as one lot at one all-inclusive price.

Joint Account. 1. A bank account of a building-society account held in the names of two or more people, often husband and wife. On the death of one party the balance in the account goes to the survivor(s), except in the case of partnerships, executors' accounts, or trustees' accounts. It is usual for any of the holders of a joint account to operate it alone. 2. In the USA a syndicate of investment banks acting together in an underwriting venture.

Joint and Several Liability. A liability that is entered into by a group, on the understanding that if any of the group fail in their undertaking the liability must be shared by the remainder. Thus, if two people enter into a joint and several guarantee for a bank loan, if one becomes bankrupt the other is liable for repayment of the whole loan.

Joint Investment. A security purchased by more than one person. The certificate will bear the names of all the parties, but only the first named will receive notices. To dispose of the holding all the parties must sign the transfer deed.

Joint-life and Last-Survivor Annuities. Annuities that involve two people (usually husband and wife). A joint-life annuity begins payment on a specified date and continues until both persons have died. A last-survivor annuity only begins payment on the death of one of the two people and pays until the death of the other.

Joint-Stock Company. An organization established by a group of individuals who act jointly to operate a business firm under an artificial name, with invested capital divided into transferable shares, an elected board of directors, and other characteristics similar to those of a corporation. In most, states, joint-stock companies operate without formal government authority. The shareholders have unlimited liability for the debts and obligations of the company, which is taxed as a corporation. Joint-stock companies, also known as *joint stock associations,* have become rare as result of the ease with which a corporation may be formed under law. In British usage, a joint-stock association is a corporation.

Joint Tenancy. In law, a single estate in property, whether real or personal, owned by two or more persons under one instrument or act of the parties, with an equal right of all to share in the enjoyment of the property during their lives. On the death of a joint tenant, the property descends to the survivor or survivors and at length to the last survivor.

Judgment Creditor. The person in whose favour a court decides, ordering the judgment debtor to pay the sum owed. If the judgment debtor fails to pay, the judgment creditor must return to the court asking for the judgment to be enforced.

Junior Mortgage. A mortgage second in lien to a previous mortgage; a subordinate mortgage. Also known as *Junior Financing.*

Junk Bond. A bond that offers a high rate of interest because it carries a higher than usual probability of default. The issuing of junk bonds to finance the takeover of large companies in the USA is a practice that developed in the 1970s and subsequently spread elsewhere.

Kk

Kaffirs. A stock exchange term for South African gold mining shares.

Kangaroo Closure. This term is relevant to meetings, particularly with closure of the meeting. This closure is applied by the Speaker of the Parliament or the chairman of a meeting, if empowered by the rules. A Kangaroo walks by jumping. This jumping principle is also applied at a meeting when the chairman faces a number of amendments. By the exercise of the closure, he selects from those amendments a few for discussion. He thus jumps from one amendment to another leaving the intervening ones undiscussed. The less important ones are 'jumped over' by the more important ones. In doing so, he chooses those which represent the viewpoints of different sections at the meeting. The act of closing a meeting in this manner is called the Kangaroo closure.

Kangaroos. An informal name for Australian shares, especially in mining, land, and tobacco companies, on the London Stock Exchange.

Kennedy Round. An extensive Renegotiation of multilateral tariff agreements, within the limits set by the General Agreement on Tariffs and Trade, initiated by the Late President Kennedy of U.S.A. 46 countries, including India, signed at the end of June, 1967 he Kennedy Round documents in Geneva. The Kennedy Round Pact is the world's biggest ever tariff cutting deal and was supposed to give a new boost to trade among developed and developing countries.

Key Accounts. In trade and commerce this term denotes the major customers of a company.

Key Area Control. A firm's Measurement of self performance in a number of vital areas such as profitability, market standing, product leadership, employee attitudes, social responsibility and productivity.

Key Lot. A marketable parcel of land one of whose sides adjoins the rear of other lots. Usually one of the least desirable lots in a subdivision because it does not offer optimum access or privacy.

Key-Man Insurance. Provides temporary protection to ensure financial solvency in the event of loss through death of a key executive. The business firm pays the premium and is the beneficiary. Premium costs are non tax-deductible; however, proceeds from the policy are not subject to federal income taxation.

Khokha. It refers to the non-convertible portion of a convertible security. A fixed rate of interest is usually paid on khokha. The term khokha is borrowed from Gujarati language meaning on empty box. The non-convertible portion of a security is termed as khokha since its content, the convertible portion has been withdrawn from it.

Kiting. An unauthorized borrowing or theft of money through the continuing action of drawing and cashing a check on one bank, following that shortly by a covering deposit in the form of an unrecorded check on another bank, that check, in its turn, being covered by a check drawn on a third bank, the process possibly continuing undetected through several banks. The success of the act depends on the time it takes for checks to clear through the banking system. The growing use of electronics in expediting and automating the transfer of funds from one bank to another is expected to have a significant impact on transactions that have depended on clearance-time delays.

Kit List. In manufacturing, a list of items that are needed to fill requisitions and that are to be from inventory and delivered to the production area.

Knock-for-Knock Agreement. A term connected with Automobile Insurance, and denoting the mode of payment by the insurance companies in an accident involving two or more cars. In such case, insurance companies generally concede to the claims of their respective clients and pay out with a view to saving the time and cost of appropriating blame.

Knot. This term is used in measuring speed at sea and equivalent to one nautical mile (1.85km.) per hour. The word itself incorporates 'miles per hour'. Hence one should say so many knots, and should not speak of 'knots per hour.'

Know-how. Specialised knowledge or skill or technique developed in producing certain things or developed for a specific use.

Know-how is the result of intensive research for years together. In commercial and industrial world it is saleable at a very high price. From the fifties of twentieth century, advanced industrialised countries of the world are selling technical know how of developing heavy projects and manufacturing sophisticated machineries to the underdeveloped countries. Transfer of know-how is an important item of foreign trade these days. This has, on one hand, increased the export earnings of the export-country while, on the other promoted rapid industrial development in the import-country.

Kondatrieff Cycle. In economic analysis, a 40-to-60 year wavelike movement in economic activity that is approximately divided between good and bad times. A theory of business cycles proposed by the Russian economist Nikolai D. Kondatrieff, born in 1892. also known as the *wave theory.*

Kuznets Cycle. In economic analysis, a 15-to-25 years wavelike movement in rates of economic growth that appears to be associated with changes in population growth.

Ll

Labour Market. US spelling of labour market.

Labour-Cost Ratio. Standard costing of direct labour divided by its actual cost.

Labor-intensive. A process or product is called labor-intensive if it uses proportionately more labor than other elements in its production. Hand-made goods with a low materials content are produced by a labor-intensive process. Service industries are usually labor-intensive.

Labor Theory of Value. The doctrine that all exchange value in economic transactions is created by labor. It is the basis of Marxian economic theory.

Lagging Indicators. Economic variables that-have been found to follow movements in the economy. The relationship between economic variables and lagging indicators is called the lagged relationship. For example, unemployment rate, capital expenditure on new plant and machinery, capital borrowing etc. are the lagging indicators which follow recession in the economy.

Laissez-Faire. The doctrine that government should let things alone and allow economic activity to go forward in response to individual and private objectives.

In the management of a particular enterprise, a style directly opposite to that of authoritarianism. The manager gives minimum direction and exercises little direct or obvious control over employees or subordinates, but rather leaves them alone to do their jobs as they think best. While this does not necessarily mean the total absence of direction or control, skillful laissez-faire managers provide it so subtly that their people are or may become highly motivated through personal commitment to responsibility. Perhaps the true skill of an effective laissez-faire manager is in selecting employees or subordinates who respond positively to this unencumbered style.

Laity. Persons in a profession who are not skilled with respect to that profession. In accounting, for example, the laity includes those who are not skilled in accounting but who might need auditors reports in the completion of their own tasks.

Land. An element of production that includes land itself in the form or real estate as well mineral deposits, timber, water, and other nonhuman or natural resources.

Landed Price. The quoted or invoiced price of a commodity including costs of loading, shipping, and unloading at its destination.

Landlord's Warrant. A legal recourse for obtaining payments for rent upon default in a lease, giving the landlord the right to possess the tenant's personal property as security until the debt is paid.

Language Sheet. A term used by central government agencies, in their accounting practice, to denote the narrative portion of an appropriation bill that accompanies an agency's submission of its budget to Congress.

Lapse. Expire, or be forfeited, as in the case of an insurance policy that is canceled or lapses on its expiration date or for nonpayment of the premium. In government accounting, the unexpended balance of an ordinary appropriation is said to lapse at the end of the fiscal year.

Last Change Date. In manufacturing, the last date on which a part was changed in a specific bill of material.

Last Cycle Count Date. In manufacturing, the date on which a particular part was counted in an inventory. This date is used to determine when the next physical inventory should be taken.

Last Material Standard Cost. In accounting, the standard cost of the material prior to the last change in its cost.

Last Material Standard Cost Date. In accounting, the last date on which the material standard cost was changed.

Last Transaction Date. The last date on which a transfer of a particular material was transacted.

Latin American Free Trade Association (LAFTA). An organization that regulates the import-export activities among eleven countries: Argentina, Bolivia, Brazil, Chile, Colombia, Ecuador, Mexico, Paraguay, Peru, Uruguay, and Venezuela. Founded in 1960 by ten countries, it took in Bolivia as its eleventh member in 1967.

Laundering Money. Processing money acquired illegally (as by theft, drug dealing, etc.) so that it appears to have come from a legitimate source. This is often achieved by paying the iilegal cash into a foreign bank and transferring its equivalent to a bank with a good name in a hard-currency area.

Law of Selective Gravity. A satirical principle holding that an object will fall so as to do the most damage.

Law of Supply. The principle that the quantity of a commodity producers are willing to supply varies directly with the price of the commodity. At higher prices, therefore, the quantity supplied will be greater than at lower prices. This "law" ignores the short-term effect of demand or non-demand.

Lay Days. The agreed-upon number of days that a marine vessel may remain in port for loading and unloading without penalty.

Leader Effectiveness. The extent to which a leader influences his co-workers in the achievement of group objectives.

Leadership. All successful organisations have one common attribute, i.e., leadership. Leadership is an important aspect of managing. By performing the functions of planning, organising, staffing and controlling, the managers can get some results. But managers could achieve better results by effective leadership. Lawrence A. Appley pointed out in 1955, that the time has come to substitute the word "leadership" for management. Leadership has become an inevitable aspect in industry during the past few decades.

Lease. A contractual agreement that transfers possession and use of property for a limited period under specified terms and conditions. A lease is an encumbrance against the title, since the rights it grants to the lessee are likewise binding on the successor or successors to the title.

Lease Assignment. A written legal document that generally conveys all rights of the assignor for the remaining term of the lease.

Leaseback. A long-term lease of real estate or equipment that has been sold to an independent agent and is then taken back under the lease agreement by the original seller.

Leasehold. An interest in land under the terms of a lease; normally classified as a tangible, fixed asset.

Leasehold Insurance. This type of policy may be written for a tenant who has an unusually favourable lease, lower in cost than could be obtained at current market prices. It provides a measure of financial protection in the event the premises are rendered uninhabitable because of fire.

Lease Purchase Agreement. An instrument whereby it is agreed that a portion of the note payments will be applied to the purchase price. The title of transferred on completion of the agreement.

Ledger. A book of accounts; any book of final entry.

Ledger Clerk. An employees who is assigned the task of posting and balancing a ledger.

Ledger Journal. A book with multicolumned pages, used as a record of transactions, functioning as both a journal and a ledger. Usually the record contains debit or credit columns or both, and is used only when the number of accounts is few and transactions are relatively few and simple.

Legal Capital. The part of a corporation's paid-in capital that becomes the par or stated value of the capital stock, as determined by law, agreement, or resolution of the board of directors. Also, the portion of net assets that is restricted from withdrawal, under corporation law.

Legal Debt Margin. In municipal accounting, the excess of authorized debt over outstanding debt.

Legal Entity. Any individual, partnership, corporation, or organization empowered by law or custom to own property or engage in business transactions.

Legal Liability. An obligations that is enforceable by law, as distinguished from a moral responsibility.

Legal List. A list of investments selected by various state governments in which certain institutions and fiduciaries such as insurance companies and banks may invest. Legal lists are often restricted to high-quality securities that meet defined specifications.

Legal Reserve. The minimum proportion of its demand deposits that a bank is required by law to keep in the form of cash in the vault or as a deposit at the Federal Reserve Bank. A decrease in the legal reserve requirement is expansionary because it enables banks to increase their loans; an increase in the legal reserve requirement is contractionary because it forces banks to reduce their loans.

Legal Tender. A currency that a creditor must by law accept in payment of a debt.

Legatee. A person to whom a legacy or bequest is given by the terms of a will.

Letter of Credit (LC). A document issued by a bank or similar institution allowing a borrower to draw a bill of exchange on it for specified purposes. In the case of international trade, an overseas buyer may arrange for a bank in the country of the supplier to issue a letter of credit to the supplier accepting a bill of exchange drawn on it upon delivery of the relevant export shipping documents. Normally, the overseas buyer opens in irrevocable letter of credit with the vendor's bank in the vendor's country.

Letters Close. Letters issued by a government or a sovereign to a private person concerning a private matter. Distinguished from Letters Patent.

Letters Patent. A writing from an official person or organization that confers on a designated person a grant (such as a right, title, status, property, authority, privilege, monopoly, franchise, immunity, or exemption) in a form readily open for inspection by all. Distinguished from Letters Close.

Letter Stock. Stock issued to founders, early executives, and investors that is not registered with the Securities and Exchange Commission and thus is not subject to restrictions on sale and disposition. It is called letter stock because a letter of intent to invest, not to trade, must be filed with the appropriate regulatory body. Also known as unregistered stock or founder's stock.

Leveling Effect. In management meeting, the effect created by a dominant person who, by force or personality or rank and title, causes others in his group or among his peers to tend to agree with his views, that is, come to his level.

Leverage. The extent to which the money capital of a firm is divided between fixed interest or fixed dividend capital (debentures, preference shares,loan capital) and equity or ordinary shares that are not entitled to a guaranteed or minimum return. A company with a high proportion of fixed interest capital is referred to as highly leveraged while one with a high proportion of equity capital has low leverage.

Leverage Ratios. A set of financial ratios intended to display the nature of the methods and sources of financing used in acquiring the corporation's assets and to indicate their impact on the earnings available to common stock-holders. Such ratios include debt to total assets, defined as total debt divided by total assets; fixed charge coverage, defined as income available for fixed charges divided by fixed charges; and times interest earned, defined as earnings before taxes plus interest charges divided by interest charges.

Levy. A tax assessment. In management, a request made on members of an organization for contributions of capital. In law, a writ of levy refers to the seizure of a defendant's property by the sheriff to satisfy the plaintiff's judgment. The word sometimes is used to indicate that a lien has been attached to land and other property owned by the defendant by virtue of a judgment.

Liability. An amount owed by one person (debtor) to another (creditor). The debtors or the creditor may also be an organization, enterprise, or business firm.

Liability Insurance. Insurance basically intended to cover the insured party's responsibility for payment obligations to others as a result of bodily injury or property damage. In order to qualify for protection by an insurer, such a liability must have been incurred as a matter of legal judgment or through voluntary or contractual agreement. Also known as third-party liability insurance; public liability insurance; liability, other than automobile, insurance; and Owners',m landlords, and tenants' (OL&T) public liability insurance.

Liability Risk. Sometimes called third-party risk or legal-liability risk, this involves the possibility that the insured party may become legally obligated to pay money to a third party.

Licensed Public Accountant. A person who has registered under state law to practice as a public accountant. In many states, the licensee must be a certified public accountant.

Lien. A right one person has to keep possession or control of the property of another in satisfaction of a debt. Among the many kinds of liens are the artisan's lien, the attorney's lien, the innkeeper's lien, the mechanic's lien, and the vendor's lien.

Life Annuity. An annuity whose payments terminate on the death of the beneficiary. In the business world, it may be an annuity derived from the purchase of an insurance policy of a special type, or the result of a special perquisite provided as part of an employment contract.

Life Tenant. A person entitled to the use of or income from property during his or her lifetime. Also applies to organizations.

Limited Access Land. Real property that is difficult to reach or is partially inaccessible.

Limited Liability. A liability that is restricted by law or valid contract. Examples include the liability of a stockholder of a corporation or of an inactive, limited partner in a firm.

Limited Partner. A member of a partnership whose liability to creditors of the partnership is limited to the amount of his or her investment. A limited partner may not participate in management. Also known as special partner.

Limited Price Order. In securities trading, an order to buy or sell a stated amount of a security at a specified price, or better price, if obtainable after the order is presented on the floor.

Liquid Asset. Cash in banks and on hand, and other cash assets not set aside for specific purposes besides the payment of current liabilities. A marketable security that is readily converted to cash may also be considered a liquid asset. Also known as quick asset.

Liquidating Dividend. A pro rata distribution to stockholders or owners by an organization in liquidation. Also, a pro rate distribution to the stockholders of a company having wasting assets, such as mines, oil wells, and timber, representing a return of paid-in capital; a return of capital to the investors.

Liquidation. The payment of a debt. The conversion of accounts receivable, investments, or inventory to cash. The settlement of an organization's debts through the sale of assets as a result of voluntary or involuntary termination of the enterprise.

Liquidation Value. The price that can be obtained from the sale of assets in a liquidation proceeding. Also known as forced-sale value. In the event of the liquidation of a corporation, liquidation value is the agreed-upon amount per share to be paid to preferred shareholders.

Liquidity. A general term used to describe the ability of a business enterprise to convert noncash assets into a resource that enables the enterprise to meet its short-term obligations.

Liquidity Preference. The theory that people prefer to hold assets in the form of money because it is more readily convertible into other forms. Money flows or can be made to flow quite readily, thus money is liquid. Also known as the theory of interest, formulated by John Maynard Keynes.

Liquidity Ratios. Ratios of financial data used as indicators of an enterprise's ability to meet its current obligations in the event of stress. The best known of these ratios are the current ratio and the quick ratio. The latter is also known as the acid test.

Listed. A term used to describe a security that has been granted the trading privileges of an exchange.

Listed Stock. A company's stock that is traded on a securities exchange, and for which a listing application and a registered statement giving detailed information about the company and its operations have been filed both with the Securities and Exchange Commission (SEC)—Unless the stock is otherwise exempted—and with the exchange itself. The various stock exchanges have different standards for listing.

List Price. A published price, intended to be the price paid by the ultimate consumer. Any trade or other discounts are calculated from the list price.

Live Load. The orders or the load of manufacturing orders that are actually available to be worked on by a manufacturing facility.

Livestock Insurance. Intended to provide coverage for groups of animals, or for individual animals such as a valuable racing horse. Insurance is available to those who professionally raise or breed game or fur-bearing animals for profit.

Load Center. A group of similar machines or work stations that can all the considered simultaneously for planning the workload. Also known as work center and machine center.

Loading. In Finance the amount sometimes added to an installment contract to cover selling and administrative costs, interest, risk, and other factors related to the contract. In an investment trust or mutual fund, it is the amount added to the market price of securities, representing administrative and selling costs, trustee's fees, and brokerage and management fees. In cost accounting, it is the addition of overhead to prime cost.

Loan Value. In insurance, an amount of money available to the owner of the policy and which the owner may borrow from the insurer. The insurance policy serves as collateral for the loan repayment.

Loan-value Ratio. In real estate, the ratio of the appraised real property value to the total mortgage loan.

Local Development Corporation (LDC). To assist small business at the grass-roots level, the federal government encourages community residents to form LDCs. Resident-organized and capitalized, LDCs solicit Small Business Administration (SBA) and bank loans to buy or build facilities for local small businesses. They raise their capital by selling shares to 25 or more local residents. After identifying small businesses in need, an LDC is eligible for one SBA loan or guarantee up to a specified maximum dollar level per year and unlimited bank loans for each small business it assists.

Lock-box System. A means of accelerating the flow of funds from the time of customer payment to the time of deposit in the company's bank account. A lock-box arrangement usually is on a regional basis, with the company choosing regional banks according to its billing patterns. The company rents a localpost office box and authorizes its bank in each of the cities in which a box is rented to pick up the remittances in the box. The bank picks up the mail several times a day and deposits the checks in the company's account.

Locked in. A security trading term. An investor is said to be locked in when a security he owns shows a profit but he refrains from selling the security because the profit would immediately become subject to the capital gains tax.

Lockout. The act of an employer in closing down a facility to keep workers out of their jobs.

Long. In securities trading terms, this signifies ownership of securities. "I am long 100 U.S. Steel" means the speaker owns 100 shares of that company's stock.

Long Term. A general expression for a period of time that extends through one more fiscal years.

Long-term Contract. Any contract for goods or services that extends beyond one year.

Long-term Debt. An obligation or liability that is due after one year, as contrasted with short-term debts or liabilities that are current and due within the next 12 months. Also known as long-term liability.

Long-term Lease. An obligation for rental payments on real or personal property over an extended period, in excess of one year.

Loss. The excess of costs over related revenues; a disadvantage. Also known as gross loss.

Loss Ratio. A term used to express the ratio between the total of premiums paid to an insurance company and the total value of claims paid out by the company.

Lost Usefulness. In accounting, the gradual dissipation from any cause or for any reason of the service life or usefulness of an asset.

Lot-book Report. In real estate transactions, a nonliability letter issued by a title company showing the last owner of record and any encumbrances thereafter. Such a letter is not a title report.

Lot-size Inventories. The quantity of supplies or materials required to support production for a specific time period, usually expressed in weeks. Also known as cycle inventories.

Lottery. In business transactions, any scheme for the distribution of goods that involves the three elements of payment of consideration: (1) a return promise, (2) an act performed, and (3) a forbearance. This involves a prize to some but not all of those who give consideration, and also involves chance. The use of lotteries to market goods is considered unfair competition. The U.S. postal laws and regulations prohibit the sending of any matter through the U.S. mails that is in the nature of a lottery.

Lump-sum Appropriation. An allotmment of funds for a specific purpose or for the operation of an economic unit without a statement of the details applicable to individual items of proposed expenditure.

Mm

M1. One of the three components of money supply in India. It is also called as "Narrow Money". M1 is the sum total of demand deposits of banks, other deposits of Reserve Bank of India, and currency notes and coins held by the public. Net demand deposits are the current account deposits and a part of savings deposits deemed to be demand liability. Other deposits with RBI are the deposits of institutions such as IDBI, ICICI, IMF and foreign governments.

M2. Refers to the sum of M1 and savings deposits with post office.

M3. Also known as "broad money", it is the sum of (i) M1 (ii) net fixed deposits with banks and (iii) portion of savings deposits not included in M1. It is a measure of total supply of money in the country which is used as a reference to set monetary targets by the RBI.

M4. The sum of M3 and total deposits with post office.

Machinery and Equipment. The category of industrial goods that includes all machines of all sizes used in production and office work, not intended for resale.

Macroeconomics. Study of the issues that pertain to the economy as a whole, to aggregates of individuals, or to groups of commodities. Examples would be total employment without regard to type of employment or skill, the income derived from such employment, or the total consumption of goods as contrasted with the consumption of a specific consumable item.

Macro Instruction. In data processing, an instruction to a computer consisting of a sequence of micro instructions; the more powerful instructions that combine several operations in one instruction.

Mail Order Selling. Selling against orders received through the post directly from consumers/purchasers or agents.

Mail-Order Wholesaler. Serving as a middleman in the distribution of goods, this merchant substitutes mail-order catalogs and order forms for a personal sales force. Such a wholesaler meets the needs of retailers who are located at great distances from regular merchant wholesalers.

Makeready Time. In manufacturing procedures, the time required to prepare machines and other facilities prior to the start of a process or of production. Also known as lead time and setup time.

Management by Objectives (MBO). MBO calls for setting of specific and verifiable objectives at different levels of the organisation. These objectives are set toward expected results for all units in quantitative terms. In this process, superiors and subordinates jointly identify the objectives and define each individual's area of responsibility. This makes everyone to know what is expected of them and motivate for higher performance.

Management by Exception (MBE). A management method under which subordinates handle normal details of their assignments and are sensitive to exceptional events that they then bring to the attention of their supervisors. Also abbreviated as MBX.

Management Control System (MCS). The scientific method by which managers set goals, measure performance in terms of results, and take appropriate action in the form of rewards, penalties, or additional training for employees.

Management Process. The whole process of management can be easily understood as a series of separate functions such as planning, organising, staffing, directing and controlling.

Manager. In the most fundamental interpretation of the word, a person who occupies a formal position in a formal organization, is responsible for the work of at least one other person, and his formal authority over that person. It is policy among some companies to set the minimum number of persons or subordinates in a group as the determining factor, or one of the determining factors, in the application of the title manager.

Managerial Effectiveness. The extent to which a manager achieves the productivity or output requirements of his or her position.

Managing Director. The chief executive of a company. The title is generally preferred in areas outside the North American continent. Broadly equivalent to president of a company, the title preferred in the United States.

Manual Rate. In insurance policies, an established premium rate, usually stated on dollars cost per thousand dollars of protection or risk.

Manufacturing Cost. Any item of expense that occurs during a processing operation. Also, the collective fixed and variable costs of a manufacturing process or operation, including raw materials, parts, direct labor, and manufacturing overhead.

Manufacturing Expense. The cost of manufacturing, other than the cost of raw materials consumed and direct labor. Also known as factory expense, indirect expense, and factory overhead.

Margin. In securities trading, the amount paid by the customer when using his or her broker's credit to buy a security. Under Federal Reserve regulations during the past 20 years, the initial margin required has ranged from 40 per cent of the purchase price all the way to 100 per cent. A stockbroker or brokerage firm may set margin limits that are below the maximum allowed by the Federal Reserve.

Marginal Cost Pricing. A method of setting prices in which price is made equal to marginal cost. Since price must be set in such a way that all output is sold, and since marginal cost varies with output, marginal cost pricing implies that the price should be set at the point at which the demand curve cuts the marginal cost curve. Marginal cost pricing is considered an appropriate policy for nationalized industries on the grounds that it maximizes economic welfare.

Margin Call. A demand on a customer to put up money or securities with his or her broker. The call is made at the time of a purchase, or if a customer's equity in a margin account declines below the minimum standard set by the Exchange or by the firm.

Margin Regulations. The authority for setting the percentage down payment required of a borrower to finance the purchase of stock. The rate is set by the Federal Reserve System's Board of Governors. An increase in margin requirements is intended to dampen security purchases: a decrease in margin requirements is intended to encourage such purchases.

Marine Insurance. Perhaps the oldest type of insurance, dating from ancient times, marine insurance indemnifies for loss or damage to vessels, cargo, or other property exposed to the perils of the sea.

Markdown. In retail merchandising, the amount by which an original selling price is reduced.

Marked Capacity. The weight limits of cargo loaded into a railroad car as stenciled on the side of the car.

Market. Any area, place, or location without geographic limits, local or worldwide, with the essential feature that buyers and sellers are free to interact so that a price is established for the commodity or service being exchanged.

Marketable Securities. A balance-sheet classification for negotiable stocks, bonds, and Treasury securities carried as a current asset in the form of investments.

Market Economy. An economic system in which the questions of what to produce, how much to produce, and for whom to produce are decided in an open market through the free operation of supply and demand. There are no pure market economies, but several specialized markets such as the organized commodity exchanges closely approximate some of the properties of a pure market system.

Market Equilibrium. The economic state in which the supply of goods is limited to the quantity already produced and placed on the market.

Marketing Development Assistance (MDA). Assistance provided by the Marketing Development Assistance Committee to an Indian exporter in developing his foreign markets. Ordinarily, grants are available to exporters for certain recognised export activities, such as (a) market and commodity research programmes; (b) export publicity and dissemination of market information; (c) participation in foreign trade fairs and exhibition; (d) trade delegations and study teams; and (e) establishment of offices and branches abroad.

The Marketing Development Assistance also provides grant-in-aid to Export Promotion Councils and other export enterprises. The expenditure on compensatory cash support to exports of selected products and the subsidy paid to the banks for providing export credit to the exporters at reasonable rates of interest are also met out of the provisions under marketing development assistance. The operation of the MDA is based on a critical examination of the proposals by the MDA Committee.

Marketing Mix. Policies or strategies in combination adopted to formulate a marketing programme.

The elements of Marketing Mix ordinarily comprise: (1) Product Planning including branding and packaging, (2) Pricing (3) Physical Distribution including physical handling and servicing, (4) Promotion including personal selling and advertising.

Marketing Research. Marketing research is distinguished from market research in that while the latter deals with the pattern of a market, the former deals with problems involved in marketing a particular product.

Marketing research begins with market research and then studies practical difficulties in selling and deciding such matter as what lines might be adopted in particular areas and what special problems might be met in any particular region. It is concerned with the problems attached to selling a particular product for a particular manufacturer.

Market Letter. A general term for short publications or newsletters issued by brokerage firms and investment advisory services to provide investors with recommendations to buy or sell securities and with other pertinent investment information.

Market Order. In instruction to a broker to buy or sell shares, stocks, or commodities at the prevailing market price.

Market Price. In securities trading, market price is the last reported price at which a security has been sold. Generally, the actual price prevailing in a marketplace at any particular moment.

Market Risk. In the securities market, the condition of uncertainty about future prices because of changes in investor attitudes.

Market Saturation. The theoretical point at which, because of decreased consumer need or disappearance of prospective buyers, few or no additional sales are likely in a marketplace.

Market Share. Sales of a product in a particular market segment as a proportion of the total sales in that segment. Also known as market penetration.

Market Theory. A wage theory whose basic tenet is that wage levels are determined by the supply of and demand for labor. Thus, if there is a shortage of qualified workers with a particular skill, those who possess that skill should be paid higher wages than workers possessing skills that are not in short supply. To some extent, this theory treats labor as a commodity, since commodity prices are determined largely by supply and demand factors.

Markup. The total amount by which established selling prices are increased during a given period in setting new selling prices. Also, an amount that is added to the purchase price of merchandise to arrive at a selling price; also known as markon.

Marxism. The theories of Karl Marx, characterized by the central claims that the ruling middle class (bourgeoisie) will be overthrown by the working class (proletariat) through revolutionary action, and that a classless society will emerge in which the principal means of production will be publicly owned. Marx did not present a clear strategy for revolution; his theory is vague as a political guide, and as a result, Marx's followers have continuously quarreled among themselves over interpretations of his speeches, writings, and scattered notes. Many still read Marx in search of an explanation of current social, economic, and political events.

Master Tariff. A tariff filed with the Interstate Commerce Commission applying to a large number of applicable tariffs.

Matched and Lost. In securities trading, when two bids to buy the same stock are made on the trading floor simultaneously and each bid is equal in price or larger than the quantity of stock offered, both bids are considered to be on an equal basis. The two bidders flip a coin to decide why buys the stock. Also applies to offers to sell.

Material Current Cost. Each time a purchase order is issued, the cost data for the relevant material are updated. The latest purchase cost becomes the current cost for the material.

Materials Control. The process of providing the required quantity and quality of material needed in a manufacturing process at the required time and place and with the lowest practicable investment.

Materials Management. A concept of organization that places under a single manager all functions concerned with the movement of materials, production control, inventory control, traffic, storage, materials, handling, purchasing, and other similarly related activities.

Matured Liability. Generally refers to bonds: an obligation that is due or past due.

Maturing Liability. Generally refers to bonds; an obligation that is about to reach maturity.

Maturity. The date on which is loan, bond, or debenture falls due and is to be paid off.

Maturity Basis. The method for calculating the values of bonds and their rates of return, based on the assumption that the bonds will be held until maturity.

Maturity Date. The date when a debt becomes due for settlement. For an Endowment Policy it denotes the date when the capital sum, with or without accumulated profits, must be paid out by the Assurance Company.

Max/min. An inventory control system under which materials are reordered up to predetermined maximum levels whenever stocks drop to a predetermined minimum level.

Medicaid. A medical aid program operated by individual states and designed to supplement the federal Medicare program.

Medicare. A federal medical aid program designed particularly for the aged.

Member Bank. A bank that belongs to the Federal Reserve System. All national banks chartered by the federal government must be members of the Reserve System. State banks may join if they meet specific requirements established by the Federal Reserve Board.

Member Firm. A securities brokerage firm organized as a partnership and having at least one general partner who is a member of the New York Stock Exchange.

Member of Companies. A person becomes a member of a company when his name is entered in its Register of Members. Subscribers to the Memorandum of Association become members automatically. Other persons become member when shares are allotted in their name on the basis of application or when shares are transferred to them. Anyone whose name does not appear on the Register is not entitled to the rights of membership.

Memorandum Bill of Lading. The third copy of a bill of lading.

Memorandum of Association. A document filed with the Registrar of Companies on the formation of a company. It is open for inspection at any time by any person at the Registered Office of the company. Memorandum of

Association forms the charter of the company and defines its objects and powers. It delimits the area beyond which the action of the company cannot go and defines the area within which the shareholders are allowed to move. It must contain the following information pertaining to a company: (1) Name—(a) It must contain the name of the company with the word 'Limited' as the last word in case of a public limited company and with 'Private Limited' as the last words in case of a private limited company. (b) While using the name, the promoters shall see that they do not adopt any name which is considered or declared as undesirable by the Government. (2) Situation—The Memorandum must mention the place in which the Registered Office of the company is to be situated. (3) Object—(a) The Memorandum must contain the object or objects of the company. (b) Except in the case of a trading company, it must also mention the area or areas to which the objects of the company would extend. (4) Liability—(a) A limited company must declare in its Memorandum that the liability of its members is limited. (b) A guarantee company must state the amount of guarantee undertaken by each member towards the liability of the company in case it is wound up. (5) Capital—In the case of a company having share capital, it must mention the amount of share capital with which the company proposes to be registered and the division thereof into shares of a fixed value. (6) Association and Subscription—(a) This would state the consent of the members as regards the formation of the company and the number of shares taken by each of them. (b) Each member is required to take at least one share of the company and to state his name, address, description and number of shares taken by him together with the name and address of the witness.

The Memorandum must be signed by each subscriber in the presence of at least one witness who shall attest the signature. A company is bound by its Memorandum but may alter it, generally by Special Resolution. The alteration must be made known to the Registrar.

Memorandum of Satisfaction. Document stating that a Mortgage or Charge on property has been discharged by repayment of the money lent. It should be signed by all parties concerned.

Mercantilism. A set of economic principles and practices intended to build national prosperity and government power by (1) accumulating precious metals through maintaining a favourable trade balance, (2) achieving economic independence through imperialism, and (3) exploiting colonies by monopolizing their raw materials and precious metals while reserving them as exclusive markets for exports.

Mercantile Agent. Agent dealing with a specified category or categories of goods. As an agent he is distinguished by the fact that, provided he has possession of the goods coming into the category or categories with the consent of the owner, he can sell and give a good Title to an innocent purchaser for value, whether or not the true owner has given his permission to sell.

Merchandise. Goods that have been purchased or manufactured for purposes of commercial sale. Also, the inventory of a merchant.

Merchant. A buyer or seller or goods who does not add to, subtract from, or in any way alter or modify the form of the goods.

Merchant Bank. Banks primarily engaged to finance foreign trade. Merchant banks assist exporters seeking assurance of payment for goods delivered abroad, and importers looking for convenient methods of settling indebtedness to overseas suppliers.

In recent years, many of the banks of India have opened merchant banking division to ease the problem of exporters of the country.

Merchant Wholesaler. A general term for a trader who takes title to goods for sale to retailers who in turn resell them to end users. Others names for a merchant wholesaler include distributor, Jobber, Merchant, and wholesaler.

Merger. Amalgmation of two or more firms under one ownership. The three common forms of merger are (1) horizontal, uniting similar plants and products; (2) vertical, uniting dissimilar plants in various stages of production; and (3) conglomerate, uniting dissimilar plants and products.

Methods Manual. Detailed information developed as sets of instructions for the routing and operations to be performed in the processing or manufacture of a part of a product.

Methods Study. A systematic procedure for the analysis of work designed to (1) eliminate unnecessary work, (2) arrange the remaining work in the best order possible, and (3) standardize the use or proper work methods.

Micro Accounting. Accounting for individual, business, nonprofit, or government organizations, or for any department or other subdivision thereof.

Microeconomics. Studies or statistics that depict the behaviour of individual issues, groups, or commodities in the economy. Examples would be an analysis of the employment data for those engaged in the manufacture of aircraft or automobiles, or of the demand for a specific commodity or consumable item.

Middle-of-the-road Style. A style of managerial leadership based on the belief that adequate organization performance is possible through balancing the need to get out the work with the need to maintain the morale of people at a satisfactory level.

Mineral Lease. A legal contract that permits the lessee to explore for and extract minerals from the leased property under prescribed conditions as to time, price, rental, or royalties. As known as mining lease.

Min/max System. An industrial procedure for stock replenishment that establishes points at which the minimum quantity on hand indicates the need to reorder so as to return the quantity to the maximum level.

Minority Shareholders. Members of a company in which the majority of the Equity Share Capital, i.e. the controlling interest, is held by another company, or a few business groups. Evidently, minority shareholders have little say in the conduct of the affairs of the company.

In India, the Companies Act, 1956, as amended up to date provides remedies to mismanagement and oppression without directing winding up. To protect the interest of the shareholders, the Act has introduced two remedies: (1) Powers of the Court (Sections 397-407); and (2) Powers of the Central Government (Sections 408, 409 and 388—388E).

In addition to above, the minority rights are being protected by the following provisions of the Act—(1) It is obligatory to have consent of the court before certain acts can be validly done, e.g. change of object (Sec. 17), reduction of share capital (Sec. 101), etc. (2) Appeal to the Central Government can be made by an aggrieved shareholder against the arbitrary action of the board in refusing to register a transfer or transmission of shares (Sec. 111). (3) Where class rights are varied, the dissentient shareholders holding 10 per cent of the issued capital can apply to the curt for cancellation of variation (Sec. 107). (4) The minority shareholder can apply to the Central Government for an investigation into the affairs of the company (Sec. 235). (5) Even a single shareholder can apply to the court for a winding up order on the just and equitable ground (Sec. 439). (6) Any member is entitled to hold up reconstruction or amalgamation of a company unless his interest is purchased

(Sec. 494). (7) The court is empowered to amend, vary, confirm, or set aside any arrangement made between the company and its creditors on the application of any creditor or contributory (Sec. 517).

Mint Ratio. Under a bimetallic standard, the ratio of the weight of one metal to another, determined by the equivalent value of those quantities of metal in terms of the national unit of currency (such as the dollar) as defined by the government. During the nineteenth century when the United States was on a bimetallic standard, the government defined the mint ratio for many year as

15 grains silver = 1 grain gold = 1 dollar

The mint ratio was therefore 15 to 1. Since the ratio remained fixed by law, it resulted in either gold or silver being driven out of circulation, depending on the relative international market values of the two metals.

Minutes. Summary of Proceedings at a meeting to be recorded for future reference. Under Companies Act, 1956, as amended up to date, every company in India is required to maintain a Minute Book (Sec. 193).

Minute Book. The register which contains the fair copy of the minutes of a meeting. It is a statutory requirement that every enterprise, irrespective of its nature of business, must maintain a Minute Book.

Miscellaneous Asset. An asset of minor significance that cannot be classified under any other heading or subheading of a balance sheet.

Miscellaneous Expense. In accounting procedures, an incidental expense, not classifiable as manufacturing, selling, general, or administrative expense. It appears as an item on an income statement below operating income or as a subdivision of income deductions.

Mixed Economy. An economic system in which the questions of what and for whom to produce are decided partially by the free market and partially by a central government authority. There are varying forms and degrees of mixed economies.

Mixed Inventory. An inventory of a class of goods whose individual items are not or cannot be identified with a particular lot.

Monetary Policy. Measures taken by the central bank and the national treasury to manipulate the money supply with the intent to influence the output of goods and services, employment the price level, the rate of economic growth, or the balance of international payments.

Monetary Theory of Business Cycles. A theory that attributes business cycles to monetary factors, such as changes in the quantity of money and credit and changes in interest rates.

Monetary Union. A situation in which two or more countries share a common currency and common financial policies and institutions.

Money. Anything that serves as a medium of exchange and thus facilitates the economic process of production, distribution, and consumption. Econometricians define money as currency and checking accounts. Superficially, credit cards appear to be money; however, credit cards do not immediately demand the movement of currency, and they may be paid for by check from the credit card holder's checking account at some time later than the delivery of the goods or services received by the consumer.

Moneylender. A person whose business is lending of money on interest. Money lending business is bound by strict regulations as: (i) The lenders must not carry on business except in their own names; (ii) They must hold a moneylender's certificate and annual Excise Licence; and (iii) They must not charge compound interest. Money is generally lent against security. An agreement is prepared and signed by both the lender and borrower before making the loan. The agreement takes into account all relevant factors concerning the loan.

Money Market. In the field of finance, a center where short-term credit instruments are bought and sold.

Money of Account. The unit in which accounts are kept and by which values are recorded. The Money of Account is usually the same as the legal tender money. The Rupee in India and the Dollar in U.S.A. are both legal tender money and the money of account. The money of account may, however, differ from the money in circulation.

Money Order. An order by a depositor of money at one post office and that sum of money payable to the addressee by another post office. Rates of commission fixed by the postal department, and revised from time to time, is charged from the depositor for rendering money order services.

Money Substitutes. Articles which serve as a substitute of money but are not regarded as 'proper money'. Such substitutes are Cheques, Bills of Exchange, Postal Orders, Treasury Bill and Bearer Bonds, used for making payments among known parties but are not generally acceptable.

Money Supply. The supply of money—or the volume of money in circulation—refers to the volume of money held by the people in the country, i.e. the individuals and business houses. The quantity of money in existence at a particular time—or the supply of money in spendable form—consists of two important items; : (i) Currency components—consisting of coins and currency notes issued by the central bank which are in circulation; and (ii) Deposit component—deposit money with the public consisting of deposits of the general public with commercial banks and with the central bank of a country.

It is to be noted, coins and currency notes, i.e. cash held by commercial banks, are to be excluded in determining money supply, since they form the basis of deposit money of the public. Secondly, the stock of monetary gold with a central bank is also to be excluded from the concept of money supply. Thirdly, the cash held by the government is also to be excluded. For, it constitutes the reserve on which the demand deposits of the public are supported.

Broadly, the proportion between currency and bank deposits to the total money supply will depend upon a) the state of the economic development of a country, b) the banking habit of the people, c) the level of income of people, d) nature of business and trade customs, and e) the level of prices.

Money Supply Rule. A guide for the expansion of the economy advanced by the monetarist school of thought, especially by Milton Friedman. The rule states that the Federal Reserve should expand the nation's money supply at a steady rate in accordance with the economy's growth and capacity to produce, approximating 3 to 5 per cent a year for the United States. More than this would lead to strong inflationary pressures; less would tend to have a stagnating if not deflationary effect.

Monometalism. The Legal Tender Money which is linked with a particular metal—gold or silver. The money is either made of the chosen metal or may be convertible into it. The value of money in use depends upon the value of metal. From 1835 to 1893, India had silver monometalism. From the middle of the 18th century to 1914, U.K. had gold monometalism. Under bimetalism two metals, gold and silver, are used for coinage purpose and the value of money depends on both metals. However, monometalism or bimetalism does not exist anywhere today. All countries have adopted the paper currency.

Monopolies and Restrictive Trade Practices (MRTP) Act 1969. The Act was introduced by the Government of India to regulate and control the share of big business houses over the production and market of a product. The Act has given the yardstick against which it is to be ascertained whether a business is big and, therefore, specific regulatory measures applicable to big businesses can also be enforceable to a company under consideration.

Monopolistic Competition. A type of market structure in which a relatively large number of the sellers of products that are similar but not identical possess some degree of control over their selling price. Product differentiation and advertising are usually characteristic of this type of competition, without emphasis on price differences.

Monopoly. A market situation in which there is a single producer or seller of a commodity or service with few, if any, substitutes. By definition the firm constitutes the industry.

Monopsony. A market situation in which a single firm is the only buyer of a product, although there may be more than one seller; also known as a buyer's monopoly. Monopsonies occur most frequently in labor markets, when a single firm is the only important employer in a locality. The early textile-mill towns of New England and the coal-mining towns of Pennsylvania were examples of labor monopsony. The improvements in and the increased availability of transportation have enabled laborers to expand their reach beyond the town in which they live or domicile, thus lessening monopsony power.

Monte Carlo Method. A trial-and-error method of repeated calculations to discover the best solution to a problem. This method is often used when a great number of variables are present with interrelationships so complex as to preclude the practicability of doing a direct analysis of the data.

Monthly Usage. In production procedures, the use of a part number on a monthly basis.

Moral Suasion. In the field of finance, oral or written appeals by the Federal Reserve Board to member banks urging them to expand or restrict credit but not requiring them to comply.

Mortality Curve. In management procedures, a curve that displays the estimated life spans of persons or things. It may also be used to display the history of actual life spans.

Mortgage. A conditional conveyance of property that operates as a lien on land, buildings, and other property, fixed or movable, given by a borrower to the lender as security for his or her loan.

Mortgage Bond. A bond secured by a mortgage against specific property or properties of the issuer of the bond.

Mortgagee. A lender of money who accepts a property mortgage as security.

Mortgage Guaranty Insurance. Insurance available to mortgagees to protect them against financial loss.

Mortgage Insurance Policy. A policy that protects the mortgagee against loss in the event that title should prove defective.

Mortgagee's Statement. A summary by the holder of a mortgage note indicating the present status of payments and the remainder owed.

Mortgagor. One who borrows money or makes a loan, using property to which he or she has title as security for the loan.

Most-Favoured-Nation Clause. This term is related with international bilateral trade agreements where each country offers 'most-favoured-nation' position to the other and a clause is incorporated to this effect in the trading agreement. In this event, both the countries agree to afford the other best available Tariff and Quota term in the course of international trade. The importance of most-favoured-nation status was pinpointed in the General Agreement on Tariffs and Trade (G.A.T.T.).

Motion Study. This area of motion and methods study has many names. It is known as methods analysis, methods engineering, methods research, work study, and work analysis. F.B. and L.M. Gilbreth define motion study as the science of eliminating wastefulness resulting from using unnecessary, ill-directed, and inefficient motions. The aim of motion study is to find and perpetuate the scheme of least-waste methods of labor.

Motivation. Motivation is a general term applying to the entire class of drives, desires, needs, wishes and similar forces that induce an individual or a group of people to work. The success or failure of a business organisation depends on the performance of people working in it. Generally, performance is determined by three factors, viz., ability, knowledge and motivation. [performance = ability + knowledge) x motivation]. Among the three, motivation is the most important factor since it deals with human behaviour. The work 'motivation' is derived from the work 'motive' which means 'to move or to activate'. Motivation is the task of making some one to act in the desired manner.

Motivational Research. An expression used in marketing for investigations of the reasons why consumers may choose one product in favor of another.

Multinational Company. A commercial firm with a financial or managerial interest in companies, affiliates, or subsidiaries in a variety of countries.

Multiple-maturity Time Deposit. A type of savings deposit that has limited withdrawal privileges and pays a higher-than-normal interest rate.

Mutual Fund. An organisation that collects savings of public for the purpose of investing in securities (debt and/or equity). The profits of the said organisation are distributed among investors after deducting managing costs. Mutual fund may be 'open end' or 'closed end'. In **open end** type of mutual fund, there is no limit on the number of shares that it can issue. As a rule it offers new shares to the public continuously and stands ready to purchase its shares at any time. The Unit Trust of India's Unit 1964 scheme is a prime example. In contrast to an open end investment company, or mutual fund, a **closed end** mutual fund rarely issues new shares after the initial offering, and it does not stand ready to repurchase its own shares. The shares issued by a closed end fund are redeemed at the end of its life. Before the expiry of its life, its shares are traded through brokers at market prices that may be higher or lower than the value of the underlying assets.

Managing an open fund is not an easy task. The maximum possible demand for redemption at any time must be estimated and the cash needed for the purpose should be maintained. Moreover, daily calculation of Net Asset Value (NAV) requires a sophisticated information system.

Nn

NAK. Negative Acknowledgment.

Naked Option. It may be a 'naked call' or 'naked put' option. In a **Naked Call Option** on a stock, the writer does not own it (the stock). Since, he can not deliver it, he bears the risk of an unpside movement in the price of the share which could be infinite Naked Put Writing is writing a put option on a stock when the writer does not have sufficient assets in his or her brokerage account to purchase the stock.

National Bank. A central bank of a country.

National Income. Not to be confused with the total income received by people from all sources (that if, personal income), national income is the total of all net incomes earned by or attributed to the factors of production: the sum of wages, rent, interest, and profits that accrue to the supplies of labor, land, capital, and entrepreneur-ship. Generally and in theoretical discussions, national income is often used simply to represent the income or output of an economy.

National Index. It is a broad based share price index compiled using a sample of 100 scrips from both specified and non-specified lists quoted nationwide at fine major stock exchanges viz. Bombay, Delhi, Calcutta, Madras and Ahmedabad. Therefore, it is called the National Inde. It is more representative of the market movement than the Sensitive Index which is compiled by using only 30 scrips are among the 100 comprising the National Index. It is calculated with financial year

1983-84 as the base year. It is a weighted index, the weights being the number of outstanding shares for each scrip. Adjustments are made to the weight and the base year for the issue of bonus and rights issues.

National Industrial Development Corporation (N.I.D.C.). An enterprise established by the Government of India in October, 1954, with the object of financing industries and promoting planned industrial development. N.I.D.C. was set up with an Authorised Capital of Rs.1 crore.

The main functions of the N.I.D.C. are to (i) formulate and execute projects for setting up new industries or developing new lines of production, (ii) provide consultancy services through its Technological Consultancy Bureau, and (iii) finance the rehabilitation and modernisation of specified industries, viz., cotton textiles, jute and machine tools.

Currently the corporation is providing mainly consultant engineering services both at home and abroad. The Corporation is rendering consultancy services for industrial development including the provision of services for design and detailed engineering of industrial projects, development planning and management consultancy services. The services of the Corporation are being made use of by individual entrepreneurs, Indian as well as foreign governments, including the United Nations.

Nationalization. The action of a government in assuming ownership of an industry; usually used in reference to an industry that was formerly privately held or operated within the private sector.

National Product, Gross (GNP). Gross Income generated from within the country plus net income received from abroad during a year. This is expressed either 'at current prices', i.e., at prices prevailing during the period to which the figures refer; or 'at constant prices', i.e., at prices prevailing during a fixed base period in the past, irrespective of the period to which the figures refer. Thus, figures 'at constant prices' discount the effect of inflation after the base period and measure the changes in real terms. Figures 'at current prices' are naturally influenced by inflation but are more useful for, say, international comparisons for the same period.

National Product, Net (NNP). During the process of production the capital equipment of the country is gradually worn out. Some machines may also become obsolete. As such, a certain part of the Gross National Product of the country must be used for the replacement of worn out and obsolete capital goods. This is not available for consumption or investment by the people. Evidently the GNP less replacements constitute the Net National Product (N.N.P.).

National Savings Certificates. A government of India Security obtainable at post offices of the country. Certificates are available in multiple units. They may be bought by anyone in his own name or that of another. Repayment follows from written application by the holder of the certificate.

Natural Business Year. A fiscal year that ends at the annual low point of business activity or at the conclusion of a business season.

Natural Financing. A sale or exchange or real property that requires no outside financing or mortgages, as when properties are traded and each party assumes the other's mortgages, or as in an all-cash sale.

Natural Monopoly. A form of business organization that occurs in a market situation in which monopoly rather than competition appears to be the most feasible and efficient arrangement for the production and distribution of a commodity or service. Public utilities are natural monopolies. Such monopolies are established by a state or federal government and are also called legal or virtual monopolies.

Natural Person. In law, an individual human being.

Natural Resources. These comprise both the raw materials and the conditions of nature that are required in production. They include mineral wealth, soil, climate, waterways, and topography. By means of foreign trade, domestic natural resources may be exchanged for those of another country or for finished products, so that productive labor therefore becomes part of the trade.

Navigational Change Principle. A principle of management decision-making that holds that a decision-maker should consider the ability he or she will have to change a decision once it is made.

Near-Money. A financial instrument with some of the qualities of money. Savings deposits, shares in savings and loan associations, U.S. Treasury bills, and the cash value of personally held life insurance policies are examples of such an instrument.

Need. A concept taken from behavioural science, assumed by many industrial psychologists to be the initiating and sustaining force of hebaviour. A positive need or desire is defined as a force that impels a person toward the achievement of a goal. A negative need is an anxiety, a force that repels a person away from certain objects or conditions, often through fear of failure. Common synonymous for need are drive and want, when positive; fear and aversion, when negative.

Needs Satisfaction. Fulfillment of a want. When a need is satisfied, it may no longer serve as a motivator. For example, a hungry person is highly motivated to acquire food and will perform a difficult task in moving toward that objective. However, once the desired amount of food has been eaten, hunger is removed as a motivator and promises of more food at that moment may not produce additional work motivation. Other needs or wants now become more important.

Negative Income Tax. Proposed government payments to a family to equalize the difference between income earned and a minimum guaranteed income level.

Negligence. In legal procedures, the failure to do what an ordinary, reasonable, prudent person would do, or the act of doing what an ordinary, reasonable, prudent person would not do. Ordinary negligence arises from errors in judgment, not from willful deceit. Gross negligence is attributable to recklessness and an extreme disregard for common standards.

Neoclassical Economics. An approach to economics that flourished in Europe and the United States between 1870 and World War I. Among its leaders were William Stanley Jevons, Carl Menger, Leon Walras, Vilfredo Pareto, Alfred Marshall, John Bates Clark, and Irving Fisher. The neoclassicists were primarily concerned with refining principles of price and allocation theory, the theory of capital, and related aspects of economics. In developing their analyses and models, they made early and extensive use of mathematics, especially differential and integral calculus. Much of the structure of modern economic science is built on their pioneering work.

Net. In accounting procedures, the amount remaining after diminution of an item by its related and associated deductions of charges, outlays, and losses.

Net Asset Value. A term usually used in connection with investment trusts, meaning net asset value per share. It is common practice for an investment trust to compute its assets daily, or even twice daily, by totaling the market value of all securities owned. All liabilities are deducted, and the remainder is divided by the number of shares outstanding. The resulting figure is the net asset value per share.

Net Avails. The net proceeds of a discounted note.

Net Change. The change in the price of a security from the closing price on one day to the closing price on the following day on which the stock is traded. In the case of a stock that is entitled to a dividend one day, but is traded ex-dividend and next, the dividend is considered in computing the change. For example, if the closing market price of a stock on the last day it was entitled to receive a 50-cent dividend was $45 a share, and if it sold for $44.50 at the close of the next day when it was ex-dividend, the price would be considered unchanged. The same applies to a split-up of shares. A stock selling at $100 the day before a 2-for-1 split and on trading day selling at $50 would be considered unchanged.

Net Lease. A lease on real property requiring the lessee to assume all operating expenses, such as maintenance, insurance, and taxes, in addition to the payment of rent.

Net National Product (NNP). Gross National Product (GNP) less capital consumption allowances, such as depreciation accidental damage to fixed capital, and capital outlays charged to current expense.

Net Proceeds. Proceeds from the sale or disposition of property or the marketing of an issue of securities less directly related costs.

Net Profit. The profit that remains after all related costs from sales revenue have been deducted. Also known as net income.

Net Profit on Sales. The balance that remains after selling and other expenses that vary directly with sales have been deducted from gross profit on sales.

Net Profit Ratio. The ratio of a firm's net profit after taxes to its net sales. One of several general measures of a company's performance.

Net Purchases. The cost of purchases of goods and services plus freight charges less returns and allowances and usually less cash discounts taken.

Net Requirements. In manufacturing procedures, the actual production or purchasing requirements for a particular item, part, subassembly, or assembly.

Net Sales. The dollar amount of gross sales less returns and allowances, freight charges, and cash discounts allowed. The general practice is to treat net sales as the net amount received from the customer after discount.

Net Worth. The aggregate dollar amount that appears on the accounting records of the equities that represent the organization's proprietary interests; the excess of assets over liabilities to outsiders. In a corporation, net worth is the total of paid-in capital, retained earnings, and appropriated surplus. In a sole proprietorship, it is the proprietor's account. In a partnership, it is the sum of the accounts of the partners. Also known as assets.

New Issue. A stock or bond sold by a corporation for the first time. Proceeds may be used to retire outstanding securities of the company, to build a new plant, to purchase new equipment, or as additional working capital. Also known as primary distribution and primary offering.

New York Stock Exchange (NYSE). Located on Wall Street in New York City, it provides a marketplace for the buying and selling of ownership shares of publicly held companies. Formed in 1792 by a group of merchants and auctioneers who decided to meet daily under an old buttonwood tree on Wall Street. The 24 men who were the original members of the Exchange handled the public's buy and sell orders in the new government's issues of stock and in the shares of insurance companies, Alexander Hamilton's First United States Bank, the Bank of North America, and the Bank of New York. In 1793 they moved indoors to a newly completed coffee house at the corner of Wall Street and William Street.

New York Stock Exchange (NYSE) Index. This compilation covers the price movements of all common stocks listed on the big board. It is based on the close of the market on December 31, 1965 as 50.00 and is weighted according to the number of shares listed for each issue. The index is computed continuously by the exchange's market data system and is printed on the ticker tape each half hour of the working day. Point changes in the index are converted to dollars and cents so as to provide a meaningful measure of changes in the average price of listed stocks. The composite index is supplemented by separate indexes for four industry groups: industrials, transportation, utilities, and financials.

No-Benefit-to-payee Clause. A clause added to their bills of lading by many transportation companies and agencies such as railroads and motor carrier lines. It provides that any insurance payable in connection with the property being transported shall be payable to the transporting company.

No-fault Insurance. In theory, replaces the traditional method of compensating automobile accident injuries, in which the victim makes a claim directly against an individual wrongdoer or, in reality, against the wrongdoer's insurance company. Under no-fault, a claim for damages is made to the victims's own company instead of to his or her opponent's. The question of who is negligent or at fault is dropped from the legal dialog.

NOI. Initials for Not Otherwise Indexed, with reference to tariff classification.

NOIBN. Initials for not otherwise indexed by name, with reference to tariff classification.

No-Load Mutual Fund. A type of mutual fund that does

not charge sales commissions. These funds are readily identified in the lists of mutual fund quotations appearing in the press because bid and asked prices are identical.

Nominal Capital. The amount of capital represented by the par or stated value of a corporation's issued stock.

Nominal Partner. An individual who lends his or her name to a partnership but is not actually a partner. The value to the partnership is in the promotional value of the nominal partner's name and reputation for which the nominal partner receives a fee in payment.

Nominal Wage. A token wage, paid in money, for services rendered by an individual.

Nonassessable Capital Stock. Capital stock that is fully paid for by the stockholder who is not normally accountable for the liabilities of the corporation. This is the common stock ordinarily issued by the U.S. Corporations.

Noncontrollable Cost. In accounting, a cost that does not fluctuate with changes in volume of production. Also, any cost that is allocated to a unit of an enterprise but is not actually incurred by that unit.

Noncumulative Dividend. A dividend on preferred stock that does no become cumulative or need not be made up at a later date, if passed (not distributed to stockholders). This may not hold in all jurisdictions, since some courts have declared that such dividends are cumulative.

Noncumulative Stock. A preferred stock on which the unpaid dividends do not accrue. Omitted dividends, as a rule, are gone forever.

Nonoperating Revenue. The revenue of an enterprise that is received from sources not classified as being within the firm's regular activities.

Nonprice Competition. The market situation that occurs among rival sellers whose goods or services are priced comparably or identically, and whose competition in the marketplace is generally concerned with claims of superiority in quality or service.

Nonqualified Stock Option. A stock option that is not eligible for capital gains tax treatment; also known as unqualified stock option.

Nonrecurring Charge. In accounting procedures, an expense or involuntary loss not likely to reoccur. If the loss is in material, it may be stated on an income statement as an income deduction.

Nonrevenue Receipts. In government accounting, collections that are other than earned income during a given accounting period. Examples are recovered expenditures and receipts from loans.

Nonstandard Material. Raw material of other goods, whose quality standard differs from that appearing in a standard engineering specification.

Nonstock Corporation. A corporation without issued capital shares. Examples include mutual savings banks, savings and loan associations, credit unions, and religious or charitable organizations.

No-par-value Capital Stock. Capital stock that does not have a specified par or nominal value.

Note Issuance Facility (NIF). A method of long-term financing issuing short-term debt instruments repeatitively. Through auctions to the most competitive bidder. It is advantageous to the borrower, since funds for the long-term are raised at short-term rate of interest. For example, 3 years funds' requirements may be met by repeatitively issuing 30-day instruments, by tapping the market upto 12 times. Noe issuance facility is more efficiently implemented by combining with Revolving Underwriting Facilitiy (RUF), i.e., the underwriting facility which is extended in every round of fund raising. The issue devolves on the underwriter, if the BIDS from investors are above the cut-off rate.

Note Payable. A promissory note of the maker held by the payee as a liability.

Note Receivable. A promissory note held by the payee as an asset.

Note Register. A book in which notes receivable are recorded in chronologic order in accordance with the date received or issued.

Notes Payable. An account showing details of notes owed to creditors.

Notes Receivable. An account showing details of notes due from debtors.

Notice Account. A type of savings account that requires the depositor to give notice of his or her intent to withdraw funds. Such accounts usually receive a premium rate of interest.

Notice Money. This refers to the borrowing and lending by commercial banks, mutual funds, co-operative banks and financial institutions for periods upto 14 days without-any collateral security. The interest rate is determined by market forces of demand and supply. The **Discount and Finance House of India** acts as an intermediary in this segment of the market.

Oo

Obligee. The person for whose benefit a promise is made in bond.

OBU. Offshore banking unit.

Occupancy Rate. The ratio of appartment units or offices rented as compared with the total number contained within the building, or the ratio of leased to total space, expressed as a percentage.

Ocean Bill of Lading. Affreightment.

Ocean Marine Insurance. The oldest form of commercial insurance; it may be obtained in either domestic or foreign ports. Lloyd's of London has gained fame as an ocean marine insurer.

Odd Lot. In the securities market, an amount of stock that is less than the established 100-share or 10-share unit of trading; from one to 99 shares for the great majority of issues, from one to 9 for the so-called inactive stocks.

Odd-lot-Dealer. A member firm of the New York Stock Exchange that buys and sells odd lots of stocks: 1 to 9 shares in the case of those traded in 10-share units, and 1 to 99 shares for those traded in 100-share units. The odd-lot dealer's customers are commission brokers acting on behalf of their customers.

Odd-Lot Theory. The notion that those who transact business in odd lots (generally less than 100 shares) are uninformed and usually do the wrong thing. Some believe that an investment strategy can be formulated by using the 'Net Odd-lot Sales' information. A positive net odd-lot sales position indicates that investors ought to by stocks.

Offence Handelsgesellschaft (OHG). A general partnership under the law of the Federal Republic of Germany.

Offer. The price names for services, goods, or securities that are ready to be sold. The price named by one proposing to buy services, goods, or securities.

Offset Statement. A report by the owner of a property or the owner of a lien against a property, which sets forth the present status of liens against that property.

Off-Setting Error. An error in bookkeeping that eliminates or reduces the effect of another erroneous entry.

Of the Books. The payment of wages for services performed but not recorded in the books or on the payroll records of the employer. Paying an employee off the books may be illegal, depending on rules and regulations pertaining to the number of employees actually working for the employer. The practice is sometimes followed by a company to reduce its costs for fringe benefits, such as social security, unemployment insurance, and medical and other types of insurance that may be required by local, state, and federal regulations. Benefits to the employee are evasion of income taxes and increased purchasing power or disposable income; but the practice is clearly illegal for the employee.

Oil and Gas Lease. A deed by which a landowner grants another party the right to extract oil and gas from the leased property.

Oligopoly. A market situation in which sellers are so few that the supply offered by any one of them materially affects the market price. Thus, each company is able to measure with a high degree of accuracy the effect its price and production decisions will have on the courses of action its competitors might follow. A perfect or pure oligopoly is one which the products of the sellers are homogeneous or undifferentiated, such as the output of copper, cement, and steel producers. Differentiated products such as automobiles, soap, detergents, and household appliances are part of an imperfect oligopoly.

Oligopsony. A market condition wherein there are few buyers for the output of several sellers.

On Account. Partial clearing of a monetary obligation, as in payment on account. Also, in credit terminology, the expectation that payment is to be made at a date later than the delivery data, as in purchased on account.

On Consignment. Transmitted to another for the purpose of sale, display, demonstration, or similar use without actual transfer of title, as in merchandise delivered on consignment.

On Hand. Owned or possessed. For example, with reference to a balance-sheet item such as inventory on hand, the value listed is for items owned by and in possession of the entrepreneur.

On Order. In manufacturing, the total of all outstanding replenishment orders. For example, the on-order balance increases whenever a new order is released and decreases whenever an order is cancelled. The releases and cancellations may be for the full quantity ordered or for partial quantities. Also, there may be receipts that do not affect the on-order balance, such as customer returns, adjustments after physical inventory counts, and production surpluses.

Open Account. An account covering the unsecured amount owed by a debtor to a creditor who has delivered services or goods without requiring payment either in advance or on delivery. Also, any account that has not been closed out.

Open Cheque. A cheque not crossed and hence it does not require to be paid into an account but may be cashed over the counter. A crossed cheque can be opened by writing 'pay cash' over the crossing and signing the alteration by the drawer.

Open-end Investment Company. An investment company that can increase its size through the sale of additional stock.

Open-end Mortgage. A mortgage agreement that permits the mortgagor to borrow additional money after the loan has been reduced, without requiring that the mortgage agreement be rewritten. Opposite of Closed-end Mortgage.

Open Indent. The Export Order is known as Indent. An Open Indent signifies carte blanche, i.e. full discretionary power given to an agent in selecting the manufacture (the question of carte blanche arises because an importer often appoints an agent to act on his behalf).

Opening Balance. The balance of an account at the beginning of a specific accounting period, usually a month or a year.

Open Market. Markets where offers to buy or sell are made to the public at large, and not to a limited number or closed doors.

Open Market Operation. Operations by the central bank intended to stabilise interest rates or adjust the quantity of money in circulation. The central bank intends to influence the level of business activity in the country in the ultimate analysis. By buying securities from the market and paying for them, the central bank increases the cash reserves of commercial banks; by selling securities in the market and getting paid through the commercial banks, the central bank contracts the cash reserves of commercial banks. For the successful working of open-market operations the central bank requires an active money market with considerable supply of securities. In fact, a developed money market helps the central bank in its open-market operations.

Open Policy. In the insurance of property, a policy in which the amount recoverable, up to the face value of the policy contract, is ascertained after a loss has occurred. Fire insurance is the most common example of an open policy. A fire insurance contract may be written for a maximum amount of $25,000, for example, but the specific amount recovered as a result of loss through fire and paid to the insured party can be determined only after the loss has occurred.

Open-to-Buy. In retailing operations, the amount of money or the quantity of goods to which a firm is limited in its purchases from vendors, the portions of a budgetary allotment remaining available for such purchases.

Open-to-buy Reports. A report of relationships between inventory and sales, used to calculate open-to-buy amounts or quantities.

Operating Account. A revenue and expense account.

Operating Budget. A budget that applies to recurrent revenue and expense items.

Operating Company. A business firm that is actively conducting transactions with individuals or outside firms.

Operating Cost. An expense incurred in the conduct of the principal activities of the enterprise. Also known as operating expense.

Operating Cycle. The period of time between the purchase of inventory and its conversion to cash receipts.

Operating Income. The excess of the revenues of a business firm over the expenses incurred in producing the revenue. Income derived from sources other than those that pertain to the regular activities of the firm is excluded, and the calculation is made before income deductions. Also known as operating profit.

Operating Loss. The difference between revenues derived from regular sources and the costs incurred in generating such revenue, when the costs exceed the revenues received.

Operating Ratio. Any comparison of an item from a financial statement with net sales; in calculations, the dollar value for net sales in placed in the denominator.

Operating Revenue. The gross sales of goods and services, less returns and allowances and cash discounts, together with gross amounts received from any other regular source of income; net revenue from sales.

Operating Statement. A detailed income statement that displays financial operations over a stated accounting period.

Operation Sheets. Precise specifications and descriptions of manufacturing methods telling in detail how an operation is to be performed. Compared with drawings that specify what part or product is to be manufactured, route and operation sheets specify how to manufacture it.

Operations Research (OR). Developed during World War II, the application of scientific methods of analysis, including mathematical models, to process complex information and arrive at decisions that offer a maximum probability for achieving organizational objectives. The British term for the procedure is operational Research.

Opinion. In accounting procedures, the written statement of an auditor with respect to the fairness of the data presented by a corporation in its report of financial results, and with respect to the corporation's use of generally accepted accounting principles in recording transactions and preparing the report.

Opportunity Cost. The return on capital that might have resulted if the capital had been used for some purpose other than the one to which it had actually been put. The term is used to indicate the best alternative use of capital.

Optimize. To rearrange the instructions of data stored in a computer so that a minimum number of time-consuming jumps or transfers are required to run a program.

Option. In securities trading, the right to buy or sell specific securities or properties at a specified price within a specified time. In business transactions, the legal right to buy or sell goods, property, or services at a specified price within an agreed-on period of time.

Optional Dividend. A dividend payable in more than one form, such as cash and capital stock, at the election of the individual shareholder.

Option Financing. The arrangement under which an individual with a stock option pays for the shares over a period of time. Financing provisions may range from a personal bank loan negotiated by the individual, at times with the unofficial assistance of the company, to low-or no-interest loans made available or cosigned by the company.

Oral Contract. A contract that is not in writing or that is not signed by the parties: within the statute of frauds, an oral contract is a real and existing contract that lacks only the formal requirement of a memorandum to render it enforceable in litigation.

Order-Notify (ON). A bill of lading term; to request surrender of the original bill of lading before the freight is delivered. Order-notify documents are usually handled through a bank.

Order Point. A level or inventory for a specific item at which it must be reordered. The order point is calculated on the basis of estimated demand, replenishment lead time, and a safety stock to cover forecast errors.

Ordinary Annuity. An annuity that is payable at the end of each period of specified time.

Ordinary Depreciation. Decrease in or loss of the usefulness of a fixed asset as a result of normal wear, tear, and aging and the normal action of the elements.

Ordinary Life Insurance. A contract between an individual and in insurer, usually a company regulated by state law. The insurance is usually offered in units of Rs. 1,000. The four most common types of ordinary life insurance are (1) whole life, or straight life, (2) limited payment, (3) endowment life, and (4) term life.

Ordinary Policy. A type of insurance policy or contract that covers property only while the property remains at the place or location mentioned in the contract.

Organisation. A sound organisation is the prerequisite for the success of any business enterprise. Organisation is the foundation upon which the entire structure of management is constructed. The term 'organisation' is viewed in two ways: (i) Organisation as a structure; (ii) as a process.

Organizational Audit. Complete and periodic re-assessment of all of an enterprise's plans, procedures, personnel, allocation of resources, etc. to determine if each of those mechanisms is being utilised most efficiently and effectively in pursuit of enterprise goals.

Organizational Development (OD). A planned process for changing a business system. Its two essential phases are diagnosis and intervention. Diagnosis begins with a comprehensive description of the organization as it presently exists; the procedures, structures, attitudes, and values of individual and group members; and the elements of interpersonal and intergroup behavior. Interventions are then designed and undertaken to facilitate the efforts of members of the organization in solving problems.

Organization Expense. A liability incurred in establishing an organization, such as the legal and accounting fees for incorporation and promotional costs created by the issuance of capital stock.

Organization for European Economic Co-operation (O.E.E.C.). The parent body of many organisations set up within Europe after the Second World War (1939-1945) to facilitate and coordinate the national and international efforts for promoting the full recovery of the European economy. In 1961 its responsibilities were taken over the by Organization for Economic Cooperation and Development (O.E.C.D.), which included the U.S.A. and Canada in addition to the original European countries.

Organization Manual. Denotes enterprise Handbook which indicates the functions, authority, duties and relationships of each major enterprise unit. The manual, properly prepared, makes possible the availability of complete information on pertinent matters about each position, thus increasing understanding and knowledge of the requirements, the limitations, and the relations of the position's components within the position itself as well as the position's external relations to the entire organisation structure.

Organization Theory. Studies of group and individual behavior, motivations, influences, and conflicts to determine more effective means of organization management and control.

Original Capital. The amount of capital paid into an enterprise at the time of organization or incorporation.

Original Entry. An accounting entry that records a transaction in a book of original entry. It may include full information concerning the transaction or refer to supporting vouchers or memoranda that contain the data on which the entry is based.

Organised Sector. All establishments in the public sector and all non-agricultural establishments in the private sector employing 10 or more workers.

Origin Period. In statistical analysis, the period of time within a time series selected as the base period.

Other Assets. On a balance sheet, minor assets not classifiable under other usual headings; generally a small part of the total assets.

Other Deductions. In accounting procedures, a grouping of minor costs shown as a single total in order to minimize the presentation of unimportant detail.

Other Liabilities. On a balance sheet, minor liabilities not classifiable under other usual headings; generally a small part of total liabilities.

Other Revenue. In accounting, income from minor sources or sources that are not the principal activity of the business. Examples include interest on customers' notes, installment accounts, and overdue accounts; dividends and interest from minor investments; and incidental profits profits from the disposal of assets other than inventory.

Outlay Cost. The cost represented by an expenditure of cash or a transfer of property.

Out-of-pocket Cost. An expense incurred by an individual, paid for in cash not charged to the individual's personal account, for which reimbursements may be sought.

Outstanding. Uncollected or unpaid, as applied to an account or a note receivable. Also, publicly issued and sold, as applied to certificates representing shares of capital in the hands of the public.

Overcharge. A charge on a freight bill based on an error in rate, weight, or rating, resulting in excessive freight charges.

Overdraft. The amount by which any type of demand payment exceeds the amount of credit against which it is drawn.

Over Freight. Freight in possession of a carrier, without way bill or identifying markings.

Overhead. In doing business, the cost that cannot be identified as a direct cost of providing a product or a service.

Overhead Rate. In accounting procedures, a standard rate at which overhead is allocated.

Overinvestment Theory. A theory of business cycles holding that economic fluctuations are caused by too much investment in the economy as business firms try to anticipate the rise in demands during an upswing, and by sharp cutbacks in investment during a downswing when business firms realize they expanded too much in the preceding prosperity.

Oversold. Characterized by prices considered too low, as when a single security or a securities market has declined to an unreasonable level.

Oversubscribed. Subscription to an issue of securities in excess of the amount sought to be raised.

Overvalued. A security whose prevailing market price is deemed to be greater than its estimated intrinsic worth based on expected future cash flows. Therefore, its price is expected to fall shortly when the market corrects its error.

This term is also used in reference to currency whose exchange rate is maintained higher than its equilibruim rate or at a rate higher than that would be determined in a free market.

Pp

PAC. Public Accounts Committee.

Panic. A widespread fear, uncertainty, and insecurity concerning the financial stability of a country. Historically, a panic results in efforts by large segments of the populace to quickly convert assets, especially securities, into cash, in runs on banks by depositors, and in the unwillingness of investors to engage in new enterprises. In the United States, federal insurance of deposits and stringent regulation of the securities markets have placed controls on the elements that have contributed to business panics in the past.

Paper Money. Paper currency in the form of Federal Reserve notes, issued by Federal Reserve Banks with the authorization of Congress. There are a few minor types of paper money in existence in the United States, most of which are being retired from use in the interest of a more uniform currency. These minor types of paper money are collectively called Treasury currency, since, at one time or another, they were directly issued by the Treasury. The coin and paper money components of the U.S. money supply are frequently lumped together and simply labeled currency.

Paper Profit. An unrealized profit on a security that has not been sold by its owner. Although the market value of a security may have increased over the purchase price, such paper profits become realized profits only when the security is sold.

Par. In the case of common stock, the dollar value assigned to a share by the company's charter. Par may also be used to compute the dollar amount of the common shares on the balance sheet. It has little significance as far as market value of common stock is concerned; many companies issue no-par stock give a stated per share value on the balance sheet. At one time par was intended to represent the value of the original investment behind each share in cash, goods, or services. In the case of preferred shares and bonds, however, par is important. It often signifies the dollar value on which dividends on preferred stock and interest on bonds are calculated.

Paradox of Thrift. The demonstrated proposition that an increase in saving may be desirable for an individual family, but for an entire economy it will lead to a reduction in income, employment, and output if it is not offset by an increase in investment.

Paramount Title. A title to real property that is superior to all others.

Parent Company. A company that controls the finances and operations of subsidiary companies. If the controlling company does not have a trade or business of its own, it is known as a holding company or controlling company.

Parity of Authority. The management principle holding that a superior within an organization has the legal and moral right to issue orders to his or her subordinates.

Parity Price. The price that yields an equivalence to some defined standard. For example, in agriculture, a price of an agricultural commodity that provides purchasing power, in terms of the goods farmers buy, equivalent to its purchasing power in a previous base period; in international economics, the price or exchange rate between the currencies of two countries that makes the purchasing power of one currency substantially equivalent to the purchasing power of the other.

Parity Ratio. In agriculture, the prices farmers currently receive divided by the prices they pay. It is used to measure the economic status of agriculture.

Par of Exchange. The ratio of one country's unit of currency to that of another country, as defined by the official rates between the two countries.

Partial Reconveyance Deed. An instrument for transferring a title, used to reconvey a portion of land encumbered by a blanket mortgage or a trust deed.

Partial Release Clause. A part of mortgage or trust deed that provides for removal of certain property from the effect of the lien on payment of an agreed-on sum. A subdivider must have such a clause in his mortgage if his tract is subject to a blanket lien.

Participating Preferred Stock. A security in a company, entitled to its stated dividend as well as to additional dividends on a specified basis at the time of dividend payment on common stock.

Participatory Leadership. A style of management in which the leader plays an active consulting and advising role but gives subordinates a considerable amount of independence in making final decisions.

Partnership. A business structure with two or more owners whose relationship is determined by mutual agreement. The partners are free to establish among themselves the features or conditions of the partnership, the contribution of each partner to the business, the divisions of authority and profits, and to some extent the limits of each partner's liabilities. There are several types of partners. Also known as Business Life Insurance.

Partnership Life Insurance. When a partner dies, the partnership is dissolved. Partnership life insurance is sup-

establishes the value of the partnership for tax purposes, assures funds to pay the heirs the established value of the deceased share, may eliminate the need for forced liquidation of the business, and preserves the business for the surviving partners.

Parts Consolidation. In manufacturing, a report showing the gross requirements, without relation to time, for a build plan, specified as a series of part numbers and quantities.

Passed Dividend. Omission of a regular or scheduled dividend.

Past Due. In accounting, descriptive of a delay in payment of an obligation beyond the time agreed on for payment.

Patent Insurance. The protective type of this insurance covers expenses a patentee might incur in legal actions to protect the patent against infringement by others. The defensive type of this insurance provides coverage against legal actions alleging that the insured has infringed on the patent of another.

Patent Monopoly. The monopoly power a firm exercises because the government has conferred upon it the exclusive right, through issuance of a patent, to make, use, or market its own invention or discovery.

Patronage Dividend. A distribution by a cooperative to its members, in the form of a rebate on purchases made by the individual member.

Payable. In accounting, an unpaid obligation, a liability, a debt owing to another.

Payback. Financial return usually related to the time required for a project, product, or other investment with measurable return in revenue to reach the dollar level of the original investment.

Payout Ratio. The proportion of earnings available for

equity shareholders distributed as dividends. Thus, for example, if a company distributes a dividend of Rs. 3 per shares out its **Earnings Per Share** of Rs. 10, the payout ratio of the company is 30 percent. Companies normally target a long-term payout ratio while setting its dividend policy, which they strive to achieve over a long period.

Payroll. A record that shows the wages or salaries earned by employees for a specific period, and the deductions for various purposes or requirements.

Penetration Pricing. A pricing policy intended to capture as large a share of the market for a product or service as early in the life of the product or service as possible. This may be done by offering the product or service at an unusually low price.

Penny Stocks. In securities trading, a low-priced issue that is often highly speculative and sells for less than a dollar a share. Although some penny stocks have developed into investment-caliber issues, the term is sometimes used to discharge a stock considered to be of low value and to offer little promise of growth.

Pension. A benefit plan that provides for payment of income to an individual who retires. Qualified pension plans are funded and must meet all IRS non-discrimination tests. The recipient of the pension is not taxed until payment actually starts.

Pension Reserve. A fund established by an employer in recognition of a future obligation to pay annuities or pensions to employees.

Percentage Order. A market or limited price order to buy or sell a stated amount of a specified stock after a fixed number of shares of such stock have been traded.

Perfection Standard Cost. A standard cost based on the best possible productivity obtained under the most favourable conditions.

Period Cost. An expenditure charged to an expense account on a time basis rather than on the basis of use or yield. In many instances the factors of time and use coincide: for example, rent, interest, real estate taxes. Straight-line depreciation may be considered a period cost.

Periodic Audit. An audit that covers an intermediate accounting period such as a month.

Periodic Income. Income that is accounted for in periods of time, such as bond interest, rent paid in advance, and profit from an installment sale.

Permission to Deal. When a company issues a Prospectus it often states that permission has been obtained, or is to be sought, for the shares to be dealt with on a recognised stock exchange.

Perpetual Inventory System. In manufacturing, a system of inventory control or measurement in which each transaction in and out is recorded and a new balance is calculated.

Perquisite. A special benefit or privilege provided as an additional, indirect form of compensation. It may take such forms as a company car, club memberships, or special entertainment allowances. Colloquially known as perk.

Personal Effects Floater. An all-risk insurance policy intended to cover the personal property generally carried by travelers. Written for a single face amount with specific limitations on payments of claims.

Personal Holding Company. A corporation the majority of whose outstanding capital stock is owned by a small group of individuals. Also known as in incorporated pocketbook.

Personal Income. With respect to individuals, PI includes moneys and taxable benefits received prior to legally authorized deductions, and includes wages, salaries, commissions, bonuses, interest and dividend payments received, and other moneys received that may be determined from time to time by the regulations of the Internal Revenue Service as subject to declarations as taxable income.

Personal Liability. An amount owed by a natural person, as contrasted with the liability of a business firm.

Personal Property Floater. An all-risk insurance contract intended to offer personal rather than business protection, it covers all perils except those specifically excluded. Unscheduled, or unspecified, property that is related to the insured's business is not covered, with the exception of personally owned professional books, instruments, and equipment at the insured's residence. The insurance covers only direct losses, and excludes property normally covered by other policies, such as automobiles, aircraft, and boats.

Personal Risk. The possibility of death or injury to an individual; covered by such classes of insurance as life, accident, and sickness.

Personnel Manager. An Official designated as manager of the personnel department of an enterprise. He assists the line and other executives in the recruitment, development and effectives use of human resources for the accomplishment of departmental objectives. He is a staff officer. He is concerned with the development and maintenance of proper relations between the interests of individuals and groups and the interests of the enterprise of which they are a part.

Functions of the Personnel Manager in an enterprise are: Recruitment and Selection, Induction, Training and Education, Job Analysis, Evolving Proper Wage and Salary Structure, Helping Management to fulfil Statutory Obligations, Encouraging Joint Consultation, Keeping a check on Labour Turnover, Help maintaining Industrial Morale, Discipline, Introduction of Suggestion Scheme etc.

Petty Cash Fund. In business accounting, a small amount of cash kept either on hand or on deposit and made immediately available for minor disbursements.

Phantom Freight. A transportation charge included in the delivery price of a commodity that is in excess of the charge for service actually performed.

Phantom Stock Option. A form of stock that simulates an option on paper. Under a phantom stock plan, a grant of stock units is made and the executive receives the appreciation in market price, and sometimes the dividends, over a period of time. Also known as shadow option.

Physical Budget. A budget expressed in units other than dollars, such as number of employees, number of worker-hours, and units of material.

Physical Inventory. An inventory determined by actual measurement of weight, or by unit count.

Pictorial Chart. A chart readily understood and enjoying widespread use by all management disciplines in charting statistics. Graphic symbols represent numerical magnitudes; quantities are compared or evaluated by means of lengths, heights, or areas of the symbols. Pictorial charts are not usually studied critically but are intended to convey an instant impression of relative values.

Planned Economy. An economic system in which the government, according to a preconceived plan, plays a primary role in directing economic resources for the purpose of deciding what to produce, how much, and possibly for whom. A planned economy may or may not be a command economy, depending on whether the government operates within a substantially authoritarian or a substantially democratic framework.

Planned Obsolescence. A marketing concept that incorporates into the original plan describing or defining the life of a product a finite time interval during which the product will be actively produced and offered for sale. At the end of the designated time interval, the product is to be deliberately made obsolete by the introduction of a new product, a different version of the existing product, or a new technology.

Planning. Planning is the fundamental function of management. It is concerned with the future activity. Future is uncertain and its prediction is always difficult. Instead of leaving the future events to chance, they are made to happen in a certain recognised manner through planning.

Planning is the determination of a future course of action to achieve the desired result. It is deciding in advance what to do, how to do it, when to do it and who is to do it. Thus, planning sketches a complete picture of things to happen in the enterprise.

Planning is the beginning of all other processes of management. Planning is basic to all the functions. No organising, staffing or control can be decided without planning. It flows through all the functions, viz., organising, staffing, directing, communication and control as their life blood.

Pledged Asset. An asset that has been placed in trust or given as security for an obligation, loan, or mortgage. Also known as hypothecated asset.

Point. In the securities market, when referring to the price of shares of stock, a point means $1. In the case of bonds, it means $10. In the case of market averages, it means a change of one whole integer; for example, if the Dow Jones average rises from 964.25 to 965.25, it has risen a point.

Policy Method. In accounting, a method of depreciation determined by financial or social policy; sometimes used in public works projects.

Political Risk. In the securities market, the uncertainty of future returns from a security because of political developments, such as revolution, currency devaluation nationalization of facilities, and so on.

Portfolio. The total holdings of securities by an individual or an institution. It may contain bonds, preferred stocks, common stocks, and other securities of a variety of enterprises.

Positive Economics. The part of economics that is concerned with propositions about what is rather than about what ought to be. The essence of a positive proposition is its concern with matters of fact, not with matters of values and ethics.

Post. In accounting, to enter an item on a record.

Postclaim Underwriting. The analysis of insurance claims for the purpose of determining whether the policy should be cancelled. It is routine practice in many companies to refer large claims to the underwriting department. The practice is often employed where the insured party has a history of a large number of small claims and future risks appear unfavourable.

Postdate. To affix a date on a document later than the date on which the document is written or executed. A post-dated cheque cannot be cashed or deposited before the date appearing on its face.

Posting. A bookkeeping process of transferring dollar amounts and their accompanying or supporting data from a book of original entry to a ledger. Also, an item in a ledger or an amount posted.

Power of Attorney. A legal document authorizing a person to act as the agent for the person granting the power. A general power of attorney authorizes the agent to act generally without restriction on behalf of the principal. A special power of attorney limits the agent to a particular or specific act, such as conveying a parcel of property or negotiating a specified contract.

Preacquisition Profits. The retained earnings of a corporation as stated immediately prior to being acquired by, or in any way having come under the control of, another corporation.

Preemptive Right. The privilege to subscribe for a pro rata share of any new capital stock a corporation is about to issue, given to a stockholder in the corporation's charter or under the common law.

Preferential Hiring. An agreement or practice under which an employer gives first choice of available jobs to members of a particular trade union. Also known as preferential shop.

Preferred Stock. A class of stock with a claim on the company's earnings before payment is made on the common stock and usually entitled to priority, or preferred treatment, if the company is liquidated. Normally entitled to dividends at a special rate, when declared by the board of directors, before payment of a dividend on a common stocks. The dividend rate depends on the terms of the issue.

Preferred-stock Dividend. A dividend paid to the registered holders of preferred stock, usually at a fixed rate per quarter and expressed as a percentage or in dollars per share.

Premium. In securities trading, the amount by which the price of security exceeds its nominal, face, par, quoted, or market value. In the case of a new issue of bonds or stocks, the premium is the amount the market price rises over the original selling price. The term also refers to a charge sometimes made when a stock is borrowed to make a delivery on a short sale. Also, it may refer to the redemption price of a bond or a preferred stock if it is higher than face value.

In wages for labour, the extra dollars paid above normal or standard rates for work performed at other than usual times, such as late shifts, weekends and holidays.

Prepaid Expense. An expenditure made for future benefits or for facilities, utilities, and goods to be used at sometime in the future. Examples, include prepaid rent, taxes, royalities, insurance premiums, stationary, and office supplies. Also known as deferred charge, deferred expense, current asset, and prepaid asset.

Prepaid Interest. The excess of the face value of a loan over the amount of money actually received by the borrower, or the difference between the two amounts: often classified as a prepaid expense.

Prepay. To pay for a service or the use of a facility before the benefit or enjoyment is actually received.

Prepayment. A business expenditure made in advance for items that will yield portions of their benefits in the present and in the future. Examples include advance premiums on insurance policies, expenses incurred in marketing a new product, and purchases of stationary supplies.

Prestige Need. In business management, the desire to be highly regarded by one's associates; the need for recognition. The need may motivate an individual to strive for higher status, inasmuch as prestige or recognition is implicit in a class-stratified society (or organizational structure) and may be made visible in the form of special privileges, perquisites, or office location and furnishings. The need may be associated with the acquisitive need and may or may not be related to the individual's need for achievement.

Pretax Income. Income reported for accounting purposes before income taxes have been deducted. Also known as pretax earnings.

Price. A ratio reflecting the exchange value of a good or a service. For example, if the price of a dressed chicken is $1 and the price of a pound of coffee is $2.50, the ratio of exchange is 2½ to 1. Two and one-half chickens have a value equivalent to one pound of coffee—in a barter system. The price system measures the value of exchange in monetary terms. This is less clumsy than the barter system on a worldwide market basis, since money is the prime and common denominator used to measure the value of goods and services exchanged within markets.

Price-earnings (P/E or P-E) Ratio. In the securities market, the P/E ratio is calculated by dividing the current market price of a share of stock by the earnings per share for a 12-month period. For example, a stock selling for $50 a share and earning $2.50 per share is said to be selling at, or to have, a price-earnings ratio of 20.

Price Index. A statistical device for comparing the amount by which prices have changed during a given period of time. A specific year is chosen as the base year and prices in all other years are measured as a percentage of the price in this base year.

Price Leader. An item or merchandise priced abanormally low. The purpose is to attract customers, generally in retail sales operations.

Price Leadership. In marketing, leadership by a dominant firm whose price sets the pace for other manufacturers to follow. The product setting the prevailing price is called the price leader.

Price System. Adherence by firms in an oligopolistic industry, often tacitly and without formal agreement, to the pricing policies of one of the members of the same industry. Frequently, but not always, the price leader will be the largest firm in the industry, and other firms will simply follow the leader, charging the same price as it charges.

Price Variance. A Variance resulting from a change in the cost of materials and labour.

Primary Account. Any account to which external transactions are first carried. At some point in the accounting period, some or all of the primary accounts may be transferred to secondary accounts.

Primary Investment. The original purchase of shares of stock form a company, the moneys derived therefrom giving the company the capital it needs to function.

Prime Cost. The cost of direct materials and direct labour entering into the manufacture of a product: the total of direct costs minus direct and indirect overhead.

Prime Rate. The rate of interest charged by commercial banks on short-term loans to preferred customers.

Principal. In securities trading, the person for whom a broker executes an order, or a brokerage firm buying or selling for its own account. The term may also refer to a person's capital, or the face amount of a bond or of a loan.

Private Carrier. An enterprise that uses its own carriers or transportation system to move its own goods. The firm is usually not engaged in interstate transportation and, when so engaged, is not regulated by the federal government but may be subject to local and state requirements. The private carrier system is feasible when an enterprise requires heavy utilization of carriers or where specialized transportation are required.

Private Corporation. The common corporation created by and for private individuals for non-governmental purposes.

Private Offering. The sale of securities by the issuer to a selected group of subscribers, usually without the intermediation of an investment banker.

Private Sector. That part of the economy not under direct government control. Included are private enterprise firms and the economic activities of non-profit organizations and private individuals. Also known as personal sector, private enterprise, and free enterprise.

Process Costing. A method of cost accounting in which costs are charged to processes or operations and are averaged over the total of units produced.

Production Planning. The phase of production control specifically involved with analyzing sales demands and developing production programs and timetables to satisfy the demands.

Productive Capacity. The potential of the economy and of companies and industries for producing useful goods and services; limited by the stock of capital goods, the available labour force, and the level of technology.

Productivity. The yield obtained from a process or product as a result of work done with or on it. Also, a wage theory holding that wages should be based on employee productivity. A chief drawback here is the lack of any generally accepted standard of productivity. The piece-rate plan of compensation approaches the theory.

Productivity of Capital. Output produced per unit of capital employed.

Product Layout. The arrangement of machines and equipment in a production or processing facility according to the sequence of operations required to fabricate and assemble the item. Machines and workers are specialized in the performance of specific operations: parts approach continuous movement. Also known as line layout. Product or line layout has found greatest application in assembly rather than in fabrication.

Profitability. Profitability seeks to establish a relation between profit and the contributory factors responsible in earning the profit.

Profitability is thus the ratio of profit, for a given period to the amount of capital invested or the value of sales. It measures the relationship of profit with certain basic business and management factors and thus serves an index of efficiency. In precise, profitability is the ratio in which profit is the antecedent and the input or resource is the consequent. It shows how the resources are utilised and how much they yield.

Profitability Index. If the discounted cash flow (or present value) method is used, the present value of the earnings of a project can be compared directly with the present value of the earnings of another, even if the investments are of different magnitudes. To compare two proposals, the size of the earnings must be related to the amount of the money that is risked. This is done by dividing the present value of earnings by the amount of investment. The resultant ratio is called the profitability index. The higher the index number, the better the project from a profitability viewpoint.

Profitability Ratios. A set of ratios of financial data focusing on the profit realized by an enterprise and its relationship to the revenue generated or the resources employed. Such ratios include the profit margin on sales defined as net profit divided by sales, and the return on total assets defined as net profit divided by total assets; sometimes analysts and investors use the ratio for return on equity, defined as earnings after taxes (EAT) divided by equity.

Profit and Loss (P&L) Statement. A business firm's formal statement of revenues, costs, expenses, losses, and profits for a given period, grouped under appropriate headings. Also known as income statement or earnings report.

Profit, Capitalisation of. Conversion of surplus accumulated profits of a company into capital, e.g., Bonus Shares.

Profit Center. A department, division, unit, or other clearly identifiable segment of a business that for purposes of financial control is treated budgetarily as an entity, enabling expenses and revenues to be accounted as a measure of the center's performance.

Profit, Paper. Increase in value of unrealised investments or assets not sold. A company may have properties which command market value well above the price originally paid for them and still recorded as of same value in its books. And since the company has no intention of parting with the property due to their need in business, the fact that it could be sold at a profit is of interest only on paper.

Profit, Ploughed-back. That part of profit of a business concern for the year not distributed but retained in the business with a view to utilising (spending) it for developmental purpose.

Profit, Pure. This term is used by modern economists to denote the actual earnings of an entrepreneur which is the result of his ability only. As such, Pure Profit = Gross Income of the entrepreneur—Interest on his own Capital + Rent of own Land and Buildings + Wages of his own Labour/effort. The outcome is the net income of entrepreneurial ability.

Profit-push Inflation. A situation in which prices and business profits begin to rise before any increase in wages or other production costs takes place. The process stimulates labour unions to seek wage increases, thereby prompting sellers to make further price increases.

Profit, Retained. That part of the net profit not distributed to the owners—shareholders in the case of a company—but reinvested in the business.

Profit Sharing. A method by which some of the profits of a business firm are distributed among employees in the form of money or shares of stock, the distribution usually being made at the end of the fiscal year. The amounts distributed may be in accordance with a predetermined formula related to years of service of the individual employee or they may be entirely at the discretion of a designated committee or of management.

Profit-sharing Plan. A formal plan under which employees share in the company's profits, usually in relation to their salary and service. Under a cash profit-sharing plan, the award is distributed each year. Under a deferred profit-sharing plan, contributions are invested and are paid out when the employee leaves the company, retires, or dies.

Profit, Unappropriated. That part of the profit of an economic enterprise not distributed as dividend nor has been allocated to any particular use.

Profit, Windfall. Unexpected profit due to sudden rise in prices of goods and articles which sometimes occurs as a result of changes in taste, fashion, war, inflation, etc. Such profits are temporary in nature.

Profit Tax. A Tax levies in addition to Income Tax on companies but not on individuals.

Pro Forma. Latin for "as a matter of form."

Pro Forma Balance Sheet. A balance sheet that depicts the status of business operations—assets and liabilities—at a specific point in time; preliminary in content, unaudited, not confirmed by a certified public accountant as to content or form.

Pro Forma Invoice. A financial statement in the form of an invoice listing goods or services considered hypothetical in that they have not yet been delivered and probably have not yet been ordered. Prices are usually entered on the invoice. Such documents are used for budgetary purposes and are generally provided by a supplier who proposes to export the items listed on the invoice to an importer who may require the document for import license and customs evaluations.

Progress Billing. An accounting procedure based on work performed under contract and allowing for the billing of work at progressive levels of completion.

Progressive Consumer. In market analysis, a consumer who would be receptive to an offer of a better product or service at a slightly higher price.

Progressive Tax. A tax whose percentage rate increases as the tax base increases. The U.S. personal income tax is an example. The tax is graduated so that, other things being equal and assuming no loopholes, a person with a higher income pays a greater percentage of his or her income than a person with a lower income. Also known as equitable tax.

Progress Payments. Payments made at stages of a construction or manufacturing program as it moves toward completion.

Projected Financial Statement. A financial statement for a future date or period of activity, as opposed to a statement of past performance, based on estimates of transactions to be conducted. Also known as a pro forma statement and giving-effect statement.

Promissory Note. An unconditional written promise, signed by the maker, to pay the bearer of the note or a person or organization so designated on the note a specific sum of money. The due date of the note may be some specified future date or may be on presentation of the note.

Proof of Loss. Generally used in the event of loss for which insurance payment is requested, a form that identifies the claimant and the relevant policy number and describes the incident and the extent of the loss. A statement may also be required as to how, in the opinion of the insured, the loss occurred. Fraud in making the proof-of-loss statement automatically cancels the policy and removes any obligations on the part of the insurer.

Purchase-Money Obligation. A mortgage or other type of debt secured by a lien that has priority over any lien subsequently created.

Purchase Order. A document instructing a supplier to deliver goods, materials, or services per specifications and at a specified price and time. On acceptance by the supplier, the purchase order becomes a legal contract.

Purchase Requisition. An internal document authorizing the purchasing department to issue a purchase order.

Purchasing Power Risk. In the securities market, the uncertainty of the purchasing power of future returns on investment because of changes in the price level.

Pure Risk. A risk in which there is no possibility for gain, only for loss. This is the type of risk generally and specifically covered by insurance contracts.

Puts and Calls. Options that give the holder the right to sell (put) or buy (call) a fixed amount of a specific stock at a specified price within a specified time period. Puts are purchased by those who think a stock price may go down, and they obligate the seller of the right to taker delivery of the stock at the specified price. The purchaser of the put may then buy stock on the open market at the lower price, delivering it at the higher price, thereby realizing a profit. A call is purchased by one who thinks the stock price will rise and that he or she will acquire it at a value higher than stipulated in the option. Put and call contracts are usually written for 30-, 60-, or 90-day periods.

Pyramid Selling. A system of selling in which purchasers buy the right to sell a product. This right usually includes a requirement to purchase a minimum quantity of the product. Titles are often part of the purchase; among them are distributor, dealer, agent sales, supervisor, representative, and area manager. The technique takes on the form of a pyramid by the fact that the first purchaser resells the product and a title to another purchaser who may do the same thing in turn. Pyramid selling has been made illegal in some countries, and where it is not directly illegal it has been repeatedly challenged.

Qq

Qualified Report. An audit report that contains one or more qualifications or exceptions.

Qualified Stock Option. A stock option plan that qualified for capital gains tax treatment. Under such a plan a stock must be awarded at market value, exercised over no longer than a five-year period, and then held for three years before it is sold; capital gains tax rates then apply.

Quality Market. Market in which quality matters more than price.

Quantity Discount. An allowance, in credit, cash, or goods, given by a seller to a buyer because of the size of an individual purchase.

Quantity Survey. A technical process for estimating the cost of a new construction, it involves detailed estimates of the quantities of raw materials to be used. The current price of the materials, and the labour costs. Also known as the price takeoff method.

Quasi Corporation. A public or municipal body or organization (as a county) not specifically incorporated or vested with all the usual powers of a corporation but exercising certain corporate functions and rights in connection with public duties.

Quasi-sovereign Yield Curve. A benechmark for yields, established by the issues of state-owned companies of a country, in international debt markets. In the absence of sovereign issues, this yield curve serves as the basis for pricing debt issues of creditworthy corporate borrowers of that country. Thus, for instance, debt issues by Indian Oil Corporation, Oil and Natural Gas Commission (ONGC) and other similar organizations would help to establish a quasi-sovereign yield curve.

Queuing Problem. The condition that occurs when the impact of demand or production facilities exceeds production capabilities.

Quick Asset. A current asset normally convertible into cash within a relatively short time period, in the order of one month. Examples are cash call loans, marketable securities, and a commodity or good that can be sold immediately on the open market at quoted prices.

Quota. In trade relations, a physical limit, mandatory or voluntary, set on the import of a product. In marketing-sales operations, the definition of a budget for orders in terms of a physical limit that becomes mandatory; a numerical quantity for performance stated in units or dollars, sometimes in both, and generally designated for a geographical region, a sales district, and an individual salesperson or sales account. The fulfillment of cumulative quotas ensures the attainment of the budget. Progress toward achievement of quotas is one tool of management for quantitatively measuring the progress of a specific effort, program, or individual in the sales activity.

Rr

Racks. Storing equipment used in warehouses and storerooms. Some of the most common types are pallet, bin, tier, cantilever, flow through, drive-through, A-frame, stationary, rollaway, adjustable-arms, fixed-arms, single-deck and double-deck.

Raider. An individual or a company attempting to acquire large block of outstanding shares of a company with a view to take its control.

Rain Insurance. Issued primarily in conjunction with outdoor events to which the public pays admission. The coverage usually extends for a brief period, possibly in the order of a few hours, and specified the perils of rain, hail, snow and sleet. Policies may cover (1) loss of revenue because the event had to be cancelled on account of unfavourable weather conditions and (2) expenses of preparing for the event, for the same reasons.

Rake-Off. Slang term for a share of the profit from a deal or enterprise particularly one paid corruptly.

Rally. A brisk rise following a decline in the general price level of stock market, or in an individual stock. Also known as upswing, upturn, and uptrend.

Rate-buster. A piece-worker who takes advantage of rates to earn high bonus payments and does not join with fellow workers in holding production back to the bogey level agreed on unofficially by the group. The unpopularity of rate-busters derives from the fear felt by the other workers that management might react to relatively high bonus payments by cutting the rate of payment for piecework. Also known as cowboy or high-flier.

Rate Group. In transportation, the group in which a given place is identified for the determination of rates in a tariff.

Rate of Exchange. The price that must be paid in one unit of currency to purchase another unit of currency.

Rate-of-Return Pricing. A method for determining a selling price for an item by adding a markup that will produce a target return on investment.

Rating. The financial or credit position of a person or a business enterprise as determined by another enterprise or by a credit-checking agency. In the securities market, the relative worth of a security as determined by any of several investment advisory services.

In the television industry, rating is the result of a survey that indicates the percentage of those television sets in use which are tuned to a specific channel or show at a specified time.

In insurance, rating is the measure of insurability, or risk taken by the insurer, and is used in the determination of the premium rate for coverage for specified perils.

Ratios. Financial ratios are derived from balanced-sheet data. Operating ratios are derived from items of income and expense. Ratios serve as a measure of merit of several aspects of an enterprise when data for one accounting period are compared with similar data from another period. Ratios may also be used to compare one organization with another or with an industry average or standard.

Raw Materials. Basic items that come from farms, mines and forests, and include such commodities as grain, wool, ore, tobacco, petroleum and wood. Also, semifinished goods purchased for use as an ingredient or component of a finished product.

Reaquired Stock. Capital stock that has been reverted in tittle to the issuing corporation, usually through repurchase, by donation, or in settlement of a debt to the issuing company. Reaquired shares that are not canceled are known as treasury stock or treasury shares.

Real Account. In accounting, a term used in double-entry bookkeeping to indicate an account that is carried over from one accounting period to another. Asset and liability accounts are examples. Also known as property account.

Real Cost. In accounting, cost expressed in terms of physical units, such as bushels, pounds, tons, miles, and workers-hours. In economics, the cost of goods and services adjusted for factors such as inflation.

Real Estate. Land and land improvements, including buildings and attachments; also, standing timber and orchard trees. Also known as real property, in contrast to personal property.

Real Estate Investment Trust (REIT). A special arrangement under federal and state law whereby investors may pool funds for investments in real estate and mortgages.

Real Gross Domestic Product. In economics, Gross Domestic Product (GDP) data adjusted for current inflation.

Real Gross National Product. Gross National Product (GNP) data adjusted for current inflation.

Real Income. Income measured in terms of the real goods and services it can buy. It can be calculated by dividing money income by a suitable index of prices.

Real Investment. In finance, an expenditure that creates a new capital asset. Real investments result in new capital formation.

Reappropriation. In government accounting, legislative action that permits the government to continue to incur obligations under an expired or soon-to-expire appropriation.

Rebate. An adjustment in a charge that has been paid to the supplier of a service or good, resulting in a return of a portion of the payment. If the adjustment was the result of an overcharge, the returned portion would be referred to as a refund. If the adjustment was made prior to payment, it may be referred to as a discount.

Recapture Clause. In a lease, a provision to terminate the lease if certain of its conditions are not met by the lessee.

Receivable. A collectible money obligation, whether due yet or not. Usually referred to as accounts(s) receivable or note(s) receivable.

Receivables Turnover. A ratio of business activity; net sales divided by average receivables during the sales period.

Receiver. A person appointed by the court for a specified time period to take charge of property while its disposition is being determined or an imposed objective is being attained. The property administered by a receiver is said to be "in receivership."

Receiving. In business and industry, the department or section responsible for receiving and identifying all incoming material and transferring the material to stores or other areas within the company.

Receiving (or Receiver's) Report. A document prepared by the receiver of a shipment as a formal record of goods received; generally used as a source document for warehouse and inventory accounting and to support shippers' and carriers' invoices. The report usually includes the name and address of the shipper, date the goods were received, name of the carrier, bill of lading number, description and quantity of goods, and signature of the person actually receiving the property on behalf of the consignee.

Recession. A downtown in economic activity, one phase of the business cycle. Decreased investment, falling incomes, falling consumption, and increased unemployment are characteristic of this phase.

Reclassify. In accounting, to break down a transaction into secondary classifications.

Reconciliation. In accounting, determining and recording the items necessary to bring the balances of two or more related accounts or statements into agreement.

Reconsignment. Changing the bill of lading provisions with respect to the consignee or destination while the goods are still in transit.

Reconveyance. Transfer of the title of land from one person to the immediately preceding owner; commonly used when the performance or debt is satisfied under the terms of a deed of trust, thus allowing the trustee to convey the title he or she has held on condition back to the owner.

Recovery Value. In accounting, estimated revenue from a resale or scrapping of a fixed asset.

Redemption Price. The price at which a bond may be redeemed before maturity, at the option of the issuing company. Also applies to the price the company must pay to call in certain types of preferred stock.

Red Herring. In finance, a colloquialism for a preliminary prospectus prepared in conjunction with a proposed security offering filed with the Securities and Exchange Commission.

Rediscount. A negotiable instrument, previously acquired by a bank at a discount, sold to a Federal Reserve Bank. The act or process of rediscounting such an instrument.

Rediscount Rate. When the Central Reserve System was originated, loans were the chief earning asset of commercial banks. Since then, buying and selling marketable securities, particularly government securities, have become significant means for obtaining added liquidity. At one time, member banks were expected to borrow at the Central Reserve when in need of funds; these borrowings were rediscounts, because loans of a commercial nature already discounted once by member banks, were the basis for rediscounting at the Federal Reserve Banks. The rate of interest charged by the Central Reserve is the rediscount rate. Also known as discount rate.

Redlining. The practice whereby banks and other institutional lenders deny mortgage credit to an entire declining neighbourhood regardless of the condition of the specific property or the creditworthiness of potential borrowers.

Reducing-balance Method. In accounting, a method od depreciating an asset. The amount to be depreciated annually is derived by applying a fixed percentage to the diminishing balance of the asset account, or by applying a diminishing rate to the original cost of the asset. For example, an asset whose estimated useful life is ten years could be depreciated each year by a constant rate equivalent to 90 per cent of the previous year's depreciation charge. Other constant rates may be selected.

Refinancing. In the securities market, new securities may be sold by a company and the money used to retire other debts. For example, the receipts from a new issue for common stock may be used to redeem outstanding bonds in order to save interest costs.

Refund. The return of an overpayment made for goods or services. The refund may be in the form of money, merchandise, services, or a credit voucher applicable to the purchase of new goods or services.

Register. The Book maintained by an enterprise to record matters of importance. Each enterprise has to maintain a number of registers for that purpose, e.g., Register of Members, Register of Directors, Register of Creditors, Mail Register, Stock Register, etc.

Register, Closure of. Every year, just before the Annual General Meeting, most companies keep the Register of Members closed for a few days in order to enable the department concerned to prepare the Annual Return and the preliminary work connected with dividend distribution, i.e., preparation of Dividend List and Dividend Warrants. Transfer may be certified and may even be deposited with the company for registration, but they will not be presented to the board for approval during the closure period.

In India, Section 154 of the Companies Act, 1956 (as amended up to date), prescribes the formalities to be complied with in regard to closure of Register of Members. Under this provision, the Register may be closed for a period of forty-five days in a year but not exceeding thirty days at a stretch or continuously. Seven days notice of closure must be given by advertisement in the newspaper. Notice of the closure may be given in the notice of the general meeting but care should be taken to advertise the notice in the local newspaper. During this closure period, no transfer of shares can be registered.

Following are the usual circumstances when the Register of Members is closed : (1) At the time of preparation of the Annual Return; (2) When the call is made and Call List is to be prepared; (3) When the dividends are declared and Dividend List is to be prepared; (4) When the new shares are offered to the members; (5) At the time of alterations and reorganisation of share capital.

Registered Bond. A bond registered on the books of the issuing company in the name of the owner. It can be transferred only when endorsed by the registered owner.

Registered Mail Insurance. This provides all-risk coverage for currency, securities, bullion, and similar valuables when shipped by registered mail. It covers the period from the messenger's departure from the insured party's premises to delivery of the item to the person to whom it is addressed. This supplements the post-office insurance limits by as much as several millions of dollars in shipment value.

Registered Trader. A member of the New York Stock Exchange who trades in stock on the floor for an account in which he or she has an interest. Also known as floor trader.

Register of Charges. Every company is required to keep a Register of Charges and enter therein all charges and mortgages specifically affecting property of the company and all floating charges on the undertaking or on any property of the company, giving in each case the following particulars: (1) A short description of the property charged (2) The amount of mortgages and charges (3) The names and addresses of mortgagees ore creditors entitled to the property charged.

Under the Amended (Companies) Act, 1974, the power of the Court to order rectification of a company's Register of Charges has been transferred to the Company Law Board.

Register of Members. As per Company law, every company must maintain a Register of Members, i.e., shareholders with the following particulars; (1) Names, addresses, occupations of members; (2) The statement of shares held— (a) Number of shares, (b) Distinctive Nos., (c)

Amount paid on each; (3) Date of entry on the register; (4) Date of removal from the register. In case the membership exceeds fifty; there must be an Index of Members to facilitate quick reference.

Registered Transfer. A transfer where the particulars of the name and address of the shareholder, date of execution and consideration for transfer appear not only on the share or scrip itself but also in the books of the company.

Registeration of Business Names. Partnership firms are required to register their names if they do not consist solely of the name of the existing partners themselves. Companies are also required to register their name with the Registrar of Companies. Where the business is controlled by a person or persons in another country—the names, nationality, etc. of the owners are also required to be registered. Undesireable names are refused registration.

Registrar. Usually a trust company or a bank—or a person employed by such an institution—charged with the responsibility of preventing a company from issuing more stock than it is authorized to issue.

Registration. Before a public offering of new securities may be made through the mails or in interstate commerce, the securities must be registered with the Securities and Exchange Commission (SEC) by the issuer. The application for registration must be filed with the exchange by the company issuing the securities. The application must disclose information relating to the company's operations, securities, management, and purpose in making the public offering.

Regulated Investment Company. An investment company that has met the requirements of the Investment Company Act of 1940 and has chosen to be regulated under this act.

Reinsurance. The sharing of risk among several insurance companies in cases where an insurance policy involves the possibility of a large indemnification and where the possibility of catastrophic loss exists. It is sometimes known as insurance of insurance. One insurance company procures insurance coverage from another, or from several others: often done without the awareness of the insured. The company buying the reinsurance is called the reinsured; the company selling it is called the reinsurer.

Release Clause. A stipulation that, on payment of a specific sum of money to the holder of a trust deed or mortgage, the lien on the specifically described lot or property shall be removed from the blanket lien on the whole area involved.

Remuneration. Payment for a service rendered. Henri Fayol, the propounder of modern management theory, emphasised in his 'General Principles of Management' that remuneration and methods of payment should be fair and afford the maximum possible satisfaction to employees and employer.

Renewal Fund. A reserve fund established for the replacement or renewal of an asset. Also known as replacement fund.

Rent. In ordinary conversation, most payments for temporary use of an item of property. Economists find it desirable to reserve the term for land rent, considering other such payments a return on the capital invested in improvements.

Replacement Method. A method od depreciation whereby an estimate is made of the cost of replacing an asset that is in use and has a limited life. The amount of the current depreciation expense, usually on a straight-line basis, is increased by a percentage derived from a comparison of the anticipated replacement cost with recorded original cost.

Replacement Theory. In accounting, a means of determining the optimum balance between the costs of breakdowns or failure versus the cost of replacement under conditions of uncertainty.

Rentier. Pensioners, annuity-holders, owners of Government Promissory Notes and others who draw a fixed income in terms of money.

Repurchased Stock. Capital stock bought back by an issuer from its stockholders.

Requirements Contract. A contract wherein one party to the contract agrees to purchase all his or her requirements of a particular product from another party to the contract.

Requisition. A formal, written request for specified articles or services; usually an internal procedure.

Research and Development (R & D or R and D). Usually used in connection with the conception and design of new products and the application of technical or engineering resources to the investigation of various alternative approaches to the physical creation of the products. Commonly abbreviated R & D or R and D.

Reserve Bank of India. The Reserve Bank of India is the central bank of the country. Indian commercial banks are controlled and regulated by the Reserve Bank under the power vested to it by the Banking Regulations Act, 1949 (previously known as Banking Companies Act). Recently under the Banking Laws (Miscellaneous Provisions) Act, 1963, the Reserve Bank has acquired wide statutory powers of regulation that enable it to control all institutions including indigenous bankers which accept deposits from the public. From the beginning of June 1964, both banking and non-banking institutions are required by the Reserve Bank to furnish details of deposits accepted from the public.

The Reserve Bank of India was established on 1st April, 1935 under the Reserve Bank Act, 1934. It originally started as a shareholder's bank with a paid-up Capital of Rs. 5 crores. From 1st January 1949 the Reserve Bank is functioning as a State-owned and State-controlled Central Bank.

Under the Act of 1949, the Directors and the Governors of the Bank are either nominated or appointed by the Central Government. At present the Central Board of the Bank consists of a Governor and three Deputy Governors appointed by the Central Government, four Directors (nominated by the Local Boards), nine other Directors and one Government official.

The Reserve Bank performs all the typical functions of a Central Bank including (i) issuing of paper currency except one-rupee notes which are issued by the Ministry of Finance, Government of India, (ii) acting as a banker to the Government, (iii) controlling credit and advances given by the commercial banks, (iv) acting as a bank of accommodation or lender of last resort, (v) maintenance of the external value of the rupee, (vi) managing public debt and raising new loans, (vii) provision of agricultural credit, and (viii) collection and publication of monetary and financial information.

Reserved Material. In manufacturing, material on hand or on order that is assigned to specific future production orders. Also known as assigned material, allocated material, mortgaged material, and obligated material.

Reserve Fund. Cash or securities separated from working capital for some specific purpose.

Residuary Legatee. One who is entitled to receive the balance of an estate after specified bequests, taxes, and other liabilities have been satisfied.

Resolutions and Agreements requiring Registration. Under Section 192 of the Companies Act, 1956 (as amended up to date), a company in India is required to register certain resolutions and agreements.

The following are the provisions requiring such compulsory registration of certain resolutions and agreements: (1) Along with every resolution to be filed compulsorily, a copy of the statement of material facts attached to the meeting in which the resolution was passed must be filed; (2) So far as resolutions are concerned, only such resolutions as have the effect of altering the Articles should be incorporated or attached to the Articles; Every resolution requiring compulsory registration need not be embodied in the Articles; (3) The list of resolutions and agreements requiring compulsory registration are the following—(a) Special resolutions and resolutions agreed to by all the members of the company; (b) Board resolution or company agreement relating to the appointment, reappoint, changes in the agreement of a managing director; (c) Resolutions passed by a company giving consent to the board to exercise powers relating to sale, lease, etc. of company's undertaking, borrowing money in excess of the paid-up capital plus free reserves as per Section 293 of the Companies Act; (d) Resolutions of the company approving the appointment of sole selling agent under Section 294.

Responsibility Costing. An accounting method that identifies costs with persons assigned to their control rather than with products or functions.

Responsibility Drift. The shifting of responsibility within an organization, caused, for example, by imperfections in delegations of authority, altered assumptions of responsibility, unforeseen overlapping of authority, changes in personnel, growth of individuals, and informal changes in objectives and in the operating environment.

Restricted Cash. Cash deposits that can be withdrawn only under special conditions or for special purposes. Usual practice is to maintain such cash in a separate bank account.

Restricted Retained Earnings. The portion of retained earnings not legally available for disbursement as dividends.

Restricter. A worker who performs or produces at a level considered to be the norm for the group of which he or she is part.

Retail Accounting. An accounting method generally used by retail stores and advocated by the National Retail Merchants.

Retirement Allowance. An annuity or pension payable to an employee who has retired from active service.

Retirement Method. In accounting, a method od depreciation formerly used by public utilities; now obsolete.

Retrogressive Consumer. In marketing analysis, a consumer who is eager to economize on an existing product or service.

Retrospective Rating. A method od adjusting the amount of a premium to the actual loss experience during the period covered by an insurance policy.

Revenue Bond. A bond issued by a government for the purpose of financing the construction or purchase of or additions to income-producing facilities. Repayment of such bonds and the periodic payment of interest on them are dependent on earnings. Familiar examples are bonds used to finance toll roads, bridges, sewers, and transit systems.

Revenue Deduction. In municipal accounting, an expense, tax, or uncollectible account receivable of a municipal utility or other self-supporting enterprise.

Revenue Receipts. In accounting, revenue that has been collected in cash for a given period of operations.

Revenue Reserves. A British expression for the portion of the net worth or total equity of an enterprise that represents retained earnings available for withdrawal by proprietors.

Revenue Sharing. A plan by which the central government turns over a portion of its tax revenues to state and local governments each year.

Revenue Tariff. An import tax usually applied to products that are not produced in the importing country, for example, tin, coffee, and bananas in the case of the United States. Typically, rates on revenue tariffs are modest.

Reverse Split or Reverse Splitup. The recall of shares by the issuer, who then reissues fewer shares in exchange. Also known as splitback and splitdown.

Revolving Fund. A fund whose resources are continuously expended, replenished, and expended again. An example is an asset available for loans the repayments of which are available for other loans. In government or institutional accounting, a revolving fund is one created by an appropriation or issue of securities for the purpose of providing working capital that is to be replenished through revenues or transfers from users of the fund's facilities.

Riparian Owner. One who owns land bounding a river or watercourse.

Risk. In insurance, the possibility of loss. Insurance tends to provide for full or partial compensation in the event an insured article is damaged or destroyed.

Risk Manager. An insurance specialist who diagnoses risks to which a project or enterprise may be subjected and prescribes appropriate action with respect to insurance coverage.

Robbery Insurance. Protects the insured from loss of property, money, and securities through robbery either on or off the premises. Robbery is defined as taking of property from a person in charge of it by force or threat of violence. Coverage may also include property on the insured's premises damaged in the course of the robbery.

Rolling Forecast. A continuing series of periods of marketing activity in the form of a budget.

Rollover. The renewal of a short-term debt at the option of the borrower under an agreement with the lender.

Rollover Bonus. A bonus partially paid out in the year in which it is earned, the remainder being paid over the following several years.

Round Lot. In the securities market, a unit of trading or a multiple thereof. On the New York Stock Exchange the standard unit of trading is 100 shares in stocks and a par value of $1,000 in the case of bonds. The unit of trading in some inactive stocks is 10 shares.

Round Sum. A figure whose final digits have been rounded off.

Route Sheets. At each stage of a manufacturing process a part is analyzed to determine the operations required and to select and specify the functions required to complete the processing. The routing of the part is summarized on route sheets. These show (1) the operations required and their sequence, (2) the machines or equipment to be used, and (3) the setup and run time per piece. For a standard part intended to be produced repeatedly to fill needs, route sheets are maintained and accepted as partially descriptive of the manufacturing methods.

Rule Off. To underscore the last entry in a journal or the last posting in a ledger account. Its purpose is to indicate that no further entries are to be made above the rule-off line and that a total of transactions has been reached.

Runaway Shop. A business organization that moves from one location to another primarily to escape unionization of its employees or the application of labour laws. It is possible for geographically centered industry to make a similar physical move for the same reasons, or to take advantage of a lower-cost labour market or more favourable taxation.

Runout List. A list of items to be scheduled into production in sequence by the dates on which the present available stock is expected to be exhausted.

Rupee. The basic unit of currency in India, Mauritius, Nepal, Pakistan and Sri Lanka.

Rupiah. The basic unit of currency in Indonesia.

Rural Bank. A Rural Bank may be described as a primary banking institution set up to serve a compact group of villages convering a population of 5,000 to 20,000 and in sparsely populated area it may cover as big an area as a development block.

In India, the concept of 'Rural Bank' scheme was introduced in the Report (1972) of the Banking Commission constituted under the chairmanship of Sri R.G. Sarayia. The Commission suggested for formation of "Rural Banks" which would essentially be co-operative in character but provide a wide range of services not usually extended by primary agricultural credit societies.

Ss

Safety Stock. An extra amount of inventory kept on hand to protects a company against delivery failures or an unforeseen increase in lead time to usage.

Salary Structure. The minimum and maximum dollar limits within which jobs are ranked according to compensation values. Usually, the structure consists of a series of coded grades, with each grade having a range of salary levels.

Sales Calls. Visits to customers or prospective customers by a sales person.

Sales Load. Commissions and other selling expenses used in determining the price of a share to an investor.

Sales Revenue. Total sales in dollars, usually for a specific period of time.

Sale Value. The price at which an asset can be sold, less any costs that are to be incurred in effecting the sale.

Salvage. The actual or appraised selling price of an asset in the form of second-hand material, junk, or scrap. The term also applies to both the sale of merchandise through channels that are not ordinarily used for the class of product and to the value received less any cost od disposition. Also, the value of an asset remaining after a disaster such as fire or wreck, or form the retirement or scrapping of the asset.

Salvage Value. The value of an asset, usually plant, machinery etc., expected to be realised on its sale or exchange on the expiry of its useful life. In insurance, it is the value of a property destroyed or damaged partly by fire, accident etc.

Sanction. Literally, enforcement. A sanction is the penalty for the breach of a law. Redress for civil injuries is called civil sanction. Punishment for violation of a criminal law is called pena sanction.

Satisfice. A concept to convey the idea that in reality commercial firms do not seek to maximize profit but rather to achieve certain levels of satiation. For example, they try to attain a particular target level or rate of profit, and they try to achieve a specific share of market or a certain level of sales.

Savings. The excess of income over consumption for a given period of time. Often referred to as current savings.

Savings Bank. A bank that accepts only savings accounts and cannot create demand deposits (checking accounts). Savings and loan associations and mutual savings banks are examples of savings banks. In 1978 tests were under way in several states wherein savings banks were allowed to create checking accounts.

Savings Bank Life Insurance (SBLI). Life insurance sold over the counter by mutual savings banks as authorized by law in some states.

Savings Bond. A debt security sold by the Treasury to individual investors. These are fully registered securities, usually sold in small amounts to make them affordable to the majority of the population.

Savings Plan. A formal compensation plan designed to provide a supplemental source of income in addition to a retirement plan for retirees, as well as a source of savings and capital accumulation for employees; also known as a thrift plan. Under the typical plan the individual contributes a percentage of pay, which is matched by the company and invested in one of several employee-selected investment options.

Scanion Plan. A cash-incentive program for employees based on sharing the savings from a reduction in labor costs from a described standard. The plan was developed in the 1930s and 1940s by Joseph Scanlon of the Massachusetts Institute of Technology and implemented with the cooperation of the United Steelworkers' Union. The plan also incorporated an employee-suggestion incentive.

Schedule Coverage. An insurance policy that defines a number of risks of the same general type to be covered under a single policy (rather then under separate policies for each risk). For example, the insured who has four properties may insure all four under a schedule policy. It is the equivalent, in short form, of four separate specific policies.

Schedule Rates. These rates are applied to insurance risks where there is enough variation to make it unfair to apply general class rates. The rates for such risks are usually determined after a physical inspection of the property by a representative of the insurance company's rating bureau. Also known as specific rates.

Scrip. A fractional or temporary share of stock or other security. It may be issued in connection with a recapitalization or reorganization and is ultimately converted into regular certificates. Also, scrip is paper "money" issued by corporations to pay wages and is accepted in exchange for merchandise by the corporations' stores.

Scrip Dividend. A dividend paid in promissory notes referred to as scrip. The notes may be negotiable, bear interest, mature at different dates, and call for payment in cash, stock, bonds, or property.

Seasonal Dating. An aspect of credit terms given to customers. During periods of slack sales, firms may sell to customers without requiring payment for sometime to come. This extension of the credit period is referred to as seasonal dating; the practice may be employed to stimulate demand from customers who cannot pay until later in the season. Seasonal dating may also serve to reduce or avoid inventory-carrying costs on the part of the firm.

Seasonal Fluctuations. Patterns of orders or sales that last for periods of less than one year. For examples, retail sales generally increase at Easter and Christmas time, and agricultural activity increases during the summer and declines during the winter. Also called seasonal variations.

Seasonal Inventories. Inventories whose levels are adjusted to absorb seasonal fluctuations in demand. Many products have reasonably predictable seasonal demand patterns. Where this is true, management has the choice of either using seasonal inventories or, if applicable, changing production rates over the year to absorb fluctuating demand. A financial analysis of the options is usually the guiding factor in decision-making.

Seasoned Security. A listed stock with narrow price fluctuations which yields regular quarterly dividends and is backed by net assets and an earning capacity considered adequate to protect the investor in such stock.

SEBI. An abbreviation for Securities and Exchange Board of India, which is a regulatory body established under the Securities and Exchange Board of India, Act, 1992. Its role is to protect the interests of investors in securities, to promote the development of securities markets and to regulate the same. Towards the achievement of these goals, SEBI is empowered to adopt various measures which include: (a) Regulating the business at stock exchanges and other marktes. (b) Registration of stock brokers, sub-brokers, transfer agents, registrars to issues, merchant bankers, underwriters and others. (c Regulating Mutual Funds. (d) Prmoting investor education. (e) Undertaking inspection and audit of stock exchanges and various intermediaries.

Secondary Account. An account that is based on internal transactions involving transfers from primary accounts and other secondary accounts. These includes a finished-product account, a bad-debt account and a retained-earnings account.

Secondary Investment. Following a primary investment, a secondary investment is the change of ownership of shares of a company's stock, such as occurs through buying and selling common shares on a stock exchange.

Secondary Offering. The redistribution of a block of stock some time after that stock has been sold by the issuing company. The sale is handled by a securities firm or group of firms, and the shares are usually offered at a fixed price that is related to the current market price of the stock. Usually the block is a large one, such as might be involved in the settlement of an estate. The security may be listed or unlisted.

Second Mortgage. A mortgage that differs from a first mortgage only in that is constitutes a second, or junior, lien or encumbrance on the property. In the case of default, the claims of the first mortgage are given priority over those of the second.

Secular Price. A price resulting from the interaction of economic forces over a period of years.

Secular Trend. A definite tendency to change in a particular direction because of long-term economic influences. Secular trends are used mainly to predict the growth rates of various industries.

Secured Account. Any account against which collateal or other security is held.

Secured Creditor. A person whose claim against another is protected by collateral, or by a mortgage or other lien.

Secured Liability. An obligation against which specific assets have been pledged or guarantees given.

Securities. An instrument that provides evidence of creditorship or ownership such as shares, debentures.

Security Analysis. Estimation of securities' risk and expected returns with a view to make investment decisions.

Security Market Line. The linear relationship between securities' expected returns and their systematic risk as postulated by the capital asset pricing model. The systematic risk of the security is measured by its beta.

Security Risk. In the securities market there are several classic types of risk that the investor must recognize.

Self-fulfilling Prophecy. A forecast that is made more realizable because special effort is given toward its fulfillment. This may happen in marketing where a decision that a particular product or market is most (or least) promising is followed by a concentration (or lack) of effort to achieve the forecast result.

Self-insurance. Often confused with non-insurance, which means not taking out an insurance policy; however, self-insurance as practiced by large companies means the actual setting aside of a reserve fund that may be used in the event of loss.

Sell-and-Leaseback Agreement. An arrangement whereby a business that owns and occupies improved real estate sells it to an investor and takes a long-term lease on the property, which it continues to occupy. The agreement may include an option to repurchase the property at the termination of the lease.

Seller's Market. A favourable condition for sellers within an industry when the demand exceeds the supply. Generally, under such conditions, prices tend to move upward.

Seller's Option. A special transaction on an exchange that gives a seller of a security the right to deliver the security at any time within a specified period, ranging from not less than six business days to not more than 60 days.

Selling Expense. Not to be confused with cost od sales, selling expense (or cost) is a class of expense incurred in the activities of selling or marketing. Examples of selling expense include advertising, sales commissions, marketing staff salaries and related costs, while cost od sales includes direct and indirect manufacturing costs.

Semitrailer. A freight-carrying vehicle that has not power of its own. It is attached to a tractor to obtain motive capabilities.

Semivariable Cost. An operating expense that varies, not necessarily at the same rate, with production rates.

Senior Security. A term that is applied to a class of securities (bond, note, or share) to indicate its preference over another class of securities in the event of liquidation. For example, a first mortgage is a senior security as compared with a second mortgage. Preferred stock is senior to common stock. A senior security is superior to a junior security.

Sensex (or the Sensitive Index) A value-weighted index compiled by the Bombay Stock Exchange authorities consisting of 30 most actively traded scrips at the Exchange. The base year is the financial year 1978-79. The method of compilation is similar to the one used in Standard & Poor's Indias, USA.

Separable Cost. A cost that may be identified with a specific product or service.

Separated Manager. A manager who is very concerned with correcting deviations. He tends to write more than talk and, partly because of this, has relatively little personal communication in any direction. He perspective tends to be dictated by past experiences. He takes great interest in rules and procedures and judges others on how well they adhere to them. He values intellect in his superiors but not in others. He does not enjoy non-routine work. The greatest fear he has about himself is that he might let emotion, softness, or dependence on others influence his judgment. His fear of others is they might act irrationally and violate the system.

Serial Bond. An issue that matures in relatively small amounts at periodic stated intervals.

Service Life. The period of usefulness of an asset to the owner of the asset. Service life may be used as the basis for calculating depreciation.

Service-yield Basis. A method od depreciating an asset whereby cost is spread over the useful life of the asset in proportion to service units consumed or outputted by the asset. Also known as production method od depreciation or unit-of-product method.

Set of Accounts. The journals, ledgers, forms, accounts, records, and files that are maintained under an accounting system.

Settlement Options. The provisions of a special compensation plan that govern the form and timing of the payout of benefits, used particularly with pension, profit-sharing, and thrift plans.

Several Contract. A contract in which each party makes a separate promise and is separately liable therefor. There may be several promises in the same contract. If the promisors make a single promise, the obligation is joint. This accounts for the use of the phrase in contracts:

"We jointly and severally promise."

Share Index. An index serving as an indicator of the overall fluctuations of a stock market. One of the best known of the various indexes of the U.S. markets is the Dow-Jones averages, a composite of four different grouping of stocks: the industrial average—30 stocks that account for 20 per cent of the value of all common stocks listed on the New York Stock Exchange (NYSE), oldest of the market indicators but no longer considered representative of the state of American industry; the utilities average—15 stocks of selected gas and electric companies; the transportation average—stocks of 20 firms, including airlines, railroads, and trucking companies; and 65 stocks—a combination of the industrial, utilities, and transportation averages. Standard & Poor (S&P) publishes a composite index of 500 stocks. The S&P-500 index is based on the aggregate value of shares of major firms with each stock's price weighted by the numbers of shares outstanding. The New York Stock Exchange index is a weighted index of all common shares listed on the NYSE, based on the close of the market on December 31, 1965, with an index of 50,00. Point changes on the NYSE index are converted to dollars and cents. The American Stock Exchange (ASE) publishes an index calculated to reflect the actual prices of all stocks and warrants listed on the ASE. The National Association of Securities Dealers Automated Quotations (NASDAQ) publishes an index of 2,350 common stocks that are traded over the counter by brokerages, rather than on a stock exchange.

Shilling. Basic unit of currency in kenya, Somalia, Tanzania and Uganda.

Shopping Goods. Consumer goods whose price, fashion, quality, and service are relatively important to the buyer. Generally bought infrequently, they are of high unit value, and the buyer may spend considerable time in shopping for price and quality, often at outlets located some distance from the consumer's residence. Items in this class include furniture,automobiles, jewellery, china and furs.

Shortage. In marketing and manufacturing, that part of a shipment that is undelivered.

Short Covering. In securities trading, the purchase of stock in order to return stock that was previously borrowed to make a delivery on a short sale.

Shortfall. The gain from a sale of an investment owned for a brief period, such as six months.

Short Rate. The disproportionate amount of an insurance premium returned when an insured cancels the policy. The insurance company retains a portion of the unused premium as a cancellation penalty.

Short Sale. Sale of shares which the seller does not own but delivers by borrowing by borrowing from or through broker. The seller later on replaces these shares by purchasing from the market.

Short-term Debt. Any current liability, including the maturing portion of a long-term liability. Short-term debts are usually payable within the next 12-month period.

Short-term Equilibrium. A time period that is long enough to permit market supply to vary within the limits of existing productive capacity.

Sight Draft. A written order drawn by one party (drawer) ordering a second party (drawee) to pay a specified amount of money upon demand (usually supported by particular documentation of a transaction) to a payee.

Sight Test. In auditing, an examination of accounts without formal analysis.

Silent Partner. A member of a partnership who takes no active part in the management of the enterprise. This type of partnership enables persons to invest in the business without taking an active part in operations but allows others to handle the day-to-day management situations. A silent partner is a limited partner, one whose financial liability in the business is limited to the extent of his actual investment; however, if the silent partner takes an active part in management the personal liability is the same as that of a full partner.

Simple Interest. The charges made by a lender for the loan of money or for a deferment of the collection of an account. It is calculated by applying an interest rate against the principal of the loan only.

Simple Journal. In accounting, a book of original entry that contains only two money columns, one for debits, the other for credits.

Simple Trust. A trust that must distribute its income currently but does not distribute capital before its termination.

Single-entry Bookkeeping. A system of bookkeeping in which only records of cash and of personal accounts are maintained. Usually, there is not a detailed record of gains and losses. In business operations where transactions are infrequent and receivables, payables, and assets other than cash are few in number, carefully maintained single-entry bookkeeping may be adequate.

Single Index Model (or the Market Model) A linear relationship between returns on a stock and returns on a market index.

Single-level Bill of Materials. In manufacturing, a list of components or raw materials for a single assembly level.

Single-line Store. A type of retail sales establishment that carries a wide variety of one line of merchandise. The goods handled are related items, such as might be found in a sporting goods shop, a furniture store, or a large men's clothing store where one could expect to find a selection of suits, ties, shirts, socks, shoes, and accessory items.

Sinking Fund. Cash or other assets, and the interest or other income earned thereon, set apart for the retirement of a debt, such as the redemption of stocks or bonds. To assure its integrity or safety, the sinking fund may be invested in such conservative areas as certificates of deposit or in government bonds, treasury notes and bills.

Sinking Fund Bond. Any issue of a bond that requires the issuer to set aside periodically a sum that, with interest, will meet the redemption price of the bond or will be equal to a specified fraction of the total.

Sinking Fund Method. A method od depreciating an asset that consists of setting aside periodically equal amounts of money that, with compound interest, will produce a sum equal to the original cost or exact replacement cost od the asset at the end of its useful life.

Sinking Fund Reserve. An appropriation or designation or earned surplus for the retirement of an outstanding obligation.

Site Audit. An audit conducted on the premises of the organization being examined, especially in financial examinations performed by government agencies such as the IRS.

Situational Sensitivity. In organizational behaviour, the skill in appraising situational elements in terms of task and relationships demands.

Slander Liability Insurance. Available to radio and television broadcasting stations, credit bureaus, and other organizations that may face accusations of oral defamation of character. Usually written with a high dollar-value deductible clause. The insured company is required to conduct its own legal defense.

Sling. A large net into which freight is placed for hoisting into or out of a ship.

Small Business. A general term related to the quantification or size of an enterprise. Definitions of small business are varied. For example, the Bureau of the Census references the number of employees within the enterprise; the Internal Revenue Service references sales volume; Dun & Bradstreet references net worth. The Small Business Administration exercises considerable latitude in defining the difference between "small" and "big"—according to type of business (manufacturing, wholesaling, retailing, service) and the dominance of the enterprise within its specific field of endeavor.

Small Business Investment Company. A privately and publicly owned but government-regulated company whose sole purpose is to provide long-term financial assistance and management services to small business firms. SBICs are licensed and regulated by the Small Business Administration, from which they may also obtain favourable financing.

Small-firm Effect. The empirical observation that shares of small firms provide abnormally high returns.

Smallest Processing Time Rule. In manufacturing, a dispatching rule that directs the sequencing of jobs in ascending order according to the time required to process. Following this rule, the maximum number of jobs per time period will be processed. The result is that the average lateness of jobs is minimized, but some jobs will of necessity be very late. Also known as least processing time (LPT) and shortest operating time (SOT).

Social Balance. The relative distribution of resources between the public and private sectors.

Social Benefits. A gain that accrues to individuals and to society as a whole, but for which the individual does not have to pay directly. Highway construction and police and fire protection are examples.

Social Costs. A disadvantage to society that may result from private production but that is not necessarily reflected in the money costs to the individual producer of acquiring the resources needed for production. Pollution is a social cost od production that the market system does not measure.

Social Overhead Capital. The capital of a society, consisting of facilities for energy production, communications, transportation and education. Also known as the infrastructure of a society.

Society Risk. In the securities market, the uncertainty of future returns from a security because of shifts in public attitudes. This may involve changing consumption patterns, pollution, and population control, for examples.

Social Security Integration. The technique whereby a pension or profit-sharing retirement plan is discounted for social security benefits. This is done by applying a formula, by excluding certain earnings from the benefits, calculation, or by subtracting social security under the so-called offset approach.

Soft Currency. A currency whose exchange rate is tending to fall because of persistent balance-of-payments deficits or because of the building up to speculative selling of the currency in anticipation of a change in the exchange rate.

Soft Loan. A loan bearing no interest rate, or a rate that is abnormally below the true cost od the capital lent. The International Bank for Reconstruction and Development, working through its affiliate, the International Development Association, gives soft loans to developing countries for long-term capital projects.

In international trade, a soft loan is a loan that is to be

repaid in the borrower's currency instead of in the lender's currency, gold, or a reserve currency. The loan is actually a disguised gift because the country that is repaid in "soft" currency cannot spend it without disrupting the borrowing country's economy. This circuitous method for making a loan is used to save the borrower's face and to counter voter objections in the donor country.

Sole Proprietorship. A form of business enterprise which is established, financed, owned, managed and controlled by an individual entrepreneur, who enjoys complete freedom of operation, bears all risks and takes all the profits earned.

Sole proprietorship is suitable when (1) the capital requirement is small; (2) the risk involved is not much; (3) quick decisions are necessary; (4) customers demand personal attention; and (5) their tastes and fashion change frequently. Of the different form of business enterprises, it is the smallest and traditional form which is found in every country od the world irrespective of the country's economic and industrial development.

Sole Trader. A person who trades on his own account, rather than in partnership or as a member of a company.

Sound Value. In accounting, the replacement cost less depreciation and deferred maintenance for fixed assets. A term generally used in appraising the present value of an asset.

Source and Disposition of Funds. A statement often included with published accounts showing the cash coming in and the cash going out during the financial year.

Sovereign. When first minted it had a value in exchange of twenty-two shillings and six pence. This fell in subsequent years but was legally fixed at twenty shillings in 1817. It ceased to be Legal Tender in 1914 even though sovereigns and half-sovereigns continued to be minted until 1975.

Span of Control. A theory and practice of management holding that a supervisor, manager, or executive cannot operate efficiently if he has more than a limited number of subordinates reporting directly to him. Generally, the higher the level of work, the smaller the number of directly reporting subordinates. For example, the span of control for a general manager might be limited to six to nine subordinates while that of a shop floor supervisor might include several hundred.

Span of Management. The concept of 'span of management' refers to the number of subordinates that a manager can manage effectively. The term of management is also called span of control, span of responsibility or span of supervision. There is a limit to the number of persons a manager can supervise effectively. So the deciding of the proper span of management is an important task of management while designing the organisation structure.

Special Assessment. Charges levied by a municipal government on those who will benefit most from an improvement or service (such as installing pavements or sewers). Often bonds are issued to finance the work, and interest and payments on the principal are included in the taxes of those who benefit from the improvement or service.

Special Audit. An audit or inspection of financial records and accounts that has a limited and specified scope. Also known as limited audit.

Special Bid. The purchase of a large block of stock on the floor of the New York Stock Exchange. In a special bid, the bidder for the block of stock will pay a special commission to the broker who represents him or her in making the purchase. The seller does not pay a commission. The special bid is made on the floor of the exchange at a fixed price that must not be below the last sale of the security or the current bid on the regular market, whichever is higher. Member firms may sell this stock for customers direct to the buyer's broker during trading hours.

Special Drawing Rights (S.D.R.). The new System of international reserves introduced in 1969 by the ten leading member-countries of the International Monetary Fund is known as the Special Drawing Rights.

Allocation of S.D.Rs to member-countries was a first attempt to create international liquidity through deliberate decisions of the international community. Member-countries, under the scheme, did not have to transfer their currency or other resources against the S.D.Rs received in allocations; the S.D.Rs were simply created to participants' accounts on the basis of their quotas in the Fund at the date of each allocation, and were then available for use in accordance with the rules of the scheme. The S.D.Rs represent entirely a new form of paper money, unconditional and automatically created as if out of thin air. The S.D.Rs allocated to participant countries thus increased the international reserves of the recipient and, consequently, the sum total of global liquidity. The new reserve asset proved readily acceptable.

Under the S.D.R. system, a member-country can use S.D.Rs to settle its debts to other member-countries. The most radical aspect is that 70% of these new units need never be repaid. They are, in fact, a newly created money. Gold, dollars and pounds and normal drawing rights with the I.M.F. would continue to be used for international payments and reserves but the S.D.Rs would serve as additional reserve units. A country running into deficit on its balance of payments need not rush for immediate aid from the I.M.F. or from other sources or take hasty restrictive action but use its S.D.Rs to pay up its deficits. Thus, S.D.Rs help to solve the problem of international liquidity.

There are so far been three principal ways in which participants could use their S.D.Rs : (a) To obtain foreign exchange from other participant countries "designated" by the I.M.F. to receive the S.D.Rs; (b) To redeem balances of their own currency held by other countries in transactions voluntarily agreed to between participants; and (c) In operations and transactions with the Fund's General Account, which is separate from the Special Drawing Account and through which the bulk of fund transaction with member-countries are conducted.

The technique followed in those matters are—(i) Transcations with Designation. (ii) Transactions by Agreement. (iii) Transactions with the General Account.

The value of the S.D.R. was previously based on gold. But it is now based on an average value of 16 world currencies of which the US dollar is most important.

Special Endorsement. A Bill of Exchange endorsed to a named person.

Special Fund. In municipal accounting practice, a fund that must be used in accordance with specified legal or administrative restrictions; also any fund other than a general fund.

Specialist. A member of a stock exchange who specializes in very few stocks or even a single stock. The two main functions of a specialist are: (1) to maintain at orderly market, insofar as reasonably practicable, in the stocks in which he is registered as a specialist, and (2) to act as a broker's broker. To maintain an orderly market, the specialist buys or sells for his own account, within reasonable limits, when there is a disparity between supply and demand. There are about 350 specialists on the New York Stock Exchange.

Specialist Block Purchase. The purchase by a specialist for his own account of a large block of stock outside the regular exchange market. Such purchases may be made only when the sale of the block could not be made in the regular market within a reasonable time and at reasonable prices, and when the purchase would aid the specialist in maintaining a fair and orderly market.

Speciality Debt. A Debt which is not barred until twelve years have elapsed, e.g., a Dividend or a Call on shares.

Specific Offer. Offer which is made to a prospective customer who enquires about the product, its price, terms of sale, etc. as opposed to a "general offer" made to all prospective customers to draw their attention in regard to use-value of the products intended for sale.

Special Offering. A large block of stock requiring special handling. Occasionally a large block of stock becomes available for sale and, because of its quantity and market, may call for special treatment. A notice is printed on the ticker tape announcing that the stock will be offered for sale on the exchange floor at a predetermined price. Member firms of the exchange may buy this stock for customers directly from the seller's broker during trading hours. The price is usually based on the last transaction in the regular auction market. If there are more buyers than shares of available stock, allotments are made. Only the seller pays a commission on a special offering.

Special Revenue Fund. In municipal accounting practice, a fund used to finance specific activities. A fund of this type may be authorized by statutory or charter provisions to pay for identified activities with some special form of continuing revenues such as specific taxes.

Special-talent Insurance. A highly specialized form of career insurance, generally providing indemnity for the loss of a member or function of the body related directly to the financial success of the insured. Examples are insurance for the hands of a well-known pianist, the legs of a famous dancer, the voice of a popular vocalist, the fingers of a dentist, or a facial or bodily characteristic of a well-known or readily recognized performer or public personality whose disfigurement might diminish or end the person's career.

Specialty Store. A retail establishment that stocks and sells a limited variety of merchandise but offers a wide selection within a category od goods. Examples include stores specializing in dinette furniture, beds, or musical records and tapes.

Speculative Risk. A risk in which there is both a chance of loss and an element of gain. A business venture and a gambling transaction are examples of speculative risk.

Spillover Effects. Benefits or costs associated with the production or consumption of a good that spill over to parties other than the buyer or seller.

Split. In the securities market, the division of the outstanding shares of a corporation into a larger number of shares. For example, a 2-for-1 split by a company with a million shares outstanding results in 2 million shares outstanding, Each holder of 100 shares before the split has 200 shares after the split; however, his equity in the company remains the same. Usually, splits must be voted by directors and approved by shareholders. One of the primary reasons for a split is that the resultant drop in price per share stimulates trading in the market and encourages new buyers, thereby increasing the demand and hopefully increasing the market value of the individual share.

Splitoff Point. In accounting, when two or more products are involved in the same or similar operation, the point at which joint costs end and costs that can be identified with individual products begin.

Spot Cash. Cash that is readily available, usually in hand, for an immediate purchase.

Spot Price. The price of a commodity available for immediate sale and delivery. The commodity is referred to as a spot commodity.

Spread Sheet. A worksheet for the analysis of a group of related accounts or classes of accounts.

Staff. The staff are experts who provide advice and service to the line officers. Their authority arises from their superior knowledge of a particular function. They do not have the power to command the line. But their advice is followed because of their higher status in the organisation.

In business organisations, two types of staff are found, namely (1) Personal staff; and (2) Specialised staff.

1. *Personal staff.* The burden of executives at higher level is reduced by personal staff. Personal staff comprises clerical and stenographic personnel. Personal staff answer routine letters, attend to phone calls, fix appointments and keep track of business agreements. They plan and supervise the routine clerical work of an executive's office.

2. *Specialised staff.* Specialised staff provide advice and service to the company as a whole. Specialised staff provide service to personnel and maintenance, counselling and quantity control.

Staff Auditor. A member of the accounting or financial division of a corporation assigned the duties of examining and inspecting the accounts of an economic unit of the corporation.

Stag. Indicates an Individual who buys heavily on a new issue of shares or stocks in the expectation that the price will rise very quickly and thus enable his to earn a large profit. Such buyers normally hold shares for a very short period. This term is connected with a stock exchange dealing.

Standard Cost Accounting. Estimates or forecasts of costs to be incurred in the production of goods or the delivery of services. Such costs become known as *standard costs.* The estimates or forecasts are based on assumptions of specific conditions. After the acquisition of experience, actual costs are accumulated and compared with standard costs as a measure of efficiency.

Standard Costing. In accounting, the process of pricing goods or services at standard cost.

Standard-cost System. A method of accounting whereby standard costs are the basis for credits to work-in-process accounts. Standard costs may be applied to charges for materials, labor, and other costs related to work in process. Physical and book inventories may be recorded at standard-cost values. Differences between standard costs and actual costs are carried to variance accounts.

Standard Labor Rate. An employee's base pay, plus any incentives and premiums in money, estimated to be attainable under efficient working conditions.

Standard Machine Time. The time allocated or forecast to be required for the use of a machine in a specific operation in a production process. It may be referenced to a specific quantity of output of units produced against a time base. Setup and teardown time may be included in the total machine time allocation.

Standard of Living Theory. A wage theory which holds that employees should be paid more than a subsistence wage. Wage level, it maintains, should be such that employees can afford higher education and some of the luxuries of life, such as recreation.

Standing Profit. The net amount that should be earned per unit of production when a job or a service is performed under an accounting method of standard costs.

Standard Order. A continuing work order that directs the production of an item to meet specified sales objectives.

Staple. The chief commodity traded in a market. Also, raw materials, or a linen, wool, cotton, or synthetic fiber.

Starboard. The right side of a ship when facing forward toward the bow.

Stated Capital. The dollars received by a corporation from the purchasers of its capital stock. Also known as *declared capital.*

Stated Value. The value given by a corporation to its capital stock for any of various taxation purposes. Also known as declared value.

State Farms. In the Soviet Union, lands that are owned and operated as state enterprises under elected or government-appointed managing directors. Workers and technicians are hired to run the farms, and are usually paid set wages as well as bonuses of their output exceeds a basic norm.

Statement. In accounting, a summary of transactions between a customer and his supplier for a fiscal period, usually a calendar month. Also, a formal presentation of classes of accounts and the related amounts, prepared as a summary of the financial condition and operating results of a company for a fiscal period, usually 12 months.

Statement of Identity. A questionnaire by which real estate title companies are helped in identifying a person; such a statement is essential, for example, when records show more than one person with the same name.

Stock. The legal capital of a corporation obtained through the issuance and sale of marketable certificates or shares.

Stock Appreciation Rights. An executive compensation plan intended to reduce the risk of market declines that may be experienced with conventional stock options. Such a plan also eliminates the need for cash investment.

Stock-clearing Corporation. A subsidiary of the Stock Exchange that acts as a central agency for clearing firms in providing a clearing operation through which transaction made on the floor are confirmed and balanced; it also provides a settlement operation to handle the physical delivery of securities and money.

Stock Company. A company organized for the purpose of writing insurance coverage and registered as a corporation owned by stockholders who need not necessarily be policyholders. The initial capital subscribed by the stockholders constitutes the company's working capital. Income must be earned from premiums paid by policyholders. In most respects, the financial operations are like those of a general corporation.

Stock Discount. The excess of par value over paid-in capital. At one time this was treated as a deferred charge. It is now generally considered a debit-valuation account to be combined, before exposure on the balance sheet, with the capital-stock account to which it is related, or to be subtracted on the face of the balance sheet from that same capital-stock amount.

Stock Dividend. A dividend paid in securities rather than cash. The dividend may be additional shares of the issuing company or shares of another company, usually a subsidiary of the issuing company.

Stock Exchange. A market in which securities are bought and sold. The principal stock exchange in the United States is knows as the New York Stock Exchange and is located on Wall Street in New York City. There are many other exchanges in large cities.

Stockholder. The person of legal record who owns one or more shares of the capital stock of a corporation. Stockholders are in effect owners of the corporation and as such have the power to establish basic corporate policies. This power is rarely exercised, however, because it is difficult for a collective of stockholders to practice direct control of the corporation. Stockholders vote annually for members of the board of directors and on other key issues.

Stockholder of Record. A stockholder whose name is registered on the books of the issuing corporation.

Stock-option Cancellation. A program under which a company cancels outstanding stock options whose exercise price is substantially higher than the current market price. The company then issues new, lower-priced options to replace the cancelled options.

Stockout. The lack of materials and supplies that are normally expected to be on hand in stores or inventory.

Stock Register. A corporate record containing the details of the issuance of stock certificates and of the disposition of those returned for transfer or for cancellation.

Stock-transfer Book. A record or journal in which transfers of capital stock are entered; maintained by the company that issues the stock or by its transfer agent.

Stop-limit Order. In securities trading, a stop-limit order to *buy* becomes a limit order executable at the limit price, or at a better price of obtainable, when a transaction in a security occurs at or above the stop price after the order has been presented to the trading floor. A stop-limit order to sell becomes a limit order executable at the limit price, or at a better price if obtainable, when a transaction in the security occurs at or below the stop price after the order has been presented to the trading floor.

Stop Order. In securities trading, an order to buy or sell a specified quantity of securities at a specified price or better. A stop order to buy becomes a market order when a transaction in the security occurs at or above the specific price after the order is presented to the trading floor. A stop order to sell becomes a market order when a transaction in the security occurs at or below the specified price after the order is presented to the trading floor. A stop order may be used in an effort to protect a paper profit or limit a possible loss to a specific amount. Since it becomes a market order only when the specified price is reached, there is no certainty that it will be executed at that price.

Stoppage in Transitu. In law, the right of a seller of goods that have not been paid for, upon learning that the buyer of the goods is insolvent, to stop the goods in transit and hold them as security for the purchase price.

Storekeeper's Burglary and Robbery Policy. An insurance policy designed specifically for small business firms. It covers low-limit losses similar to those described in a comprehensive crime policy.

Stores. Supplies and raw materials used in the manufacture and distribution of goods; also, such items used in the maintenance of a plant and its equipment.

Stores Ledger Cards. In manufacturing, cards on which are maintained records and data related to material on hand and on order.

Straddle. The purchase of a put and a call for a single security at the same market price; also known as a *double option.* The purchase of two puts and one call is referred to as a *strip.* and of one put and two calls as a *strap.* Speculators in securities make use of straddles as one means of protecting holdings whether the prices of the securities go up or down.

Straight Deductible. In insurance, the most common form of deductible clause; it provides that there is no coverage for small losses, typically in the amounts of $25, $50, or $100. In some policies the deductible clause is mandatory. In others, it is optional and may be inserted into the policy with a corresponding reduction in premium payments.

Straight Lease. A lease for a fixed, agreed-upon price for a specific period, with regular payments of equal amounts. Also known as *flat lease.*

Straight Life Insurance. Premiums are paid by the insured throughout his or her lifetime. When death occurs, the face value of the policy is paid to the beneficiary. This type of policy has cash surrender or loan value. Also known as *ordinary life* and *whole life* insurance. A variation is the limited-payment contract wherein premiums are paid for a finite number of years, usually 20 or 30. After that period, protection continues for the life of the insured without further payments of premiums. Also, the single-premium payment life policy may be offered, which requires only one payment for lifetime coverage.

Straight-line Method. A depreciation method that assumes that assets depreciate at a uniform rate, in equal amounts for each year of the asset's useful life. Thus, if a machine is estimated to have a ten-year life, one-tenth of its cost is taken as depreciation in the first year, one-tenth in the second year, and so on until the tenth year, when the residual value is estimated to be at zero dollars.

Street Name. Securities held in the name of a broker instead of the customer are said to be carried in a *street name.* This occurs when the securities have been bought on margin or when the customer wishes the security to be held by the broker.

Style Flexibility. In organizational behaviour, the skill of a manager in varying his or her basic style of behaviour appropriately to meet a changing situation, so that managerial effectiveness is increased.

Style Resilience. In organizational behaviour, the tendency of a manager to maintain a single, appropriate basic style, so that his effectiveness as a manager is increased.

Subassembly. In manufacturing, a low-level assembly or minor assembly of individual components or materials later combined with other subassemblies to form a high-level assembly or an end product.

Subjective Value. In accounting, a value assigned to an asset by management without supporting verification from an independent source, possibly without relation to market value, and usually based on opinion or experience rather than or hard data.

Subordinated Debt. A debt that ranks below the actual amounts owed to general creditors. In times of financial embarrassment, an arrangement is sometimes made between a creditor and a debtor to subordinate a specific debt, where the creditor has faith in the business future of the debtor.

Subrogation. The right of an insurance company, after paying the insured's loss in accordance with the amounts described in the policy, to take over all the insured's legal right against negligent third parties. If not for subrogation, the insured might attempt to collect twice for the same occurrence, once from the insurance company and again from the negligent third party.

Also, the transfer of a legal claim or right from one person to another. For example, when a creditor is unable to collect on a promissory note, the note may be transferred to a third party, who pays the original creditor and sues the debtor who defaulted on the loan.

Subscribed Capital Stock. The part of the capital stock of a corporation against which unpaid subscriptions are outstanding. As subscriptions become fully paid, capital stock in issued.

Subsidiary Accounts. A group of similar accounts that related to the same activity or object and that are maintained in a separate record and controlled by an account in the general ledger.

Subsidiary Ledger. A supporting ledger containing a group of accounts. Examples are an expense ledger, customers' ledger, creditors' ledger, and a departmental ledger.

Subsidy. A grant of financial aid, usually by a government agency, to a person or institution. One form of subsidy, called a *grant-in-aid* is restricted to special purposes.

Substitution Effect. As the price for a commodity, good, or service is increased beyond a critical level, consumers will seek lower-priced alternatives or substitutes. When such phenomenon occurs and is súccessful, the tendency is for the original commodity, good, or service to become reduced in price in response to overproduction, high inventories, or the law of supply and demand.

Summary Prospectus. A prospectus in short form permitted by the Securities Exchange Commission under regulations relating to promotional activities of dealers in SEC-registered securities.

Sum-of-the-Years Digits Methods. A method of depreciation of a fixed asset that allows depreciation to be taken at an accelerated rate in the early years of the asset's useful life. To calculate the depreciation rate that is to be taken each year, a fraction is developed in which all the years of useful life (n) of the asset are added together (1+ 2 + 3 + ... + n) and used as the denominator. For the first year, the numerator is *n*, for the second year it is *n — 1*, for the third year, n — 2 and so forth. For example, for an office machine with a useful life of five years (n = 5), the denominator of the fraction is 15. Depreciation the first year is 5/15th of the acquisition cost of asset; it is 4/15 the second year, 3/15 the third year, and so on. In the final year the total remaining value of the asset may be fully depreciated, ignoring for purposes of this example any recoverable market value for the asset. Also known as *sum-of-the-digits method*.

Sunk Costs. In accounting, costs that have been incurred and are not reversible in the event of a decision to discontinue an incompleted project.

Sunspot Theory. A theory of business cycles proposed in England during the late 9th century. It held that sunspot cycles (disturbances on the surface of the sun) exhibited an extremely high correlation with agricultural cycles for a number of years; therefore, sunspots must affect the weather, which influences agricultural crops, which affect business conditions. This theory received worldwide popularity when it was first introduced, but then fell into disrepute because the high correlation between sunspots and agricultural cycles did not endure; it was the result of accidental rather than causal factors.

Superintendent. A title sometimes used to denote the manager of a factory or a division; equivalent to *general foreman* or *works manager* in some countries.

Supermarket. The supermarket initially was intended to appeal to people with limited incomes by offering low prices and minimum services. The first supermarkets were located in warehouses, had poor lighting, and offered extremely simple displays of goods, primarily foodstuffs. Modern supermarkets are generally large, well lit, and air-conditioned, with well-organized displays of assorted goods, including a wide variety of household merchandise. Except for the feature of self-service, they have come to resemble large versions of the old-time *General Store.*

Supervisor. In general, any person who directs the activities of others. Often this title is applied to a group leader who heads a section within a department.

Supplemental Appropriation. In government accounting, a Congressional grant of funds that has the effect of increasing an appropriation that has been previously approved.

Supplementary Cost. In accounting, the cost of a product that is not included in prime-cost data.

Supplies. Materials that are essential to the operation of a business but are not physically incorporated into the products or parts manufactured by the firm. Supplies include wrapping paper, machine oil, cleaning materials, and fuel for the operation of the machinery.

Support Deed. An instrument used in the transfer of property in which the consideration is the support for life of the grantor by the grantee.

Supporting Style. In organizational behavior, the basic managerial style a manager uses next most frequently after the dominant style.

Surplus Value. According to the theories of Karl Marx, surplus value is the difference between the value that a worker creates as determined by the labour time embodied in the goods he produces, and the value that he receives as determined by the subsistence level of the wages. This surplus, Marx contended, is appropriated by the capitalist, and is the incentive for the development of the capitalistic system.

Surrender Value. The portion of premiums paid or another amount recoverable on an insurance policy if the policy is canceled immediately after having been issued.

Surviving Company. A company operating as an entity that has acquired the assets of other companies and continues the operations of those it has acquired but under its own name.

Suspense Account. An account in which receipts or disbursements are carried on a temporary basis, pending classification or identification.

Synergy. Notion that value achieved by combined two or more complementary/competitive businesses exceed the total of individual values of these entities. For Example, some years ago Brooke Bond Lipton India Ltd. was merged with Hindutan Lever Ltd. to reap the benefits of synergy. These days, merger is being used worldwide to consolidate business and improve market value of companies.

Systematic Risk. The portion of a security's total risk that is related to the movement of the market as a whole. Major political, economic and social events affect almost all the stocks in the market, therefore, systematic risk (or alternatively market risk) cannot be diversified away. It is also termed as 'Undiversifiable Risk'. However, there is a way to reduce systematic risk; by diversifying internationally when the correlation coeficient between the movement of different markets is very less. Systematic risk of a financial asset is measured by beta coeficient, i.e., the ratio of covariance of the stock's return to the variance of the market return. It shows the sensitivity of the stock's return to changes in the market return.

Tt

Takeout Loan. A long-term loan that replaces an interim construction loan.

Takeover. The acquisition of a business by another through purchase, exchange of capital stock, or any other device.

Tangible Asset. Any asset that exists physically, as opposed to an intangible asset.

Tangible Value. The worth of tangible assets such as plant and equipment and current assets.

Tare Weight. The weight of packing material; in carload shipments, the weight of the empty freight car.

Tariff. A schedule of duties authorized by a government and imposed on commodities imported or exported. The intent may be to generate revenue for the government or to protect domestic supplies. Also, in transportation, a publication that sets forth the charges, rates, and rules of transportation companies.

Tax-anticipation Note. In municipal accounting, a note issued in prospect of the collection of property taxes and scheduled to be repaid from the collected taxes.

Tax Avoidance. The management of financial matters so as to lower taxes as much as is legally possible.

Taxable Equivalent Yield. Taxable return which is after payment of tax is equivalent to a given tax-free return. The taxable equivalent yield is calculated by using the formula:

$$\frac{\text{Tax-free rate of return}}{1 - \text{tax rate.}}$$

For example, an investor would have to earn more than 14.29 percent rate of return on a taxable security to prefer it to 10 percent tax free rate of return if he is in the bracket of 30 percent tax rate.

Tax Base. In economics, the object on which a tax is levied, such as sales, property, income, and so on. For example, the base may refer to objects owned by an individual or to the aggregate real estate of a community.

Tax Certification. The confirmation by city and country treasurers that no taxes remain unpaid prior to the acceptance of a warranty deed for recording; required in some states in real estate transactions.

Tax Receivable. In municipal accounting, the uncollected portion of current and delinquent taxes.

Tax Evasion. Taxes owed by deliberately not paid; an illegal position.

Tax-exempt Bond. A debt security of a state, city, or other public authority, the interest receipts of which are exempt from federal income taxation.

Technical Analysis. A form of security analysis that attempts to predict future price trends on the basis of charts, indexes, price, volume or other market statistics.

Tender. In securities trading, an offer to purchase outstanding stock from the stockholders. Usually made by a corporation or an individual to gain control of a company or to simplify the corporate structure of the company making the tender. The price offereced is usually above the market price. However, if there is no limit to the number of shares the maker of the tender will pruchase, the market price rapidly moves to the higher price represented by the tender.

Tentative Balance Sheet. A balance sheet in work form, intended for discussion, review, or any other managerial purpose prior to its publication in final form.

Terminal Account. A general or expense ledger account appearing as an item on a balance sheet or income statement. Also, any account that is not changed; in which transactions are not transferred, reclassified, or reallocated; and that is considered closed as entered in its classification.

Terminal Charge. A charge made for a service performed in a carrier's terminal area.

Term Insurance. Provides protection for a specific period of time, without savings, investment, or cash-value features. Usually written for 5-, 10-, or 15-year periods, although some companies issue policies for longer terms than 15 years.

Test Check. The verification of selected items in an account as an indication of the probability of, or the development of an opinion concerning, the accuracy of the entire account or record.

Thin Market. A securities market in which there are comparatively few bids to buy or offers to sell, or both. the phrase may apply to a single security or to the entire stock market. Price fluctuations between transactions are usually larger in a thin market than when the market is liquid (opposite of thin in trading terminology). A thin market in a particular security may reflect lack of interest in that issue or a limited supply or a limited demand for stock in the market.

Third-party Rights. An insurance contract is generally between two parties, the insured party and the insurance company. Under certain conditions, such as where an insurance company offers a life insurance contract that specifies a beneficiary who would eventually receive the payment, the rights of the third party, the beneficiary, are recognized.

Third World. The entirety of the poor nations that are burdened by problems of underdevelopment, poverty, illiteracy, and technological backwardness.

Throughput Accounting. An accounting system that enables original expenditures recorded in primary accounts to be identified in secondary accounts and financial statements.

Tie-in Sale. A practice whereby a seller requires the buyer to purchase one or more additional or *tied* products as a condition for purchasing the desired or *tying* product. Also known as *tying contract*.

Tight Money Policy. The policy of making credit dearer by controlling its expansion using various techniques of credit control. The techniques used to control expansion of credit are:

1. Increasing the **Bank Rate**.
2. Selling securities of the RBI in the open market to decrease level of funds with banks. This technique is known as the Open Market Operations.
3. Increasing the Cash Reserve Ratio or the Statutory Liquidity Ratio.
4. Raising interest rates.
5. Using **Qualitative techniques** of credit control for controlling credit for a particular sector.
6. **Moral suasion**.

Time Deposit. A deposit in a financial institution requiring at least 30 days notice before a withdrawal may be effected. Most savings accounts are time deposits; however, few financial institutions exercise the 30-days notice requirement.

Time Draft. A draft payable within a specified time—usually 30 days—after acceptance by the drawee.

Time Order. An order to buy or sell a security that becomes a market or limited price order at a specified time.

Title Company. A company that insures titles and issues title insurance policies to property owners.

Token Money. A government-issued object, either paper or metal, whose value as money is greater than the market value of the materials of which it is composed. Examples are pennies, nickels, dimes and dollars.

Toll Bond. An indigenous vesion of the Revenue Bond which provides for payment of interest and principal from the inflows on a specific project such as a prt, bridge or ohter infrastructure schemes. The toll bond has been engineered in India by Infrastructure Leasing & Financial Services Limited; it is being issued to mobilize funds for the Rao-Pithampur Road in Madhya Pradesh. It is estimated that the toll charges from vehicles traversing the road will be sufficient to pay the coupon and redeem the bonds whose tenure is 10 years.

Trace. An auditor's term for the process of ascertaining whether or not an item has been disposed of in accordance with the facts as reported.

Traceable Cost. A cost element whose origin can be identified even though it may have been transferred from one account to another.

Trade Acceptance. A bill of exchange drawn on the buyer by the seller of merchandise and unconditionally accepted by the buyer. Made out in accordance with the terms of the contract between the seller and the buyer.

Trade Account Payable. An amount owed to a supplier by a company that has received goods or services provided by the supplier.

Trade Account Receivable. An amount owed to a supplier by a company to which the supplier has delivered goods or provided services.

Trade Balance. The difference between the value of goods exported by a nation and those it has imported.

Trade Development Authority. A 'Service Institution' set up by the Government of India for providing package assistance to enterprises at the micro-level after identifying the potential of their products and their requirements of assistance.

It undertakes selective export development of industrial products with both short-term and long term prospects of growth to selected markets. In the discharge of this function, the TDA identifies technically competent and commercially viable units, particularly in the small and medium sector, assists in the expansion of export-oriented production facilities in the selected product and areas, undertakes product development/adaptation and helps in raising the technological levels of selected industrial exports. The units, products and markets are chosen by the TDA after collecting and processing all relevant information and after a careful study of the factors relevant to a sustained build-up of exports with minimal deployment of scarce resources. It arranges for commercial contacts between selected Indian units and potential foreign buyers of standing and repute, and facilitates conclusion of contracts. A special function of the TDA is to attract international subcontracting of engineering and other components from India and promotion of export-oriented joint ventures in the country in conjunction with the Indian Investment Centre.

Trade Discount. A discount allowed by their suppliers to a class of customers, such as electrical appliance or business machine dealers. It is based on a published list or suggested end-user price, is usually offered on the basis of volume purchases by the dealers, and is not related to date of payment.

Trade Fair Authority of India. A 'Service Institution', came into existence on March 11, 1977, after unifying three organisations, namely Directorate of Exhibitions and Commercial Publicity, the Indian Council of Trade Fairs and Exhibitions and Commercial Publicity and the Trade Fair Organisation.

The objectives of TFAI are : (1) to promote, organise, and participate in industrial trade, other fairs and exhibitions; (2) to set up show-rooms and shops in India and abroad; (3) to undertake trading activities in commodities connected with or relating to such fairs and exhibitions; and (4) to develop exports of new items for diversification and expansion of India's exports.

The TFAI brings out four journals, providing in it information on the country's economy, business possibilities offered by foreign markets, government's trade policies, facilities available for exports and important tenders floated by other countries.

Trade Investment. In the United Kingdom, an investment by one business firm in another for the purpose of protecting or expanding the investor's activities. Usually represented by a minority ownership of capital stock.

Trademark. A word, name, symbol, device, or any combination of these, adopted and used by a manufacturer or merchandiser to identify its goods and distinguish them from those manufactured or sold by others. The primary function is to distinguish one entrepreneur's goods from another's. A trademark may be owned by an individual, a firm, a partnership, a corporation, or an association or other collective group. Application for registration of a trademark is made to the Commissioner of Patents, Washington, D.C. If granted, the trademark registration is valid for 20 years, renewable so long as the mark is still in use in commerce. In the event of transfer of business ownership, a trademark may be assigned, sold, or traded as an asset along with the goodwill of the business using it.

Trade Name. The name by which a product or a service is known. It may or may not be registered as a trademark.

Trade Note Receivable. A customer's promissory note, pledging payment for goods supplied or services rendered.

Trade Payable. An amount of money owed to a creditor for goods or services received. Also known as *account payable.*

Trade Price. The price charged to regular customers who purchase continuously or in large volume for resale to their own customers. It is usually the list price or suggested end-user price less an applicable discount.

Trader. One who buys and sells goods, commodities, or securities for his or her own account for short-term profit.

Trade Receivable. An amount of money invoiced to a customer for goods delivered or services rendered. Also known as *account receivable.*

Trading Certificate. The Certificate issued to a public company by the Registrar of Companies enabling it to commence business. Trading Certificate is also known as Commencement Certificate.

Trading Company. A company organized to carry on commerce with foreign nations or with other trading companies in overseas territories.

Trading Limit. One of the prices above or below which trading on commodity exchanges is not allowed during any one day. Also, the maximum number of contracts an individual is allowed to hold at one time in commodities covered by regulation.

Trading Market. A securities market that does not exhibit a definite price trend and with few traders who are other than professionally engaged in the trading of securities.

Transfer Payment. A disbursement by the government for which it receives no goods or services. Items such as Social Security payments to the aged, unemployment compensation, and certain business subsidies are included because they channel tax revenues back to businesses and households without directly absorbing resources.

Traveler's Check. A draft issued by a bank or express company that is payable on presentation by an correspondent of the issuer.

Traveling Auditor. A staff auditor whose functions is to examine branches and divisions of a corporation at outlying locations as an aid to corporate control.

Traveling Requisition (TR). A purchase requisition made up once and refused each time the raw material or product is to be recordered so that new requisitions do not have to be written repeatedly.

Traveler's Check. A draft issued by a bank or express company that is payable on presentation by any correspondent of the issuer.

Traveling Auditor. A staff auditor whose functions is to examine branches and divisions of a corporation at outlying locations as an aid to corporate control.

Traveling Requisition (TR). A purchase requisition made up once and reused each time the raw material or product is to be reordered so that new requisitions do not have to be written repeatedly.

Treasury Stock. Stock issued by a company but later reaquired. It may be held in the company's treasury indefinitely, reissued to the public, or retired. Treasury stock receives no dividend and grants not voting right when held by the company.

Trial Balance. A term applied to the preparation of a list of account balances abstracted from a customer's ledger or other subsidiary ledger for the purpose of testing their totals and comparing them with those in the related control account. The trial balance is the basic summary of the total debits and total credits in a ledger preliminary to preparing a financial statement.

Trust. The right of property, real or personal, held by one for the benefit of another.

Trust Deed. A conveyance of a title to a trustee to be held until a loan or a performance secured by a note is paid or completed, at which time the title is reconveyed.

Trustee. On who holds property in trust for another to secure the performance of an obligation.

Trust Estate. An estate subject to a trust or being held in trust.

Trust Fund. A fund held by one person, the trustee, for the benefit of another, the affairs of the trust being conducted in accordance with the provisions of a formal trust agreement. Various states have passed legislation governing the conduct of the trustee.

Trust Mortgage. A mortgage to a person or a corporation as trustee, who holds the security for the benefit of others in accordance with the terms and conditions set forth in the instrument. Such a mortgage may be given to secure an issue of bonds sold by the mortgage to various persons and transferable at their will. The mortgage is given to a trustee who acts for and on behalf of all bondholders.

Turnaround. The situation wherein a company's trend of declining sales and/or earnings is reversed.

Turnover. In accounting, the number of times in a stated period that various assets are consumed and replaced. When used in ratio analysis, one of the indicators of the specific performance of management and the firm. Also, the financial statements of companies in the United Kingdom use the term as the equivalent of the U.S. term gross sales, the first item on an earnings report.

Uu

UDEAU. West African State Customs Unions.

Unadmitted Asset. An asset determined to have little or no liquidation value. In reporting the financial position of an insurance company, such assets are segregated and deducted as a group.

Unallotted Appropriation. In government accounting, the remainder of an appropriation available for purposes defined by the original appropriation determination.

Unamortized Debt Discount. The portion of debt discount that remains and is to be spread over future fiscal periods. Usually appears as a prepaid expense, if related to a bank loan, or as a deferred charge, if related to a long term bond issue.

Unapplied Cash. In municipal accounting, cash not reserved for specific purpose and available for use within the fund of which it is part.

Unappropriated Budget Surplus. In municipal accounting, the excess of the estimated revenues of a fund over the original appropriation for a given period of time.

Unappropriated Earned Surplus. The part of earned surplus that has not been transferred to a subordinate account or earmarked for a specific purpose. Such surplus therefore remains available for distribution in the form of dividends.

Unappropriated Income. An account set up for budgetary control to which is credited the excess of income, according to a related and approved expense or earnings budget.

Unavoidable Cost. A cost that cannot be eliminated but must be continued even under a program of business retraction. Also, a fixed cost.

Unbilled Cost. A recoverable cost that may be identified with specific and uncompleted contracts for goods and services. Such uncompleted contracts are classified as assets or receivables.

Unclaimed Dividends. The dollar amount of the dividend checks not yet cashed by stockholders or not yet in their hands.

Unclaimed Wages. Wages earned but not claimed by employees. although cash is available to make the payments. Also wage checks not yet presented for payment.

Uncontrollable Cost. An item of expense that is beyond the control of a specified executive of a business.

Uncrossed Cheque. A cheque which has not been crossed, and which can be cashed anywhere.

Undated Stock. Government loans for which there is no stated redemption date, e.g. consols. The holder receives an annual income of a fixed interest rate on the loan. The stock may be dealt in on the market.

Under Bond. Denoting imported goods stored in a government warehouse awaiting payment of duty on re export.

Undercut. To offer a product or service at a lower price than competing suppliers.

Underdeveloped Nation. In comparison with the more advanced countries, a nation that tends to exhibit (1) a poverty level of income and hence little or no savings, (2) a high rate of population growth, (3) a substantial majority of its labour force employed in agriculture, (4) a low proportion of adult literacy, (5) extensive unemployment that may be disguised, and (6) heavy reliance on a few items for export. Also referred to as *less developed nation*.

Underemployment. A situation where is not enough work for workers in a company to do. 2. A situation where there is not enough work in a country to occupy all the workforce.

Underlying Company. A company that is part of a larger consolidated organization and is kept in existence only because of non transferable rights or franchises that it possesses.

Underlying Security. A security issued by a subsidiary company and guaranteed by the parent company.

Underpriced Security. A security which is trading at a price less than its intrinsic worth as calculated by a security analyst.

Underwriter. In the securities market, an agent acting between a corporation issuing new securities and the public. The usual practice is for one or more underwriters to make an outright purchase of a corporation's new issue of stocks or bonds and to from a syndicate to sell the securities to individuals and institutions. Underwriters also distribute very large blocks of securities, perhaps held by an estate. Thereafter, the market in the securities may be over the counter, on a regional stock exchange , on the American Stock Exchange, or on the New York Stock Exchange.

Undischarged Bankrupt. A bankrupt who has not received from the court a certificate of discharge whereby normal business and personal rights are restored.

Undisclosed Factoring. The collection of debts by a factor whose role is hidden from the public. The factor sells the goods as the undisclosed principal of his client and is responsible for any bad debts.

Undistributed Profits. Profits which are not distributed to shareholders as dividends but which are retained by the company as reserves.

Undivided Interest. The interest of co owners in a property in which their individual interests are undistinguishable from one another.

Undivided Profit. The undistributed amount of a corporation's net income not yet formally transferred to retained earnings; a term generally used on the financial statements of banks where undivided profits are often combined with earned surplus under the heading surplus and undivided profits.

Unearned Increment. In accounting, any increase in the value of property due to circumstances beyond the control of the property owner and not attributable to direct expenditures or efforts. An example would be the increased market value of a piece of real property caused by improvements made to neighbouring properties.

Unencumbered Allotment. In government accounting, the portion of an allotment or allocation that has been neither expended nor encumbered.

Unencumbered Appropriation. In government accounting , the portion of an appropriation that has been neither expended nor encumbered. Also known as *unencumbered balance.*

Unexpended Appropriation. In government accounting, the portion of an appropriation that has not yet been expended, although it may be committed in whole or in part. Also known as *unexpended balance.*

Unexpired Cost. An expenditure, including prepaid expenses , whose benefits will be realized in the future.

Unenforceable Contract. Strictly speaking, they are not at all contracts, either because they are promises not supported by consideration, or because the formalities of the law have not been compiled with.

Uniform Accounting System. A system of accounts common to similar organizations. Trade associations, for example, propose accounting systems that are uniform in application to all members of their particular associations. Federal and state regulatory agencies, such as public utility commissions, may develop and strongly recommend; uniform accounting systems for organizations and institutions that come under their purview.

Unintended Investment. Unforeseen buildup of inventories in the economic system. Actual saving and actual investment are brought into equality in the economy by this means.

Unissued Capital. Capital in the form of shares which a company is authorized to issue but which it has not done so.

Unitary Demand. A state existing when quantity bought varies with price charged so that total revenue remains the same.

Unit Cost. The cost of a single unit of product or service. It is equivalent to average cost.

United States Rule. A method of identifying the amounts of interest and principal included in a partial payment of an interest-bearing debt. Also known as merchant's rule.

Unitization. The concept of containing a variety or quantity of goods within a single unit to facilitate carriage, handling, etc.

Unit Trust. Unit Trust is known as Fixed Investment Trust also. In the case of fixed investment trusts, there is no discretion given to the management to choose and select any type of securities but investments are confined to a fixed list of representative and diversified securities irrespective of industrial and financial variations. The principle of unit trust is that permanent investment in certain definite shares will prove profitable in the long run, whatever may be the changes in the market conditions.

The special characteristic of Unit Trust is that it buys a block of specified shares and securities in a number of companies and divides this block into small units and sub-units which are then sold to the public. A person gets a certificate to the extent of his ownership and receives an appropriate portion of profits earned by the trust on the block of investment. Among the many merits claimed for this type of investment trust, some are : (1) Investors have a definite idea about the investment of their funds; (2) The units are subunits of a block of securities are small enough to enable even small savers to invest in them; (3) Securities are lodged with reputed and trust-worthy banks and, therefore, there is no possibility of deceiving the investors; (4) Manipulation by management is ruled out.

Unit Trust of India (U.T.I.). An Autonomous enterprise, set up by a special statute on December 5, 1963 which started its activities from July 1, 1964. The initial Capital was Rs. 5 crores contributed by the Reserve Bank of India (Rs. 2.5 crores), Life Insurance Corporation of India (Rs. 75 lakhs). Central Government (Rs. 75 lakhs), scheduled Commercial Banks and other financial institutions (Rs. 1 crore). It is managed by a Board of Directors comprised 9 members.

The main functions of the Trust are: (1) To set units to small and medium savers of the country and to invest the money, thus collected, in selected industrial and business enterprise. Keeping in view the financial condition of the small and medium savers, the Face Value of the Units have been kept in between Rs. 10 and Rs.

100; (2) To invest money in such a manner that, on an average, not less than 6% income accrues to the enerprise; (3) To arrange selling of units through the branches of the State Bank of India and 36 other commercial banks; (4) At the end of each financial year, to distribute among the unit holders 90% of the Net Profits as Dividend Income from Unit Trust to the extent of Rs. 2,000 is exempted from Income Tax; (5) To publish regularly in the newspaper the daily buying and selling price of Rs. 10 Face value of unit; (6) To give loans keeping units as security; (7) To keep note of the fact that in no circumstances more than 5% of the investable fund is being invested in any particular enterprise; (8) To distribute the investment in many enterprises; (9) To mobilise and turn small savings through the units into productive investment.

United Nations Conference on Trade and Development (UNCTAD). The United Nations Conference on Trade and Development (UNCTAD) was established in 1964 in order to provide a forum where the developing countries could discuss the problems relating to their economic development. This was set up due to a feeling that the existing institutions like GATT and IMF were not properly organised to handle the peculiar problems of developing countries. At present, UNCTAD is the only body where developing, developed as well as centrally planned countries are members.

Unlimited Company. A company whose members bear full personal liability for the company's debts. It need not issue shares. Compare limited company.

Unlisted Securities. Shares which are not listed on the official Stock Exchange list, but which are traded on the Unlisted Securities Market.

Unpaid Dividend. A declared dividend that has not yet been paid; an unclaimed dividend. Also, a passed dividend on cumulative preferred stock.

Unquoted Investments. Shares and stock of a company not having a stock exchange quotation and which are held by another company. Such investments must be recorded in the holding company's balance sheet at cost or at an estimated current valuation.

Unredeemed Pledge. An item given as security for a loan which has not been redeemed by repaying the loan.

Unrequited Exports. Exported goods whose value is used to repay a previous debt. Additional foreign exchange earnings are thus not generated by the exports.

Unsecured Creditors. Individuals or companies who have loaned money without obtaining a charge against the borrower's assets. Such creditors rank equally with each other and, upon bankruptcy of the borrower, are paid parri passu according to the size of debt after the secured creditors have been fully paid.

Unsecured Account. A personal account supported only by the general credit of the debtor, without collateral or other tangible guaranty.

Unsecured Liability. A liability for which the creditor holds no security.

Upset Price. In the case of equity proceedings in a bankruptcy, the amount established by the court as the lowest acceptable price for a firm's assets when offered at public auction.

More generally, the lowest price at which a seller is willing to sell. Also, the initial price asked at an auction before bidding is started.

Up Tick. In securities trading, a transaction made at a price higher than the preceding transaction. Also called a *plus tick.* A stock may be sold short only on an up tick or on a *zero-plus tick.* A zero-plus tick is a transaction at the same price as the preceding trade but higher than the preceding different price.

Usance Bill. Refers to the fixed maturity Bill of Exchange.

Uses of Funds. Application of funds for the purchase of non-current assets and payment of non-current liabilities, dividends and taxes.

Usufruct. The right to use property owned by another while refraining from actions which might diminish the value of the property or alter it materially.

Vv

Valuation Account. A reserve account that relates to and partly or wholly offsets one or more other accounts, including accumulated depreciation, allowance for bad debts, and unamortized debt discount.

Valuation Reserves. An amount deducted by a creditor from the book value of debts due to him, in the expectation that some of them are likely to be defaultered.

Value Added. The difference between the income received from the sale of the products or services of a business and the expenditure incurred in buying materials from outside sources to produce those products.

Value Added Statement. A financial statement prepared by a business relating to its value added during the accounting period. The statement identifies the value added and shows how this value has been appropriated to various claimants, for example the government (taxes), employee wages and salaries, and providers of finance (interest and dividends).

Value Added Tax. A method of taxation of goods and services whereby tax is levied on the extra contribution to the value of a good or service rendered through a business's operations. The tax rate is applied to the value added, as calculated by subtracting the invoiced cost of its supplies from the invoice price charged by the business for the goods or services it produces.

Value-Added Tax, Modified (MODVAT). Modified scheme of "Value-added Tax" introduced in India by the then

Finance Minister V.P. Singh and came into force on March 1, 1986.

The MODVAT allows manufacturer to get almost immediate and almost complete reimbursement of the excise duty paid on inputs and intermediary products. The MODVAT has been introduced as a measure in cutting costs and ultimately in reducing the prices of the final product through the availability of internal relief of the duties.

Value Analysis. Usually performed by the purchasing department, the study of materials, parts, or components, purchased or manufactured. The purpose is to determine the value received for the dollars spent and to start specific action intended to improve that value.

Value Buying. This term stands for buying of materials by the purchase department of an enterprise which looks to quality and economy. It is expected that any purchase of materials should satisfy the quality required by the production department, and the quality should also ensure safe storage without any wastage and deterioration in value. Of course, it may not always be possible to buy best quality of materials at the lowest price. But, at the same time, it is not too difficult to ensure quality and economy in buying. As such, the purchase department will study production requirements and trends of the market and accordingly adjust its purchase policy to suit the needs of the situation. In other words, it will look to 'value buying'.

Valued Policy. Insurance usually issued for property whose precise value may be difficult to establish, such as a work of art, a coin collection, or a rare book. Such a policy establishes a face amount for the value of the insured property, and in the event of loss within the terms of the policy, the face amounts is paid. Another example is a life insurance contract under which the dollar amount is fixed and becomes payable on the death of the insured.

Value Weighted Index. A share price index in which each share's price is assigned weight equal to its market capitalization.

Variable Annuity. A pension benefit plan that fluctuates in value with the changes in the worth of the assets, typically common stocks, in which the pension fund is invested. The variable annuity was designed to provide an adjustment mechanism for inflation on the theory that stock prices would rise over time.

Variable Cost. Items of costs that vary in direct proportion to changes in production or activity. For example, direct material and direct labour costs are usually variable costs with each unit manufactured require a certain quantity of material and labour. The use of the term **variable** in accounting is distinguished from its simple meaning **changeable**. In accounting, variable refers not to changes in costs over time or due to seanonal variations but changes which are associated with the level of production. If an item of cost increases with the increases in the volume of production, it is a variable cost; otherwise, it is not.

Variable Cost Ratio. The ratio between sales revenues and variable costs. One of many ratios by which the performance of management or a business may be measured.

Variable Price Option. A form of non qualified stock option under which the exercise price decreases as the stock price increases in relation to the stock price at the time of the award. Also known as *yo-yo* option.

Variance. In accounting, the difference between corresponding items in comparative balance sheets or in income or other operating statements. Also, the difference over a period of a year or less between standard costs and actual costs; the difference between the expected or planned and the actual.

In statistics, mixed positive and negative quantities can be converted to all positive quantities by the process of squaring. The average of the squared deviations from the mean, used as a measure of dispersion, is called variance.

In law procedures, a discrepancy between what is charged or alleged and what is proved or is offered as proof.

In real estate zoning, an exemption from the application of a zoning ordinance or regulation, permitting a use that varies from what is otherwise permitted. The exception or variance is granted by the appropriate authority in special circumstances to protect against an undue hardship wrought by strict enforcement of the zoning regulations.

Variety Store. A store carrying a wide range of relatively inexpensive goods for the household. Small appliances, dry goods, stationery, and notions are typical of the items offered. Also known as five and ten five and dime store and five and ten cent store.

Vendeee's Lien. The encumbrance of a buyer for the return of his or her deposit in the event a seller defaults on a contract.

Vendor. An outside company selling or supplying material or services.

Vendor's Shares. Shares in a company which are issued to the seller of a business which is converted into a limited company. The shares are issued as consideration for the sale of the business.

Venture. A business enterprize or project undertaken, often in association with one or more partners, with a view to making profits, but in which there is a risk of loss.

Venture Capital. Capital for investment in projects which have a high risk potential.

Verify. 1. To check the accuracy of the recording of accounting entries in books of account. 2 To check the accuracy of data which has been recorded on to input media by transfer from the basic documents. Such verification is usually by means of mechanical duplication, such as punching, where discrepancies between the initial input and the verifying process give rise to warning signals or else the tape stops.

Vertical Disintegration. The switching from own production to external purchase of certain components, induced by circumstances in which optimum production requires large resources than can be provided by the company. Specialist manufacturers are thereby established, serving the needs of all the businesses in a particular industry.

Vertical Filling. A system of filing in which documents or holders are stacked on edge one behind the other in some particular sequence.

Vertical Integration. The merger of firms engaged in different stages of production of an item. 'Backward integration' would be used to describe the merging of a tyre manufacturer with a rubber plantation. 'Forward integration' would be used to describe a merging of a brewer with a hotel chain. Motives for vertical integration include the desire to secure sources of supply or outlets for the finished product.

Vertical Market. A business environment in which the ownership of natural resources, their manufacture and the ultimate use of the finished products are vested in a single organization.

Volume Discount. An allowance, in credit, cash, or gods, given by a seller to a buyer because of the aggregate size of the purchases in a series of transactions over a specific period of time. Distinguished from a quantity discount which is usually related to a single transaction rather than a series.

Volume Rate. In motor carrier tariffs, any rate to which a volume minimum weight applies.

Voting Trust. The transfer by two or more persons of their shares of stock of a corporation to a trustee who is to vote the shares and act for such shareholders.

Voucher. A document serving as evidence of the disbursement of cash. A document authorizing the disbursement of cash. Written evidence of a business or accounting transaction.

Voucher Audit. An authorized individual's examination of a proposed disbursement. In government accounting, the postaudit of individual disbursements made by the comptroller general.

Voucher Check. A document showing details of a payment made, including date, amount, discount, deductions, invoice number, and other references to goods or services for which payment has been or is to be made. A voucher check may combine the features of a check, a formal receipt, and a detachable remittance record.

Voucher System. The systematic treatment of documentation used in accounting, designed to ensure the proper recording of transactions.

Ww

Wage. Payment for employment normally made weekly and related to output or hours worked.

Wage Differentials. A difference between the price of one form of labour and another, arising through a particular demand and supply situation for each type of labour. Reasons for differentials vary, but include experience, skill and geographical location.

Wage Drift. The tendency for earnings from employment to increase, despite an official fixed level of pay, through overtime working and bonus payments.

Wage Freeze. A period when wages are not allowed to increase.

Wage Incentive. A monetary encouragement paid to stimulate greater production, better quality of work, etc. Incentives may be part of the pay structure (e.g. piece rates, relating earnings to output, with bonuses for extra output) or may take the form of annual awards depending on business performance in the year (e.g. profit-sharing or annual bonus).

Wager. A contract between two parties involving the staking of value upon the outcome of an event, past or future, on which the parties differ. Neither party must have any interest in the event except in the stake. In Britain wagering contracts are void, although not illegal.

Wage Rate. The rate of remuneration earned by an employee. The rate may be expressed in terms of hours, units produced, etc.

Wages Spiral. The continuing upward movement in wage levels, occasioned by the attempt through wages increases to offset the effects of inflation on living standards.

To the extent that wage increases themselves induce inflation (through price rises needed to cover increased wage costs, or through the expansion of monetary incomes with an upward effect on demand) a continuous interaction between price rises and wage rises results.

Wage Theory. Any of the varying approaches to or theories for determining the wages paid to employees.

Waiver. The voluntary relinquishment of a right or privilege without causing the insurance policy to be canceled. A premium waiver may become part of the contract terms, as when an incident temporarily prevents a business firm form conducting its affairs. The insurance company may have voluntarily relinquished or waived its right to premiums for the specified period of time.

Waiver Clause. A clause in a marine insurance policy whereby either the insurer or insured may take action to minimize a loss arising from an accident without prejudicing their position vis-a-vis the insurance policy.

Wants Primary. The requirements of food, clothing and shelter, which must be satisfied to ensure survival.

Warehouse. A building in which goods are stored, pending distribution for sale, collection for despatch to a factory, etc.

Warrant. 1. A receipt for goods deposited in a warehouse providing all details necessary to identify the goods and the date from which charges are payable. Such a warrant may be transferred by endorsement. 2. A judicial document empowering a person or authority to perform such acts as are specified therein. 3 A document entitling the holder to certain money or property.

Warranty. 1. Express or implied undertakings or declarations made by an insured party to an insurance contract which, if not followed or if incorrect, invalidate the contract. 2. An element or statement of fact contained in a contract which, if broken, does not invalidate the contract. The aggrieved party may, however, claim damages.

Wall Street. 1.The street in New York where the New York Stock Exchange is situated. 2. The US financial world in general.

Wash. In accounting, a transaction that is reversed or offset by another transaction in a short period of time.

Wash Sale. The sale and purchase of substantially identical securities within a 30-day period. Losses from such transactions are not legal deductions from income subject to federal income taxes.

Wasting Asset. A fixed asset with a limited useful life and subject to depreciation. Examples include assets from which natural products such as ore, oil, and timber are extracted at a rate exceeding the natural replacement rate, thereby causing a gradual diminution of the value of the asset.

Watered Capital. The excess of capital stock issued, at its par or stated value, over the fair value of the assets contributed in exchange.

Watered Stock. Any class of the capital stock of a corpmoration containing watered capital.

Waybill. Issued by a carrier to the shipper, a record of details describing a unit of freight. Copies may be provided to all interested agents of the carrier.

Wealth. In economic theory, an individual's total stock or inventory or tangible or intangible possessions having a definable market value and capable of being exchanged for money or other goods through a transfer of ownership. The same principle may be applied both to a business firm and to an economy as a whole, measured at a single instant in time.

Welfare State. A country which provides through the central government and its agencies minimum standards of living for the population in terms of income, health, education, housing, etc.

Welfare Theory of Taxation. The theory of taxation based upon the maximizing of community welfare by minimizing the total loss of satisfaction resulting from taxation. The loss of satisfaction to a poor man resulting from a tax of £x will be greater than the loss of satisfaction to a rich man Therefore, to ensure equality of sacrifice the wealthy must pay a progressively higher tax.

Wharfage Charge. Any charge made for receiving and removing goods on a wharf.

Where-used Report. In manufacturing, a report that displays, for each part, all assemblies that contain the part in their single-level bill of material.

Whole Life Insurance. A type of life insurance that provides protection throughout the entire life of the person insured. Premiums are spread over the life of the insured and hence this policy is least expensive.

Wholesale Price Index. A measure of the average prices of commodities purchased in large quantities in transactions between firms.

Wildcat Strike. An unofficial labor strike called on short notice or without notice and without going through contractual procedures for settling grievances.

Withdrawal Account. A type of mutual fund account that pays a certain amount of money periodically to the owner of the account; often used by retired persons as a source of income.

Withdrawal Provisions. In a savings plan and occasionally in a qualified profit-sharing plan, the timing and terms under which either individual contributions or a portion of the accrued company contributions can be withdrawn by the participant.

Withholding. In business accounting, the process of automatically deducting from salaries or wages the amounts of money specified by law or regulation, as in the case of government income taxes, and specified by contract with the employee, as in the case of voluntary contributions to pension or employee stock purchase plans.

Withholding Tax. (1) A tax which is deducted from interest or dividends before they are paid to the investor. (2) (US) Income tax which is deducted at source.

Without Prejudice. A form of words written in a letter to indicate that the writer does not consider himself legally bound to do what he offers to do in the letter.

With Profits Policy. A type of life assurance policy in which, in return for higher premiums than on an ordinary life policy, a bonus is paid, being a share of the surplus in the life fund on its revaluations.

Working Capital. Refers to the deployment of funds in current assets such as cash, inventory, accounts receivables, raw material, marketable securities, etc. Two types of working capital are distinguished — Gross working capital and net working capital. The working capital defined above is **Gross Working Capital**. Net working capital is the difference between current assets and current liabilities. This is a measure of the extent to which a firm is protected against liquidity problems. When accountants use the term working capital, they are generally referring to the net working capital. From a management view point, however, it makes no sense to actively manage the difference between current assets and current liabilities. They have to manage total of current assets and current liabilities.

Current assets may be financed with short-term and/ or long-term sources. Short-term sources are known as current liabilities. Examples of current liabilities include creditors, bills payables, bank finance. These are payable within one year. Normally, permanent working — the amount of current assets required to meet long-term minimum needs, are financed by long-term sources of finance such as share capital, retained earnings, long-term loans etc.

Working-Capital Turnover. The ratio of net sales to working capital. One of many ratios by which the performance of management or a business may be measured.

Working Control. Theoretically, control of a corporation requires ownership of 51 per cent of the corporation's voting stock. In practice, effective (working) control may be exercised through ownership, individually or by a group acting as one, of less than 50 per cent.

Work Order. In business and industry, an internal document that authorizes the performance of a specific task or job. Also known as *work ticket*.

Works. In many countries outside the United States equivalent to the word factory.

World Bank. The International Bank for Reconstruction and Development—the IBRD or World Bank, for short—was founded at the International Economic Conference held at Bretton Woods in July 1944 and started functioning in June 1946. The World Bank is an international co-operative organisation associated with the

United Nations having the status of a specialised agency. Its aim is to assist the economic development of its member-countries and to raise the living standard of the people of the world.

The objectives of the Bank, as set forth in the Articles of Agreement, are as follows: (1) To assist in the reconstruction and development of territories of members by facilitating the investment of capital for productive purposes; (2) To promote private foreign investment by means of guarantee or participation in loans and investments made by private investors; (3) To promote the long-range balanced growth of international trade and the maintenance of equilibrium in balance of payments by encouraging international investment.

The initial Authorised Capital of the World Bank was $10,000 million subscribed by its members according to their economic strength. U.S.A. is the largest subscriber followed by the U.K., and India is the 5th subscriber from the top of the list.

The Bank is managed by a Board of Governors which consists of one representative appointed by each country. Normally once in a year the meeting of the Governors are held. But, however, the Governors have delegated most of their powers to a Board of Executive Directors which usually meet once a month. At present there are 20 Executive Directors—5 are appointed by the top five subscriber-nations, and 15 are elected by the Governors of the remaining members for a two-year term. The President of the Bank is also the Chairman of the Board of Executive Directors.

Write-Down. The transfer of a portion of an asset account to an expense account; the deliberate reduction of the book value of an asset.

Write-off. The transfer of the remainder of the value of an asset to an expense account; the act of reducing book value.

Write-up. The recording of an increase in the book value of an asset without incurring additional outlays of cash or other property and without producing an inflow of cash; the act of setting down an unduly high value.

W-2 Form. A statement of document in a standardized format that all U.S. employers must give to their employees. The form contains the dollar amounts of wages and other compensation paid to the employee, contributions to Social Security (FICA tax), federal taxes withheld, state taxes withheld (where applicable), and a "yes" or "no" as to whether the employee participated in a qualified pension plan. A copy of the W-2 form must be attached to the employee's income-tax reports to the federal and state governments. The data given on the W-2 form cover the calendar year for the tax return.

Xx

X-Efficiency. The efficiency of a firm in buying and using inputs. Most firms do not operate a maximum X-efficiency.

XR or XR or Ex-Right. It is a method of quoting shares in a stock exchange whereby the current purchase is not entitled to a right of issue by the company which is contemplated or announced to be issued.

X-Theory. A traditional view of human motivation that, because of an inherent dislike of work and responsibility, people prefer to be directed, coerced and financially induced within a closely controlled organizational structure.

Yy

Yankee Bond. A bond in dollars issued in the United States by a foreign company.

Yankees. A Stock Exchange term used to describe US Securities.

Year-end Adjustment. Where indicated, a review and modification of a ledger account at the close of a fiscal year. Not related to corrections of clerical errors, but referring to adjustments made necessary by accruals, prepayments, changes in accounting policies, inventory data, or other transactions that may have occurred without being completely recorded.

Yen. The basic unit of currency in Japan.

Yield. (1) The actual rate of return received or obtainable from an investment, generally expressed as the annual income calculated as a percentage of the purchase price of the investment. (2) The rate of return for a capital investment project, which equates the net capital expenditure with the discounted value of future net cash inflows. 3 The output of a process.

Yield Curve. A graphic presentation of the term structure of interest rates. In the graph, yield to maturity are plotted against time to maturity. For example, following table depicting time to maturing and yield to maturity may be plotted on graph:

Term (years) to maturity on Government Securities as on March 31, 1995	*Yield to Maturity (%)*
1	11.23
2	11.73
3	12.23
4	12.47
5	12.71
6	12.77
7	12.83
8	12.88
9	12.94
10	13.00

Yield Gap. The difference between the dividend yield obtainable from ordinary shares and the yield obtainable from fixed interest stock, the variation being due to the greater risk associated with ordinary shares and the likely future growth of the company.

Yield Variance. That portion of a material's usage variance that is due to the difference between the standard yield specified and the actual yield obtained.

Yield to Maturity. The discount rate that equates the present value of future promised cash flows from the security to the current market price of the security. It is the compound rate of return on investor will earn if the security is purchased at the current market price, all payments are made according to schedule, and all interest payments are reinvested at a rate equal to the yield to maturity.

York-Antwerp Rules. Regulations designed to establish international conformity in the administration of matters relating to the carriage of goods by sea. The regulations may be included, at the option of the contracting parties, in general average clauses relating to charter parties, marine insurance policies and bills of lading.

Y-Theory. A theory of human motivation based on the premise that people are interested in work, want responsibility and will direct themselves without the need for coercion by management.

Zz

Zero-base Budgeting (ZBB). A method of drawing up budgets with initial expenditure under various heads assumed to be zero. That is, expenditure incurred during the previous year/years is not taken as a base for the allocations for the current year. Proper justification of the budgetary requirements are needed for allocation of funds. Therefore, managers are forced to critically examines their ongoing programmes and activities which leads to curtailment of non-essential expenditure.

Zero-Coupon Bond. A bond that is issued at a discount, makes no periodic payments of interest and redeemed at the face value on maturity. The return to the investor consists of the discount i.e., the difference between the face value and the issue price, zero-coupon bond offers advantages to both investor and the borrower. Since investor does not receive periodic payment of interest, he does not have to worry about their reinvestment. The borrower is not required to make arrangement for meeting regular payment obligations. Zero coupon convertibles have been issued by some companies in India. ICICI, IDBI and some financial institutions have also issued deep discount bonds which also belong to the zero-coupon bond category.

Zero-rating. The allocation of 0% VAT to a certain type of good or service.

Zip Code. The US postcode. Each address has a five figure-number.

Zollverein. A customs union characterized by the abolition of duties between member states and the establishment of a common tariff policy in respect of non-members.